"Raise Up a Child"

Also available from Lyceum Books, Inc.

HUMAN BEHAVIOR FOR SOCIAL WORK PRACTICE: A DEVELOPMENTAL-ECOLOGICAL FRAMEWORK, by Wendy L. Haight and Edward H. Taylor

ADOPTION IN THE UNITED STATES, by Martha J. Henry and Daniel Pollack

DIVERSITY, OPPRESSION, AND CHANGE, by Flavio Francisco Marsiglia and Stephen Kulis

CRITICAL MULTICULTURAL SOCIAL WORK, by Jose Sisneros, Catherine Stakeman, Mildred C. Joyner and Cathryne L. Schmitz

CROSS-CULTURAL PRACTICE; SOCIAL WORK WITH DIVERSE POPULATIONS, by Karen V. Harper and Jim Lantz

SOCIAL WORK PRACTICE WITH FAMILIES: A RESILIENCY-BASED APPROACH, by Mary Patricia Van Hook

THE ETHICS OF PRACTICE WITH MINORS, by Kim Strom-Gottfried

HUMAN DEVELOPMENT IN
AN AFRICAN-AMERICAN FAMILY

"Raise Up a Child"

EDITH V. P. HUDLEY,
WENDY HAIGHT, AND
PEGGY J. MILLER

LYCEUM
BOOKS, INC.
Chicago, Illinois

© Lyceum Books, Inc., 2003, 2009

Published by

LYCEUM BOOKS, INC.
5758 S. Blackstone Ave.
Chicago, Illinois 60637
773+643-1903 (Fax)
773+643-1902 (Phone)
lyceum@lyceumbooks.com
http://www.lyceumbooks.com

All rights reserved under International and Pan-American Copyright Conventions. No part of the publication may be reproduced, stored in a retrieval system, copied, or transmitted in any form or by any means without written permission from the publisher.

ISBN 978-0-925065-47-6

Library of Congress Cataloging-in-Publication Data

Hudley, Edith V. P., 1920-2007
  "Raise up a child" : human development in an African-American family / Edith V. P. Hudley, Wendy Haight, and Peggy J. Miller.
      p. cm.
  Includes bibliographical references (p.) and index.
  ISBN 0-925065-47-1
  1. Hudley, Edith V. P., 1920-2007 2. African American women—Biography. 3. Grandmothers—United States—Biography. 4. Hudley, Edith V. P., 1920-2007—Family. 5. African American families. 6. Child rearing—Philosophy. 7. Child development—Philosophy. 8. Texas—Biography. 9. Oakland (Calif.)—Biography. 10. Salt Lake City (Utah)—Biography. I. Haight, Wendy L., 1958- II. Miller, Peggy J. (Peggy Jo), 1950- III. Title.
  E185.97.H836H83   2003
  973.9'092—dc21
                                                          2002155626

Dedication

This book is dedicated to the memory of Aaron Franklin Patton (1880-1946) and Mamie E. Scott Patton (1889-1930), and to our children: Matthew and Camilla, and Kurt and Kathleen.

Contents

Preface **vii**
Acknowledgments **ix**
Introduction **xi**

PART 1: CHILDHOOD 1

Chapter 1. Family **5**
Chapter 2. Watching, Listening, Questioning **10**
Chapter 3. That Little Switch **15**
Chapter 4. Mamie's Death **19**
Chapter 5. Other Mothers **25**
Chapter 6. Community **28**
Chapter 7. Racism and Resistance **34**
Chapter 8. The Dead Return **41**
Interlude 1: Religion and Spirituality **46**

PART 2: YOUTH 59

Chapter 9. Eighth Grade **61**
Chapter 10. Working for Miz A. **64**
Chapter 11. Protection against Predators **69**
Chapter 12. Keeping to the Right Path **73**
Chapter 13. Segregation and Integration **76**
Interlude 2: Oppression and Resistance **81**

PART 3: MARRIED LIFE 91

Chapter 14. Courtship **94**
Chapter 15. Outsmarting Mr. Bill and Cousin Oscar **96**
Chapter 16. Working in the Shipyards **101**
Chapter 17. Aaron's Death **106**
Chapter 18. Family Troubles **108**
Chapter 19. No More Babies **113**
Chapter 20. Storekeeping **117**
Chapter 21. Edna and Kathareen **120**
Chapter 22. The Accident **125**

Chapter 23. Mother Ewing 130
Interlude 3: Mentoring 134

PART 4: RAISING CHILDREN 143
Chapter 24. Raising Sand about School 146
Chapter 25. Working with the Teachers 151
Chapter 26. Chastising Children 154
Chapter 27. Two Different Children 160
Chapter 28. Fathers 163
Chapter 29. Other People's Children 170
Interlude 4: Physical Discipline 173

PART 5: LATER YEARS 185
Chapter 30. Meeting Floyd 187
Chapter 31. Floyd and His Sons 192
Chapter 32. Little Edith and Lulu May 196
Chapter 33. Reaching Out in Salt Lake City 203
Chapter 34. Thoughts about Death 205
Interlude 5: Narrative 207

Epilogue 217

Appendix A: Chronology of Important Events in the Life of Edith V. P. Hudley 219
Appendix B: Important People in the Life of Edith V. P. Hudley 222
Appendix C: Notes for Students 225

Index 229

> Train up a child in the way he should go: and
> when he is old, he will not depart from it.
> —**Proverbs, 22:6 (King James version)**

> I KNOW the conditions under which you were born, for I was there. Your countrymen were NOT there, and haven't made it yet. Your grandmother was also there.... I suggest that the innocents check with her. She isn't hard to find.
> —**James Baldwin**, *The Fire Next Time*
> **(emphasis in the original)**

> The individuals who are part of that beloved community are already in our lives. We do not need to search for them. We can start where we are. We begin our journey with love, and love will always bring us back to where we started.
> —**bell hooks,** *Salvation*

PREFACE

When we first met Edith Hudley, we were struck by her passionate commitment to children and her ceaseless storytelling. Two intertwined desires animate Mrs. Hudley: to raise up children in the way they should go (to paraphrase her favorite passage from the book of Proverbs) and to bear witness to the lessons learned from a lifetime of caring for children. As developmental psychologists with an interest in narrative, we were fascinated.

Once we got to know her better, we realized that her life story is especially timely, given the currents that are reshaping the field of human development. Scholars and practitioners are more aware than ever that human development cannot be reduced to a single trajectory, that different social and cultural conditions create a multiplicity of developmental experiences for children. As the world grows smaller and local communities grow more ethnically and culturally diverse, there is heightened interest in building a foundation of knowledge that is deeply pluralistic.

The impetus for these changes comes from theoretical advances within developmental psychology and allied fields. And it comes from the changing nature and needs of the constituencies who enroll in human development courses: the increasingly diverse college student population, many of whom will become parents in the not too distant future, and the aspiring practitioners—social workers, teachers, clinicians—who want to be better informed about differences so that they can better support children's development.

How can we as teachers of human development adapt to these changes? What can we do to offer our students in the fields of social work, education, and psychology a more inclusive understanding of how people develop?

Scholars have responded to these questions by revamping their lectures to include research from a broader range of cultures and communities. They capitalize on the diversity in their classrooms by inviting students to reflect on their own upbringing and by encouraging them to listen to one another across the boundaries of culture, race, gender, and class. They use textbooks that weave findings from different groups into the discussion of standard topics and include "sidebars" that take up issues germane to particular groups.

All of these innovations help. And yet we often feel dissatisfied with our efforts to diversify the material that we teach: a glimpse of African-American families, a snapshot of Chinese classrooms, a gesture toward ethnic identity, dwarfed by the discussions of self-concept, self-esteem, and personal identity. These additions feel piecemeal, haphazard, and peripheral to a substantive core that remains stubbornly mainstream. Where are the in-depth treatments of other ways of life that would stir students' imaginations? What could be done to encourage students to recognize the cultural nature of their own experiences and to enter vicariously into other people's experiences?

This is why we need Edith Hudley. As James Baldwin said of another grandmother, she was *there*. We can check with her if we want to learn about the conditions that shaped her life and the lives of her offspring. Her story, presented and responded to in the pages that follow, offers readers the opportunity for sustained engagement with her world. It is a world in which children's experience and parents' child-rearing practices are inflected through African-American and Christian systems of meaning. Although her story is autobiographical, encompassing the whole sweep of her life, it is not, strictly speaking, an autobiography. It is instead a life story or oral history, which is to say, a set of stories told orally and subsequently translated into written form by us, her coauthors.

Mrs. Hudley's story is considerably longer than the research reports that we have offered our students in the past. However, length is not really the point. The pedagogical value of her contribution lies in its narrative power. Often narrative is thought to mirror an external reality. From this vantage point, Edith Hudley's story provides a window into historical events—what was it like to grow up in rural Texas in the pre-Civil Rights era?—or subjective experiences—how did she cope with the loss of her mother?

But this reflective view does not do justice to narrative as a creative act. Conjuring trumps reporting for Mrs. Hudley, as for all master storytellers. She crafts scenes and populates them with living, breathing people. She mounts arguments and orchestrates perspectives and personas. Before long, readers find themselves inhabiting these scenes, hearing these voices, imagining these ways of raising children. And they come to know Edith Hudley herself, who she is and has been and what she stands for. We hope that these encounters will move readers to enter into a conversation with her about how to cultivate children's development.

ACKNOWLEDGMENTS

Many people have had a hand in bringing this book to fruition, and it is a pleasure to acknowledge them here. Barbara Bowman, Jean Briggs, Suzanne Gaskins, Artin Goncu, Randolph Potts, Julian Rappaport, Jill Kagle, and Joseph Tobin discussed the project with us at various points along the way or provided feedback on early drafts. We appreciate their careful reading, incisive criticism, and generosity.

We are also grateful to our colleagues in the Language and Culture Group at the University of Illinois at Urbana-Champaign, especially Michele Koven, Daena Goldsmith, Janet Keller, and Irene Koshik for their encouragement and their constructive criticism of portions of the book.

Carl Johnson, Edward Taylor, and Karen Wyche served as formal reviewers of the manuscript. Their commentary was invaluable: comprehensive, penetrating, and sympathetic.

We began to write this book in 1998-1999 when Peggy Miller was on sabbatical from the Departments of Speech Communication and Psychology at the University of Illinois at Urbana-Champaign, and we completed the final revisions in 2001-2002 during Wendy Haight's sabbatical from the School of Social Work at the University of Illinois at Urbana-Champaign. The initial draft of the introduction was written while Miller was in residence at The Poet's House in New Harmony, Indiana, in the spring of 1999. During her sabbatical year, Haight was a visitor at Brigham Young University, where she benefited from many thoughtful discussions with psychology faculty, especially Erin Bigler, and generous access to excellent facilities. We gratefully acknowledge the support of these institutions.

We thank Cindy Workman for her meticulous transcription of the audio recordings of Edith Hudley's stories, Dorothy Anderson for her expert copyediting, and Susana Vazquez-Weigel, who provided able and cheerful assistance with every phase in the production of the manuscript.

Finally, we owe a debt of gratitude to David Follmer for his unstinting support of this book and for his patience. We especially appreciate David as a creative thinker. In his role as publisher he seeks out and embraces innovative, interdisciplinary projects, and we have been the beneficiaries.

INTRODUCTION

Edith Valerie Patton was born in 1920 on a small family farm in Kennard, Texas. The sixth of eight surviving children and the youngest girl, Edith was her mother's helper and apprentice. At an age when many children are still in preschool, Edith washed diapers on a washboard, churned butter, pieced quilts, and baked cakes. "Honey, I was a worrisome little child coming up. I wanted to know *everything*. My mother used to say, 'Lord, Mr. Aaron, that's the nosiest little child we've got.' I could hear them talking, and I would try to get to where I could eavesdrop."

When Edith was ten, her mother, Mamie, died from complications of childbirth, and she was called upon to help her father raise her younger brothers. Aaron realized that he would have to be father and mother to Edith, but, he did not face this challenge alone.

When his daughter brought him questions that he found inappropriate for a father to answer, Aaron would say, "I'll have to get back to you on that one." A little while later, a female relative or one of the women from the community would approach Edith with the answer. These "other mothers" played a crucial role in guiding Edith through the perils of impending womanhood. Their devotion set into motion what would become a lifelong pattern. Later, when Edith moved to Houston and then to Oakland, she sought out "other mothers," stalwarts of the church, who were willing to provide the support and guidance that she needed. Eventually, Edith became an "other mother" to younger women, thereby claiming her rightful link in the chain of mothering.

This book tells the story of Edith Hudley's life, largely in her own words. Because she has spent much of her life caring for children—her brothers, sons, grandchildren, and "adopted" offspring—this book is also about child rearing.

Why do we need another book about child rearing, and why would readers want to learn about Edith Hudley's experiences? Our answers are rooted in our commitments as developmental psychologists and social work educators. There is growing awareness that children cannot be understood apart from the cultural and historical contexts that shape their lives. This is true of all children, but because African-American children and other minorities have been underrepresented in studies of child development, the need to imagine the contexts of their lives is especially urgent.

We believe that Edith Hudley's story will stimulate readers' imaginations. It may prompt you to question, enlarge, or reaffirm certain assumptions about child rearing or take a second look at what you thought another parent or child was up to. These imaginative forays are critical for understanding human development and for cultivating the kind of perspective taking that is fundamental to social work.

A compelling storyteller with a prodigious memory, Mrs. Hudley brings past and present contexts to life. Indeed, her storytelling demonstrates that it is impossible to segregate the two. A danger or a grief experienced decades ago or a word of wise advice from a long-dead parent intermingle with the present, informing what a parent does in the here-and-now. Although Edith's experiences of growing up in the deep South and of raising her sons elsewhere have much in common with others of her generation, they are uniquely hers. She tells a personal story, and personal stories invite personal responses.

A Life Grounded in Religious Faith

Edith Hudley has strong opinions about child rearing. At the most basic level, however, her message to her many offspring is the same message that she received from the family and community into which she was born: religious faith is the most important force in life, the compass by which all conduct is oriented. It is impossible to be in Mrs. Hudley's presence without becoming aware of the strength and radiance of her religious conviction. This is no vague abstraction; her faith is alive in the moment-by-moment play of her thoughts and feelings, her ceaseless storytelling, her daily actions.

At the heart of Mrs. Hudley's religious conviction is a bred-in-the-bone belief in the power of love to anchor and transform. Edith Hudley always knew that her parents loved her. That experience has remained a lifelong touchstone, fueling her determination to put love to work wherever possible. Her life story speaks to bell hooks' (2001) call for a return to an ethic of love in child rearing and in the struggle for racial justice. Hudley redeems hooks' faith that "unrecognized visionaries" are in our midst (p. 255).

Although Mrs. Hudley's commitment to love is evident throughout her life story, it is most clearly articulated in response to the racism that she and her family experienced. "[My parents] taught us all the time, 'Don't hate nobody.' Now, that was one thing I praise God for, that they brought that to us, 'Don't hate people, regardless of what they do to you. . . .' Leave it to God and He'll fix it. I used to wonder, 'Why do they tell us to leave it to God? How come God haven't fixed it already? Well, Papa, how come He haven't already fixed it?' He said, 'He'll fix it in his own dear time.' "

As Edith Hudley's adult life unfolded, male-female relations severely tested her commitment to love. This motivated her to raise her sons to respect women and to make sure that they got the sex education that they needed.

For Edith Hudley, expressions of faith arise in connection with specific personal experiences, both positive and negative. One of the most striking features of her life story and approach to raising children is that she does not sentimentalize or deny the realities of life, however ugly. The concrete brutalities of racism and of male domination are acknowledged so that children can be forearmed with knowledge and with practical strategies for handling predictable dangers. We marveled at the frankness with which she—and her parents before her—discussed with their children matters that many families keep hidden.

How This Book Came to Be Written

This book owes its existence to the long-standing relationships among the three authors. Wendy Haight first met Edith Hudley in June 1992, three days after the birth of her daughter, Camilla. "My husband and I had moved to Salt Lake City with our three-year-old son, Matthew, the previous year to begin new jobs. We were apprehensive about moving our biracial family to this area. Upon our arrival, we were directed to First Baptist Church, a center of the African-American Utahn community.

"When Camilla arrived, somewhat earlier than we expected, the pastor, as well as Camilla's godmother, Alzie, both urged us to speak with Mrs. Edith Hudley. The pastor informed us that Mrs. Hudley had done more for children than anyone he knew. She was an old-fashioned church mother who took responsibility for all of the children in her community. Alzie said that Mrs. Hudley loved children and that she would always be there for the whole family. Needless to say, I immediately sought her out. She told me to bring the babies by her house. Of course she would care for them while I worked. And, she would teach them to call her, 'Grandma.'

"Over the next three years, I came to enjoy my time at Grandma Edith's house as much as my children did. As we cared for Matthew and Camilla, Edith recounted her own experiences as a child, parent, and grandparent. Listening to these stories, I worried about how my children, or children of any ethnicity, could grow up healthy in racist America. As I listened more closely, it became clear that for Edith, socialization is rooted in spirituality, strongly held and deeply felt personal beliefs about the meaning of life, including an ultimate love, which all may receive, and an ultimate justice, to which all are accountable.

"Subsequently, I began to do research, in my professional role of developmental psychologist, on the spiritual socialization of African-American children [Haight, 1998, 2002]. I wanted to understand how individuals like Edith have thrived despite profound, ongoing stress and then to consider the implications for parents, teachers, and social workers involved in the day-to-day socialization of children. Very little systematic research has explored the strengths of African-American children, their families, and communities, including the ways in which African-American adults, like Edith, socialize resilience. However, at this point, my research did not focus specifically on Edith but rather on the Sunday School at First Baptist Church."

Wendy introduced Peggy Miller to Edith in September of 1997. Edith had come to Urbana to visit with Wendy and her family, and Wendy thought Peggy would be fascinated by Edith's storytelling. Peggy and Wendy had known each other for a dozen years. Peggy was Wendy's advisor in graduate school, and the two have been friends and colleagues ever since (Haight & Miller, 1992, 1993).

"Wendy brought Edith to my house for tea one morning. Although I have studied oral storytelling for much of my career, I had never before met anyone with such a passion to share her experience. The purpose of her storytelling, she soon made clear to me, was didactic. She wanted the next generation to learn, as she had done, from her exemplary parents. And she wanted to pass on lessons from her own life so that younger people could see, and be nourished by, how God has worked through her.

"I was reminded, as I listened to Edith, of the book *Motherwit* that I have used in my courses in communication and psychology at the University of Illinois. *Motherwit* is Onnie Lee Logan's (1989) life story. Born in 1910 into a large African-American family in rural Alabama, accorded few opportunities for formal education, Logan spent her life delivering babies in and around Mobile. "I'd rather see a baby be born in the world than to eat if I'm hungry," she said (p. 48). Like Logan, Edith has had a profound effect on many children and sees her life's work as an expression of her Christian faith. In my classes, I found that Logan's life story struck a chord with students from a variety of cultural backgrounds. What is it about her that these young adults find so arresting? Perhaps her sense of vocation."

"In an e-mail conversation the next day, we came up with the idea of writing a book with Edith. Wendy broached the matter with her. Would she be interested in working with us to write a book about her life and experiences raising children? We were not surprised when she agreed enthusiastically: she had enjoyed talking to Wendy's psychology students at the University of Utah and was delighted when Wendy quoted her in a paper that she wrote about First Baptist Church. These activities allowed Edith to reach a wider audience, and a book would do the same.

"Interviewing" Edith Hudley

A few days later we sat at Wendy's kitchen table, with two tape recorders and the few remaining slices of Edith's sweet potato pie. (She had baked and distributed a dozen pies to Matthew and Camilla's classrooms.) We asked her to tell the story of her life any way she wanted to tell it. She proceeded to talk nonstop for four hours. During this time, she did not eat or drink or get up to stretch. In fact, she barely moved except to use her hands to picture events she was narrating. We listened and drank tea, and occasionally Wendy managed to interject a question. Three hours into the recording session, we devoured the pie. When Peggy left an hour later, walking home in a daze, Edith was still going strong. After a break for dinner, Edith talked on to Wendy, with Matthew and Camilla occasionally in attendance. Wendy had had the foresight to purchase a large supply of audiotapes. By the end of the day, twelve were filled.

This first recording session taught us that one does not really interview Edith Hudley. Although she had never before narrated so much of her life in a single sitting, her stories had a shape that had been honed over multiple tellings. We tried to respect the integrity of her tellings by not interrupting or redirecting her talk. Such interventions would not have worked, anyway. Interviewers usually worry about how to get the interviewee to talk; with Edith the challenge is to figure out how to get the floor.

A few months later, in January 1998, we visited Edith in Salt Lake City. Our daughters, Camilla, age five, and Kathleen, age ten, accompanied us. We collected another eleven hours of recording. Again, our goal was to listen and to keep our interventions to a minimum. This time, however, we had some questions that we were determined to ask. We wanted to check our understanding of certain events in Hudley's life, and we had a concern that we wanted to discuss with her.

Two (White) Coauthors?

The concern was this: How did Edith feel about teaming up with two white women to tell her life story? Did she have any reservations or second thoughts about this project and our role in it? These questions arose from issues within the academic disciplines that have shaped our commitments as scholars and teachers. (Behar, 1993; Clifford & Marcus, 1986; Fine, 1994; Wolf, 1992). One of these issues concerns who can rightfully study whom. Given the realities of race and class is it acceptable ethically for a white person to study a black person, for a formally educated person to study one without formal education, for a person who has access to certain forms and audiences of professional discourse to study someone who does not? Would it even be *possible* for a person whose background and life experiences are radically different—who did not grow up in the deep South, who has not experienced racism firsthand, who is from a younger generation—to come to know that other person?

Wendy broached our concern toward the end of our four-day marathon recording session in Salt Lake City. She told Edith that some of her colleagues had objected to this project on the grounds that it is inherently exploitative for two white women to work with a black woman on her story. How did Edith feel about this?

> Edith: Well, you know what? We are all his children. He created us all, regardless of what color we are, we are sisters in Christ. So, He didn't say, "I'm gonna make you this color and I'm gonna make you this color and you sisters this color and you sisters that color." We all was created through Him and by Him. So, if we all was created by him, why can't we all be sisters? You see what I'm sayin? God created us all—we have the love for each other—that we can't we be sisters? You see?

> Wendy: Well, some people, when they read our book are going to have a hard time with that.

> Edith: Well, they'll just have a hard time with that. They just got to pray a little bit more and search their hearts a little bit more, you see what I'm sayin? Because, God created everybody. Now, He didn't create me to hate you, He didn't create you to hate me, it's the individual that do that.... He said, "Love ye one another as I have loved you."

> Wendy: Some people are gonna criticize this though—

> Edith: Well, I don't care! If they criticize it, they need to go back there on their knees and ask God to forgive them.

Wendy pursued this line of questioning further, but Edith would not give an inch. She simply will not grant that the racial divide necessarily makes a whit of difference between individuals, a position that coexists comfortably with her unflinching recognition of racism and of the toll it has taken on her life. Edith's enthusiasm for this project, her conviction that we could work together, and her trust in our judgment have allayed our doubts about our role in this undertaking and have sustained us throughout.

It may sound odd to say that Edith had to allay *our* doubts. This seems to deny the very power differential between researcher and subject that scholars have rightly insisted must be acknowledged. But the issue of power is never simple, and in this case, the greater power that we have, by virtue of our education and professional status, could not diminish another asymmetry in which the greater power, indisputably, lay in Edith's hands. Within the structure of moral authority that Edith has always recognized—in which the older and wiser instruct the younger—we are the ones in need of guidance. What was Wendy thinking, taking a three-day-old baby to church? The reason that Peggy can't make pie dough is that she has no patience!

And there is still another circumstance that allowed us to work together. Edith embraced this project from its outset because it dovetails with the animating purpose of her life: to share her wisdom and to make a difference in other people's lives: "I thank God for what He did for me, for keepin this within, that I can tell somebody else. And maybe it can help somebody else 'cause that's the way my parents brought me up." From this standpoint, we are not so much researchers as midwives. Our role is to assist Edith in bringing forth her vision—a vision that is already fully formed—to a larger audience.

Audiences for This Book

Because Edith Hudley's understandings about how to raise children are deeply rooted in African-American experience, we hope that her story will be interesting to parents and grandparents of African-American children. Christian believers—especially those who affiliate with the Baptist church—will hear familiar echoes and may find inspiration in a child rearing philosophy that is informed by faith. Yet Edith Hudley's message is not limited to black Americans or to Christians. Her understanding of how to combat racism (or hatred of any kind), of how to raise adolescents to be respectful of the opposite sex, of how to discipline children—is worthy of consideration by anyone who wants to raise strong and loving children in twenty-first-century America.

Introduction

As scholars, we hope to reach several professional audiences as well, especially social workers, but also educators and clinicians, who daily face the challenges of enhancing children's growth and wellbeing. In each of these fields there is a growing effort to ground policy and practice in knowledge of the variety of pathways toward healthy development that different cultural and ethnic traditions promote. We provide examples of how we responded to Mrs. Hudley's story and sketch some of the questions and implications that her life poses for social workers: differentiating between physical discipline and physical abuse, coordinating mentoring for teen mothers, and making religious resources available to ill children.

We also provide examples of how to integrate two important research traditions within social work: quantitative research, a cornerstone of modern, empirically based social work, and qualitative, case-based understandings. Many of our students have difficulty relating quantitative and qualitative approaches, often referring to quantitative "or" qualitative approaches and identifying themselves with a perceived superior tradition. This is hardly surprising since scholarship in the social sciences is similarly polarized. For us, however, the boundaries between quantitative and qualitative approaches are blurred. Effective practice requires a dual focus on the context of particular cases and on group trends.

It also requires a broader and deeper understanding of the plurality of developmental trajectories, particularly those that are available to children from minority backgrounds. Practitioners and policymakers look to the field of human development for insights into how socioeconomic and cultural contexts shape children. However, as developmental psychologists by training and cultural psychologists by inclination, we know that African-American voices are heard too little in these fields of inquiry. The latest edition of the preeminent reference volume on child psychology reports that the number of studies involving African-American samples in mainstream developmental journals is very small and has decreased from 1970 to 1990, a state of affairs that itself deserves study (Fisher, Jackson, & Villarruel, 1998). When African-American children and parents are studied, they are often portrayed as disadvantaged or at risk. Although many of these studies originate in a desire to address the poverty that disproportionately affects African-American children, the focus on vulnerability risks reinforcing powerful negative stereotypes of black Americans. Accurate, compassionate, and unbiased understanding of children's lives and life conditions—isn't that what scholars of child development hope to promote? And yet this goal, as it applies to African-American children and their families, is undermined by several other patterns in the literature: the lack of study of middle-class black children, invidious comparisons of minority children with their more privileged counterparts, and descriptions that fail to take into account the socioeconomic, cultural, and historical contexts that would render children's and parents' actions intelligible.

Although the importance of context is widely acknowledged, scholars sometimes dismiss as "unobjective" work that attempts to understand the experiences of African-American families on their own terms. When such work prominantly portrays individuals' strengths, it may be treated as especially suspect: the researcher must be operating out of a biased political agenda. Yet, in a curious case of myopia, when research systematically omits the experiences and meaning systems of poor and minority children, it may not be recognized as serving, however inadvertently, its own political agenda.

Fortunately, there are some studies that do portray African-American families on their own terms. Edith Hudley's enduring ties to family and to other "kin" who are not related biologically (her beloved "other mothers") will remind some readers of Carol Stacks' classic work *All Our Kin* (1974). Her prodigious storytelling can be seen as her own continuation of African-American traditions of oral narrative, of which many fine studies and compendiums exist (Etter-Lewis, 1993; Davis & Gates, 1991; Goss & Barnes, 1989; Goodwin, 1990; Heath, 1983; Labov, 1972; Shuman, 1986; Smitherman, 1986; Sperry & Sperry, 1996). The ways in which she finds strength in spirituality and religious community can be linked to an incipient literature on the role of spirituality in children's development (Coles, 1990; Haight, 1998; Hale-Benson, 1987; Zimmerman & Maton, 1992). Her commitment to education may bring to mind Diana Slaughter-Defoe's studies of middle-class black families as well as James Comer's biography of his mother (Lee & Slaughter-Defoe, 1995; Slaughter & Johnson, 1989; Comer, 1998).

A great deal can be learned by asking the larger question—how do African-American children and their families create meaningful lives?—instead of focusing narrowly on the difficulties of growing up black. The larger question is likely to lead toward a more capacious vision of child development and a more interesting set of research questions.

In short, we believe that as Edith Hudley narrates her experiences as daughter, wife, mother, divorced mother, "other mother," and grandmother she takes her place amidst the growing chorus of African-American voices who inform developmental psychology and allied arenas of practice. The study of child development will remain impoverished, and social work and educational and clinical practice will remain handicapped until these voices are heard. This does not mean that Edith stands as "spokeswoman" for an entire group. Like every human voice, hers is distinctive; shared values and interpretive frameworks are personalized within the idiosyncrasies of her experience. She speaks from her own corner within her own communities, but she reaches beyond, inviting other voices to respond.

Listening to Edith Hudley

The best way to hear Edith's stories is face-to-face in a familiar kitchen or at the back of the sanctuary after church. If one listens more than once, certain recurring themes will become apparent; key events in her life, some dating back more than seventy years, will be evoked again and again. Like many gifted storytellers, Edith has an uncanny ability to evoke the past. Who could be better than she at calling forth the people who shaped her life and fashioned her outlook: her mother, Mamie; her father, Aaron; her "other mother," Mother Ewing? By the end of our second recording session, they were nearly as alive as she was.

Encountered on more formal occasions, even once, Edith's words can leave a powerful impression. Following are typical excerpts from the ungraded, anonymous journals of undergraduate students—everyone was white and most were from middle-class backgrounds—following Edith's appearance in their child development class.

> It was really weird, but immediately I felt this great love for her. I don't even know her but I just felt absorbed by the love she radiated. She touched my life and I will never forget her....

> I was sort of amazed at how similar her beliefs were to mine. I mean, seventy-three-year-old African-American women don't usually have as similar belief systems as twenty-year-old white girls! That was a pretty stereotypical answer, but that was what I was thinking! I did come out of class being very inspired to keep on pushing forward and upward and to not let others make me feel inferior to them.

> Today's class was the most memorable period this quarter for me. Mrs. Hudley's philosophy of life and her exuberance were refreshing. I'm amazed that a person who has walked the road that she has walked can stand up and express such a powerful faith in her God and in herself. That she came from such a destitute and humble background and yet has a cheerful, can-do attitude that would make any middle-class, glad-handing motivational lecturer blush with envy. It is refreshing just being around her....

> Mrs. Edith Hudley came to class and spoke for about an hour. It was extremely interesting and quite entertaining. I laughed out loud several times. But, more importantly, I was affected by some of the thought provoking words of her father. Her father said, "Never get angry, and never hate—hate will destroy you." She went on to say that she was always told that God created [each of us] and left part of himself inside each person. If you hate, you lose that part....

These undergraduates said that they were touched, inspired, refreshed, provoked to think anew by their encounter with Edith Hudley. They spoke in terms that mesh with Mrs. Hudley's own intention of helping others by sharing her life experiences. Although they inhabited different worlds, these young (privileged, white) adults and this elderly (African-American) grandmother, both seemed to recognize that a particular genre—the inspirational life story—was in play.

Hearing and Not Hearing Edith Hudley

Is there a danger here? Might readers absorb Edith Hudley, the inspirational figure, into their stereotype of the virtuous, strong, black grandmother, facing innumerable obstacles, buoyed by religious faith, and ultimately undaunted? Might they thereby dismiss her as a stock character inhabiting a well-trod racial landscape? Some of our colleagues who share our goal of diversifying the study of child development argued that the match between Hudley's perspectives and white readers' stereotypes of how elderly black women think, talk, and raise their children is so close that it is bound to affirm racial stereotypes. From their perspective, there is an insuperable rhetorical challenge entailed in using Edith's life to discomfit racial stereotypes. Thus, our hope that readers (at least white readers) will be moved to take her words seriously, to respond to her unique voice, is hopelessly unrealistic. One colleague also raised the problem of age stereotypes, arguing that Hudley's advanced age "means that for young readers her wisdom will come across less as the beliefs of contemporary black Americans and more as an oral history of a quaint but antiquated and bygone era."

We were startled by these comments, because we had been thinking about Hudley's life story as a counterweight to the master narrative of risk and disadvantage. We saw her story as combating a racial stereotype implicit in a scholarly literature that tends to elide the strengths of African-American children and families. But by seeing Edith's story as a challenge to that master narrative, had we romanticized her?

Everywhere one looks, Edith Hudley's story keeps company with other stories, some of them deafening—master narratives of race, gender, and age; oral histories; inspirational tales; realist fiction. Mikhail Bakhtin (1981, 1986), the well-known discourse theorist and philosopher of language, said that our words are never entirely our own. To wrest one's own meaning from the discourses that surround and inhabit us, each of which is saturated with value and with the history of other people's voices, is next to impossible. In *Playing in the Dark*, Toni Morrison (1992) says, "there is no escape from racially inflected language" (p. 13).

This being the case, we can only forecast the challenge of active engagement with Edith Hudley's story and hope that readers will want to make that effort. Our hope rests, in part, on Hudley's exceptional powers of expression. Her eagerness to do this book implies a confidence in her own ability to command the attention of her audience. And why not? She has been doing that all her life in homes, churches, PTA meetings, and, more recently, college classrooms.

In this last venue, many of the students heard her words as relevant to their own lives—not as relics of some bygone era. In her memoir, *Talk to Me*, Anna Deavere Smith (2000) says that the problem is not so much that black people identify with white people but that such acts of empathy are seldom reciprocated. The fact that these students were moved to identify with Mrs. Hudley, again, prompts us to hope that others will do likewise. And although her inspirational message was appreciated by these students, it was not necessarily the only message discerned. Some responded to her playfulness.

It may be this quality—her vitality and sense of fun—that children find so compelling. During one of our visits, Camilla begged Grandma Edith to do her hair in corn rows. The hair braiding session lasted about two hours during which time Camilla had to sit very still. Wendy offered to read a story, which Camilla rejected. Instead, with a naughty gleam in her eye and in excellent imitation of the church mothers, she intoned, "Dear *Lord*, help me sit still!" Edith clapped her hands, bent double giggling, then stood up and proceeded to elaborate (with a straight face), "Lord *Jesus* help my baby sit still so I can do this pretty braid straight!" Camilla picked right up on this, and they continued to "pray" back and forth for several minutes. Then Edith looked at Wendy and instructed, "Now, *this* is what ya'll should be taping!"

Edith Hudley, In Her Own Words

The experience of reading Hudley's stories cannot be the same as hearing and seeing her in the flesh, with all the tonalities, textures, and rhythms of real-life, whole-body communication. We have tried, nonetheless, to stay as faithful as possible to her own words. Twenty-three hours of audio recordings were transcribed verbatim, yielding 346 typed, single-spaced pages. As transcripts got done, we passed along copies to Edith. Although much is lost in reduction to the verbal medium alone, the transcript does preserve the flavor of spoken language and of Edith's individual style of expression. We are aware that there are complex sociolinguistic issues at stake in translating vernacular speech and performed oral narrative into written form (Bauman, 1986; Jaffe, 2000). We have aimed for expressive rather than linguistic accuracy, adopting conventions for rendering oral discourse (e.g., "gonna," "makin"), retaining repetitions and not altering grammatical constructions. These choices are intended to convey the artfulness of Edith Hudley's storytelling.

The biggest challenge as coauthors, has been to envision how a book could emerge from this mountain of transcripts. How to prune in a way that retains the essence of Edith's message and the conviction of her telling? Is there any way to accomplish this without intermingling our voices with hers? Obviously, this introduction is nothing if not an intermingling. Again, our words are never entirely our own (Bakhtin, 1981). In the chapters that form the body of this book we try, nonetheless, to let our voices recede as much as possible, to let the only audible voices be hers and those whom she invokes.

Still, our shadow voices are there in the choices that we made. How many chapters should there be? Which topics should be covered? Which passages should be included and which excluded, and how should these passages be juxtaposed? Should the book follow some overarching principles of organization, chronological or topical? Again, these choices were ours and even though Edith approved them, there is no denying that our hands shaped her story as it appears in this book.

Luckily for us, her tellings are not without signposts. Her habit of repetition was especially useful in highlighting which events were most significant to her. We heard Edith tell certain stories—about her mother's death, about the time that Mother Ewing pulled her back from the brink—again and again. Some of these stories recurred daily, and although each telling may have been nuanced differently, key phrases were sounded each time. This habit of repetition does not bespeak a faltering memory. Quite the contrary. It is closer to a kind of prayer or meditation, a way that Edith reminds herself of the timeless meanings and consolations of her life. In addition to these always relevant stories, other stories were revisited for several days running because of their aptness to current circumstances.

We have tried, then, to render Edith Hudley's storytelling in a way that preserves its origins as an oral text. Those who are unaccustomed to such "speakerly" texts may be surprised by the "sound" of casual speech, by unfamiliar grammatical constructions and turns of phrase, and by other features of her narrative performance. Like many accomplished storytellers, Hudley not only repeats favorite or momentous stories but also uses repetition as a stylistic device. For example, in the course of telling a story she might draw attention to a dramatic moment by recycling that moment, or she might repeat a choice line from a quoted conversation. Listen closely, and you may get caught up in the rhythms of her speech and hear echoes of the storytellers in your own life.

One additional quality of Edith Hudley's speakerly stories needs to be pointed out. Like many works of modern fiction, Hudley's stories do not necessarily follow a straight narrative line. She relates the mystery of Kathareen's parentage from several temporal vantage points. When invoking an event that happened in mid-life, she interposes advice received decades earlier. Sometimes Hudley steps back and surveys the whole of her life. Sometimes she notes how the meaning of an early event ripened in the wake of subsequent events. Although Edith Hudley's story is a story about the past, it is not just about the past. It is told and listened to in the perishing present and oriented to the future, undertaken in the hope that it will interest and enlighten.

Constructing a Hybrid Text

We hope to reach both a general readership and a more specialized audience of scholars and practitioners. How, then, to balance the needs of this dual readership? How to create a text that is accessible—

unencumbered by technical reference—yet locates her stories and reflections in a scholarly context?

Our solution to this dilemma, as it pertains to those who simply want to hear Edith Hudley tell her life story, was to create chapters that stand alone and to allow her words to flow, without interruption, from her childhood in rural Texas, through her adolescence, marriage, work in the shipyards of Oakland during World War II, raising her sons, divorcing her husband, remarriage, and so on. These numbered chapters are organized by chronologically ordered phases: "Childhood," "Youth," "Married Life," "Raising Children," and "Later Years." We preface each phase with a prelude that orients the reader to the setting, historical context, events, and people who figure importantly in this phase of Hudley's life.

For readers with a professional interest in child development, we punctuate Edith Hudley's life story with a series of scholarly interludes: each phase of her life is followed by an interlude, a pause for reflection on the cluster of chapters that preceded it. For example, after the several chapters comprising "Childhood," the reader encounters the first interlude: "Religion and Spirituality." The book thus follows a call and response structure. Mrs. Hudley tells a portion of her story, and we respond with perspectives from the relevant literature. Our intention is to enter into a dialogue with Hudley's story. Once again, Bakhtin has been our guide: If active understanding is a joint creation, then our task as listeners is to prepare a rejoinder (Morson & Emerson, 1990).

Other interludes take up the topics of oppression and resistance, mentoring, physical discipline, and narrative. In settling on these topics, we left out many others that deserve attention. We chose topics that represent a mix in terms of the distance between Mrs. Hudley's life story and the topics and issues currently in play in the fields of social work and human development. In *White Teacher*, a meditation on race and difference, Vivian Paley (2000) speaks of "unasked and unanswered questions" (p. 122). The first two interludes, "Religion and Spirituality" and "Oppression and Resistance," are oriented to these kinds of questions. These interludes invite readers to see how the ways in which Edith Hudley's life and perspectives on child rearing raise questions that rarely, if ever, get asked in the developmental literature. They point to whole arenas of life that are largely uncharted from a developmental perspective.

By contrast, the succeeding interludes on mentoring and physical punishment reveal a closer match between Mrs. Hudley's concerns and the concerns of scholars and practitioners. These interludes invite readers to revisit questions that have been asked but that deserve deeper answers. These are the interludes that speak most directly to social workers. Hudley's life story does not furnish recipes for intervention, but it does provide much needed context and perspective for some of the most vital issues in the practice of social work. For example, Edith Hudley enters into the debate about spanking as a passionate advocate for physical punishment. Some readers will not agree with her. However, her memories of what happened to black boys in rural Texas in the 1930s or in Oakland decades later whose parents did not discipline them show how she came to hold this position and what is at stake for her. They provide the context that allows readers who grew up in different worlds to imagine their way into hers.

The final interlude provides an opportunity to reflect on Edith Hudley's life story as a story. There are many different literatures on narrative; Hudley's story fits neatly in some and not so neatly in others. Once again, it raises fresh questions for developmental researchers and practitioners.

In sum, this book is constructed to allow readers to enter the text by two routes—as listeners to the story of Edith Hudley's life and as partners with her and with scholars and practitioners in a conversation about human development. Once readers enter her world, many pathways are opened.

References

Bakhtin, M.M. (1981). *The dialogic imagination*. Austin, TX: University of Texas Press.

Bauman, R. (1986). *Story, performance, and event: Contextual studies of oral narrative*. New York: Cambridge University Press.

Behar, R. (1993). *Translated woman: Crossing the border with Esperanza's story*. Boston: Beacon Press.

Clifford, J., & Marcus, G.E. (Eds.). (1986). *Writing culture: The poetics and politics of ethnography.* Berkeley: University of California Press.

Coles, R. (1990). *The spiritual lives of children.* Boston: Houghton Mifflin.

Comer, J.P. (1998). *Maggie's American dream: The life and times of a black family.* New York: Plume.

Davis, C.T., & Gates, H.L., Jr. (Eds.). (1991). *The slave's narrative.* New York: Oxford University Press.

Etter-Lewis, G. (1993). *My soul is my own: Oral narratives of African-American women in the professions.* New York: Routledge

Fine, M. (1994). Working the hyphens: Reinventing self and other in qualitative research. In N. Denzin & Y. Lincoln (Eds.), *Handbook of qualitative research.* Thousand Oaks, CA: Sage.

Fisher, C., Jackson. J., & Villarruel, F. (1998). The study of African American and Latin American children and youth. In W. Damon (Ed.), *Handbook of child psychology.* New York: John Wiley.

Goodwin, M.H. (1990). *He-said-she-said: Talk as social organization among black children.* Bloomington, IN: Indiana University Press.

Goss, L., & Barnes, M. (1989). *Talk that talk: An anthology of African-American storytelling.* New York: Simon and Schuster.

Haight, W. (1998). Gathering the spirit: Spiritual socialization as a protective factor in the lives of African American children. *Social Work, 43,* 213-222.

Haight, W. (2002). *African-American children at church: A sociocultural perspective.* Cambridge: Cambridge University Press.

Haight, W., & Miller, P. (1992). The development of everyday pretend play: A longitudinal study of mothers' participation. *Merrill-Palmer Quarterly, 38,* 331-349.

Haight, W., & Miller, P. (1993). *Pretending at home: Development in sociocultural context.* Albany: State University of New York Press.

Hale-Benson, J. (1987). *The transmission of faith to young black children.* Paper presented at the Conference on Faith Development in Early Childhood. (Henderson, NC, December 8-11).

Heath, S. (1983). *Ways with words: Language, life, and work in communities and classrooms.* New York: Cambridge University Press.

hooks, b. (2001). *Salvation: Black people and love.* New York: William Morrow.

Jaffe, A. (2000). Introduction: Non-standard orthography and non-standard speech. *Journal of Sociolinguistics, 4* (4), 497-513.

Labov, W. (1972). *Language in the inner city.* Philadelphia: University of Pennsylvania Press.

Lee, C., & Slaughter-Defoe, D. (1995). Historical and sociocultural influences on African American education. In J. Banks & C. Banks (Eds.) *Handbook of research on multicultural education.* New York: Simon & Schuster Macmillan.

Logan, O. (1989). *Motherwit: An Alabama midwife's story.* New York: Penguin.

Morrison, T. (1992). *Playing in the dark: Whiteness and the literary imagination.* New York: Vintage Books.

Morson, G.S., & Emerson, C. (1990). *Mikhail Bakhtin: Creation of a prosaics*. Stanford, CA: Stanford University Press.

Paley, V.G. (2000). *White teacher*. Cambridge, MA: Harvard University Press.

Shuman, A. (1986). *Storytelling rights: The uses of oral and written texts by urban adolescents*. Cambridge: Cambridge University Press.

Slaughter, D., & Johnson, D. (Eds.). (1989). *Visible now: blacks in private schools*. New York: Greenwood Press.

Smith, A.D. (2000). *Talk to me: Listening between the lines*. New York: Random House.

Smitherman, G. (1986). *Talkin and testifying: The language of black America*. Detroit, MI: Wayne State University Press.

Sperry, L., & Sperry, D. (1996). Early development of narrative skills. *Cognitive Development, 11*, 443–465.

Stack, C.B. (1974). *All our kin: Strategies for survival in a black community*. New York: Harper & Row.

Wolf, M. (1992). *A thrice told tale: Feminism, postmodernism, and ethnographic responsibility*. Stanford, CA: Stanford University Press.

Zimmerman, M.A., & Maton, K.I. (1992). Life-style and substance use among male African-American urban adolescents: A cluster analytic approach. *American Journal of Community Psychology, 20*, 121–138.

Part 1

Childhood

Part one of Mrs. Hudley's oral history encompasses her childhood from 1920 to 1935, which she spent "in the country" on a small family farm. The farm included a four-room home built by Edith's father, Aaron, which housed his wife, Mamie, and their eight children. The house did not have indoor plumbing or electricity and was heated by a fireplace. The family farm was on the "Patton tract," land set aside by the "white Pattons" (former slave owners) at the end of slavery to be passed along to the "black Pattons" (former slaves) over the generations. From this land, Aaron and Mamie fed their family and raised cotton for cash. Aaron also did a variety of jobs within the community for cash, including making railroad ties, digging wells, and picking cotton. The farm faced the woods and was surrounded on three sides by fields. From her home, Edith could see four other homes, the family farms of relatives. Transportation was by foot, mule, or mule-drawn wagon. Mrs. Hudley estimates that when she was growing up, her community consisted of twenty families who had lived on the land from slavery times. Some owned their land as did the Pattons, and others were share croppers, that is, tenant farmers who received a share of the value of crops minus charges for housing, seeds, tools, and so on. Throughout this community, Edith was known as "Aaron Patton's baby daughter" or "Little Mamie."

The Patton tract was approximately 16 miles outside of Kennard, Texas, in Houston County. Kennard was settled in the 1850s around a small sawmill that shut down the year of Edith's birth. Much of the area eventually was sold to the federal government and reforested in the 1930s to become part of the Davy Crockett National Forest. Although the closing of the mill had a profound impact on the economy of Kennard, the population remained stable through the 1930s. During Edith's childhood, Kennard had a population of approximately six hundred and had eight general stores, a bank, a hotel, a drugstore, and a school (Bishop, 2001). This is the town to which Edith and her family traveled to shop and do their business.

Edith Hudley grew up during segregation times. As a child, Edith wondered why it was that she worked alongside of whites in the fields but she was not allowed to attend the same school. She did not question that the whites attended a different church, but wondered why they would come to her church to hear the singing. In town, Edith was not permitted to try on shoes in the white-owned store or to drink, eat, swim, or use toilets in "whites only" facilities.

During Mrs. Hudley's childhood, blacks were excluded from the political system. For example, in some places blacks (but not whites) had to pass literacy tests in order to vote. In Texas and many other southern states, poll taxes eliminated most blacks from the voting rolls. Blacks also were kept from participating in the political system through terrorist activities, including those of the Ku Klux Klan (Johnson, 1997).

Mrs. Hudley's childhood occurred in the heyday of the Ku Klux Klan. In the early 1920s, the Klan numbered over 3 million people and had expanded to become nearly a national organization. Its goal was to reassert the dominance of the white Protestant community through whipping, torture, and even murder (Johnson, 1997). Nationwide, Mrs. Hudley's home state of Texas ranks third (behind Mississippi and Georgia and ahead of Louisiana and Alabama) in the number of recorded deaths by lynching. In the 1920s and 1930s lynching was considered by whites to be a form of interracial social control and recreation rather than crime, and hence law enforcement was uneven and ineffectual. Although the number of recorded deaths by lynching declined in the twentieth century, there nevertheless were seventy-six black deaths in 1919, twenty-three in 1926, and twenty-four in 1933. Note that these statistics refer to *recorded* lynchings resulting in *death*. Some lynchings were not recorded, and some "only" involved torture and dismemberment (Zangrando, 1991). However, it is important to note that the Klan of the 1920s and 1930s, for all of its hype and hatred, failed to deflect the nation's progress toward a pluralistic, democratic society (Trelease, 1992).

Edith's experience of this cultural and historical context was complex. She describes whites and blacks in her rural, southern community as "tied" by common ancestors. From an early age she recognized that this common ancestry was a result of the rape of her ancestors (e.g., Aunt Sarah) by white men in slavery times, and she also enjoyed the kindness of the white Pattons of her own childhood. The "white Pattons" recognized the "black Pattons" as relatives and assisted them in times of need. For example, after Mamie's death they employed Edith's older brothers, looked out for Edith when she conducted errands in town, and helped the family with transportation. Although these people and many other whites treated Edith's family with kindness and humanity, she reports that other whites were "salty"—they would "look right through you." Some were even dangerous.

When reading part 1, you may find it helpful to refer to Appendix A, which outlines several key events in Mrs. Hudley's childhood. Edith enjoyed her position as baby of the family until the birth of a brother in 1926 and another brother in 1928. In 1927, at the age of seven, Edith enrolled in an all black elementary school. In 1930, Edith's mother, Mamie, died at the age of forty-one from complications of childbirth. In 1931, the family home burned down, and extended family and other community members housed the family and provided food and clothing until Aaron could rebuild.

Appendix B lists a number of people who figured prominently in Mrs. Hudley's childhood. Mrs. Hudley's parents, Aaron Franklin Patton (1880-1946) and Mamie E. Scott Patton (1889-1930), were deeply loved and have remained powerful role models throughout her life. There were a number of other adults who stepped in to help the family after Mamie's death, including Edith's godmother, Mama Carrie, and Aaron's sisters, Aunt Mollie and Aunt Martie. During Mamie's two year illness, Edith loved and cared for her baby brothers, Oliver Wendell and Willie Oscar, beginning her lifetime passion for raising children. Nor was Edith, herself, without the care and guidance of older children and adolescents, including her older siblings—Ruth, Andrew, Percell, Mary Sterling, and Margie Louise—and her beloved and admired godbrother, Harvey.

For students and teachers, Appendix C raises a variety of topics for thought, discussion, and further study. These issues are designed to complement coursework in social work (especially Human Behavior in the Social Environment and Women, Society, and Social Welfare Issues), education, human development, and developmental psychology.

References

Bishop, E.H. (2001). Kennard, TX. *The Handbook of Texas Online.* http://www.tsha.utexas.edu/handbook/online/articles/view/KK/hlk6.html

Johnson, P. (1997). *A history of the American people.* New York: Harper Perennial.

Trelease, A. (1992). Ku Klux Klan. In E. Foner & J. Garraty (Eds.), *The readers companion to American history.* Boston: Houghton-Mifflin.

Zangrando, R. (1991). Lynching. In E. Foner & J. Garraty (Eds.), *The readers companion to American history.* Boston: Houghton-Mifflin.

Chapter 1

FAMILY

Mother's father died when she was young, and that is one reason why Mother married as young as she did, 'cause Grandmother remarried. She [Edith's mother, Mamie] had had three brothers that died—Aaron, Alfred, and Solomon. They was young. And I asked Papa, "What did they die from?" And he said, "Baby, it was hard times," he says, "and them children just didn't get enough to eat and develop like they should. And that was what they died from." Grandma was havin a hard time, and she had a big family when her husband died, and these three kids went behind him. And then she turned around and married again and started havin a family again. And Papa said that man [Grandmother's second husband] wasn't doin nothin but goin fishin and killin the rabbits and squirrels and feedin Grandma and those children. [Laughs] Lord have mercy! I hate to laugh about it, but Papa said he was the laziest man! He said, "I went and helped Mama [his mother-in-law] lots of times"—he called her "Mama"—, "I went and helped Mama lots of times with the farmin and everything," he said. And that's what caused my mother to want to get out and marry at a young age. Mother was sixteen when she married my dad, and at that day and time, a man had to be twenty-one before they considered him of bein a man to marry. Not like the young kids now, say nineteen and twenty. He was twenty-one and Mama was sixteen. And see, Mama start in havin childrens too young. That's what cut her life short.

My dad's family was very close, they was very close. Both Mother and my dad's side of the family was very close. When one needed, the other was there. I remember some of my dad's sisters that had growed up before I was born and that was away from home. And if one said, "I need you," they made it their business for somebody in their family to get to them. I remember several of my dad's relatives that passed away when they was away from home. And I don't know why they always got in touch with my [dad]. My dad was one of the main ones that would have to go and see that this is done, or that's done, or they'd get their body back home.

So, that's the way they brought their childrens up to, if one was in need, you reach out and you help. Because I remember times when my dad had a sister and she was, I think she was livin in Houston or Conrow. But, at that day and time, that was a long way from home, when you didn't have no way of gettin around to get there. And, she needed to come home. And the way money was flowin, you had to work—a grown man makin 75 cents a day. And sometimes it was less, dependin on the type of work you'd do.

Well, my dad, he would dig wells, he'd do cisterns and things like that. And if he wasn't doin that, he was makin railroad ties. My daddy kept himself busy. Somebody needed some wood and most all of the whites had these wood stoves, and my daddy was cuttin wood. He would cut wood for them, or for the stove and the fireplace.

So he would make extra money where other peoples wasn't makin any money. So, my dad was keepin this little change comin in. But Mother was the best manager. She could manage and handle the money better than my dad. So, when he'd make it, that was to Sweetheart. Sweetheart was home havin babies and raisin a family when he was out from one job to another. He knowed how to do so many things that when he wasn't doin one, he was doin the other. Sometimes it wasn't that much, but it was enough to keep the family goin.

But, all in all, the families was tied. When they marry in this family and this family, they was tied. The whole family. If one needed, they all needed. That's the way they was, and they would go to each other's rescue. And that's the way my daddy and my mother brought us up to be.

And, from a child, where I was born—if I could go back and take those pictures—ya'll would be *shocked*. I was born in Texas, back in the woods, where my daddy built this house himself. And I can see that house. It was a four-room house with a hall in between. It was two rooms on one side and two on the other. When you come in, you enter into the first room. We called it the big room. It had a fireplace in this room, that was the main sittin room. And it was two beds in that room. Mama's sewin machine was in that room, chairs. From that room there was a door goin to the kitchen. And in the kitchen was a window that you pushed over—we didn't have no glass—it was made from these wooden swingin windows.

My daddy made the table. We had a long table. He made this bench on one side that was next to the wall on that side. Then he had a glass window on this side, where the table was, where the bench was along this length of the table. And this end of the table was near a door that went outside in the hall, and then on the other end was another window, but it was a swing window where mother could open and swing back. And her workin table—she had another table that was where she worked—and the stove sit over here in this corner.

My dad was a wonderful dad. He got a fourth grade education. He was his daddy's oldest son. He was from a large family. My mother's from a large family. He used to have to stay home and help his dad, but other brothers and sisters was goin to school. He got a fourth grade education, but I want you to know, my daddy could count money fast, and I used to laugh at him. [Laughs] "Two bits, four bits, six bits. Two bits, four bits, six bits," and he could count in his head faster than I could put it on paper. But, now he couldn't put it on the paper as fast as I could. But Papa could count anything in his head, faster. Honey, my daddy had it. I said, "Oh, if I had the brains that he had when he was comin up!"

Papa could tell you how many pounds of cotton it was gonna take to make a bale. When they got seeds in it, you know its heavy. All right, you got to go and gin that cotton. He could tell you how many pounds of cotton it gonna take, with the seeds in, to have a bale of cotton with the seeds out. How much it would have to be to weigh so much. He could figure all that out. He was *good* with his head. Oh my dad was good! A fourth grade education!

And my daddy could tell you things, and he'd say, "Just watch my word!" Now when he'd say, "Watch my word," I didn't want Papa to say that! 'Cause whatever he said would come true. It would come true now. Papa said, "Now just watch my word." And when he'd tell you something, sayin, "Just watch my word. Just watch it. 'Cause it gonna come true." And I used to ask him, "How do you know this?" He said, "Well," he say, "if you stay close enough to the Master, he'll warn you of things." And I think he had that inner connection there. That he felt things, and he could tell you things. And his sister, he'd go to his sister with the same thing.

I remember one time she came to my dad's house and she was all upset, and she say—she called him Bud—and she said, "Bud," she said, "We're gonna get some bad news." Papa said, "Sister, don't say it." She says, "Yes," say, "We gonna get some bad news." Say, "Some of our family is gonna be brought in here." Papa say, "Sister, don't say that." She said, "Bud, I seen it last night, and I'm comin to tell you. We got to get together, 'cause one of our sisters or brothers or somebody is gonna be brought in here." And, honest to God, it wasn't long before one of those sisters passed away. Auntie saw it, and came in and told her brother. Said we've got to get ready.

I don't know how they could see all these things! But they had that gift, I guess. Those were the two oldest, her and my dad. My dad was the oldest son, and she was the oldest daughter. And Papa didn't get the education that the others got because the family was large, and his daddy kept him out of school, helpin him to provide for the family.

But he was the master of a lot of things. There wasn't nothin that my daddy couldn't take in hand. And he was a good farmer, he was good. And just like you see these boards that people put—instead of shingles, they got boards—my daddy, he did all of that and built his own house. Every house that I can remember my dad built it. And Mama called him a jack-of-all-trades. (Laughs) She used to tickle me sometimes. She'd get angry about it, "He's a jack-of-all-trades and good at none." "Well, Sweetheart"—that was his word—"Sweetheart, why would you want to say that?" Like he done made her angry about somethin and that's the way she would get back at him.

But my dad was a sweet dad. If I could just bring those two [Father and Mother] back and give them what they deserve! I'd tell Him, I'd say, "Lord, please forgive me for sayin that, but they just went too soon. I didn't get to give 'em what I could."

Chapter 2

WATCHING, LISTENING, QUESTIONING

I used to watch my mother cook, and I used to be the little girl that keeps the wood in the stove. See, that was the way I got to be so close in the kitchen all the time. Because I was the youngest girl, and I liked to be around her cookin. And sure enough, if she's cookin somethin sweet, I'd want a taste. So therefore I was in the kitchen with her more than any of the other girls. And I think that's where my cookin came from.

Plus, my dad's older sister, I stayed with her one time when Mother and Dad was workin at Lufton, Texas. They had to leave home. They was goin over there workin. My dad was cookin for a hotel when I was small, and I stayed with dad's sister.

I wanted to cook so bad. She had a man to bring her a little tin stove, and the little dishes and all. And I was bein anxious, tellin how I wanted to help cook. She'd put 'em in my little cup, tell me to fix it all up, and she'd say, "OK, you can go out and put it in the stove," and I'd put it in the stove. Then she'd say, "Well, you go out, and I'll watch it for you." I'd go out to play. She'd put it in her stove [laughs] and cook it, then put it back in my stove and tell me, "Well, you better come see about your food." And I'd come in, "Oh, it's done!" "Yeah, you better take it out." So she was foolin me all along, but yet still she was encouragin me to cook, and that was her idea, to cook. So I got a lot of that from my dad's older sister and my mom. Those were the two that instilled in me, small, of startin up cookin. And my dad, my dad was a good cook. He was a good cook.

I was a little girl and they was buildin a chimney. They used to get this, they called it "post oak soil" and mulch, and that's what my daddy started to build these chimneys to the house. And Mama had this baby. It was a pretty baby, and I was at the house. But they had a hall in between—two rooms on this side and two rooms [on the other side]—well, they let me stay in the kitchen, and Mama was in the room when the baby was born. That was the prettiest baby. It had a head full of hair! And the baby died—or was born dead.

And I went and I was a lookin at the baby, and Papa had to stop buildin the chimney to build a little box to go bury the baby. And I was there watchin the baby, and I was just lookin for the baby to say somethin. And I said, "Mama, the baby ain't sayin nothin!" I was listenin for the baby to cry. And Mama said, "Well, the baby won't be sayin anything. The baby's goin back to Jesus," she said. That's the way she told me the baby's dead. But she had, if I'm not mistakin, it was five kids [who died in infancy] 'cause she told me she woulda been a mother thirteen times, and there was eight livin. I was a nosy child, and I asked her, "Mama, how many children?" She said, "I been a mother thirteen times."

∾

My mother taught me how to wash baby diapers on a washboard. She taught me all the things that, I don't know how I can put it in words. My mother was a mother, and she was teachin me before she had her last two babies. My mother taught me how to make a cake. We had those old granite pans, with the big spoons, and she put that sugar in there and the butter. We had milkin cows, and we had butter. She learnt me how to churn. She learnt me how to pick up the butter, how to work the milk out of the butter.

And she taught me my ABCs, and she started teachin me from the school books before I was old enough. You had to be seven years old in order to go to school. The first day I went to school I went through two books that the teachers had that I was supposed to be startin at. Mother had taught me at home.

Now I told that teacher, I said, "I know all that." And she said [laughs], "You do?" I said, "Yes, Ma'am!" She said, "Well, OK, you want to

Chapter 2

stay in recess with me?" I stayed one recess and read her that whole book. Then I said, "Now I know how to spell those words." She said, "You do?" "Yeah." She said, "OK." Well, she said, "Another book, borrow it." I brought it home, "Mama," I said, "Mama, she give me the same book you done taught me." She said, "Well you has to go back and tell her you know that book." So I went backs the next day. I said, "I know this book." She said, "You do?" "Yes. Yes, Ma'am, I know this book!" "Well how you know?" "My mama taught me this book." And so, she said, "OK, you want to stay in?" I stayed in. I read that book through to her. Then I say, "I can spell all the words too." She said, "Well, OK, I'll take your word for it." [Laughs] She didn't want to spend all that time inside too.

So, she gave me another book. I went home with that book, I said, "Mama, I'm tired of this woman givin me these *same* books." I said, "Mama, won't you come go to school with me? So you can tell that teacher what book I need!" So Mama said, "Well, maybe I'll go down there with you."

So, she took—I heard her tellin my dad one night—I was a eavesdropper. I was a big eavesdropper. I'd hear 'em talkin, and I'd get to where I could hear, and I was takin all of it in, too. And I heard her tell my dad, "Mr. Aaron, I think I'm a goin"—she called him "Mr. Aaron"—"I think I'm gonna have to go to school with these kids tomorrow. Can you hitch up the wagon? And so I can go down there and talk to their teacher. Valerie [Edith's middle name and nickname] is not satisfied. She's comin home every day complainin about this same book that she done read." Papa said, "OK." He was always good about things like that.

He fixed up the wagon the next mornin, and we all got in there and we went to school. Mother was in school with us all day. It was too far for her to go by that wagon back and forth, or to walk, so Mother stayed in school with us all day. She fixed—that was one thing about her, bless her heart—she'd fix a big pan, so we could all eat together at school that day.

When school was out, we all came home, but in the time she was down there, her and the teacher was havin a conference about what was best for me, and for her to keep me busy. 'Cause mother had to tell her everything that she had been teachin me. And see, you had to be seven years old. And that was borin to me to be home. And everybody's goin to school, and I'm still at home. So mother just had to teach it. Mother started me on mathematics too. And then she had me learnin my time tables. Before ever I had went to school I was learnin all of that.

So she let the teacher know how far she had gone, and that woman told her, she said, "I wish all of the mothers was like you. And any day you want to come in here and help me with these children—." 'Cause it was a two-room school, and it was two teachers, and each teacher had a bunch of grades they had to teach in a day's time. She said, "Anytime you feel like you want to come and help me with these," she says, "you are welcome." Said, "All parents can come. Anytime." So, that made it good for my mother.

ಌ

But, Honey, I was a worrisome little child comin' up. I wanted to know everything. I wanted to know everything. They called me nosy. My mother used to say, "Lord, Mr. Aaron, that's the nosiest little child we've got." I was nosy. I could hear 'em talkin, and I would try to get to where I could eavesdrop and hear what they sayin. And now if I didn't understand everything they was sayin, I was still tryin to hear. And mother called me "Nosy." She named me "Nosy." But, I was glad that I was nosy because of the age that I was when she passed. She had taught me a lot. And that helped me a lot with my kids when they's comin on. And with my brothers under me. They was two under me. So, it helped me a lot. To know things that was good and things that was bad and things that we shouldn't do, and all like that.

I was nosy [laughs]. And I seen things happenin but they didn't tell me. And I goes and I asks my Mama one day. 'Cause I had seen my sisters and them havin their period. And that time, they didn't have money to buy pads. They used those flour sacks and cut 'em up, you know, and then they would wash 'em. Oh, Lord, mmm. So, I went and asked mama one day, what was wrong with one of my sisters? And I said, "Mama, somethin *wrong* with her, 'cause—" [Laughs] I went to tellin her what I had saw, and Mama said, "Well, that's all right. I'll see about it." Now that's what she told me.

Because durin those times, it was certain things you just didn't ask. You had to sort of figure it out. They wouldn't come out plain with you—like they do now—and talk [to] the children about things. But if they wanted to know somethin, they'd say, "Tell Valerie to go ask Mother." So, I didn't have no better sense, whenever they'd tell me to go ask Mama—"Go ask Mama so-and-so and so-and-so"—and sometimes she'd look at me, she'd say, "Who told you to ask me that?" [Laughs] She knew the way I was askin I didn't know what I was talkin about. And I'd say, "Mary told me to ask you that," or "Margie told me to ask you that," or "Purcell told me to ask you that." Whatever! Mama said, "Mmm hmm, well you tell 'em I said come and ask me themselves." I'd go back, and "Mama says you come ask her." [Laughs] Then sometimes she'd give me the answer, and I'd go back and I'd have it all twisted up. [Laughs] And they'd say, "What?" I'd say, "Oh, go ask her yourself!" [Laughs] So, it sort of broke it down to me, then, that Mother was there *for* us, regardless, and she wanted us to come to her.

Chapter 3

THAT LITTLE SWITCH

If you did somethin wrong, you'd get that little switch. And it sting. But now when we was goin to school, the teachers had what they called a rattan. They used to plat [braid] it. They made a switch out of it. Now I didn't think that rattan would ever wear out, but thank God, I didn't get to get no whippin with that rattan. 'Cause I was afraid of that rattan.

But, the children was obedient, more obedient. They didn't come back to the teachers like children do now. I have been to school since my kids been in school. And to hear the childrens talk back to the teachers—I feel so sorry for those teachers I almost went into tears. And the way they [children] would talk—my mother and father wouldn't allow us. You'd better not disobey that teacher. And they'd get the word when I was goin to school.

The parents and the teachers worked together with the kids. They didn't [have] parents' and teachers' meetings, like, you know, the PTA. I didn't know anything about that until my kids was in school. But my parents would meet with the teachers to see how the childrens was comin along and if there that was anything they could do. Now if the parent got a note from the teacher about that child—if it was somethin the child had [done] and if they'd do it again—they would write a note [to ask] if it's all right for the teacher to chastise that child. Then, if that parent say "Yes," that teacher was gonna chastise that child when they do somethin wrong again. Then the teacher would ask the parents to come and visit the school and sit in and see how your child was doin.

∾

Well, we were brought up reachin out, see. If you seen me doin somethin wrong, you speak to me, "Now you know your mother don't allow you to do that. I'm gonna report you to your mother. You better stop. I better not see you back with no lip!" Oh, no, no no. That was a no-no. I [as a child] better say, "Yes, Ma'am, I'm not gonna do it anymore." That was, that was the thing we'd be sayin. So you wouldn't tell Mother. Because if I act up, and you go tell Mother, when I get there, "Sister so-and-so tell me you did such and such a thing, and she spoke to you and you acted up. Now, what must I do?" And that spankin was gonna come. I better honor you. That was one thing. You had to honor your elders. If you chastise me, I didn't want to get another one. You can chastise me, give me a spankin. "You know your mother doesn't allow you to do that!" I'd better not go tell Mother. I'd get another one! So, that's the way it was. It was the love, I think it was, the community love. All the mothers was lovin to their children. They was bondin together.

One of the old ones in the family could say, "I'm gonna tell your mother on you, 'cause you know your mother don't allow you to do that." Better not give you back no lip. Uh uh. That older one tell you that, you better listen. And you'd better not give back no lip. That's the way they brought us up. Even if you was workin for somebody, in the field or where[ever]—and whoever we was workin for seen you doin somethin wrong—"I'm gonna report you to your mother." And you won't say nothin back to them neither. You're workin for 'em, you bet you better not say nothin back to them neither. "Now, if you want to work for me, you better do just what I say. Now if you can't do that, you can't come back." You better be quiet and do what they say. That's the way it was. It seemed like everybody was for everybody. Tryin to help each other.

∞

I can remember my dad chastisin one lady's son. She was a single mother, and this was a funny thing. She was a single mother, and she had three boys and one girl that she was raisin them. She had a grown daughter that was gone by at that particular time. And that oldest boy would take one of those twins, and one of those twins would follow him anywhere. And I remember they was livin in the back of where we was livin, on another road. But our field went to that road. And Papa had watermelons. Oh we raised watermelons, and we had sugar cane, all that. We had a good field. Peas, and all of that. And we had milk cows and everything.

The oldest boy, he didn't know what to get into. He'd take one of his twin brothers, come over to our house, turn out our calves, the calves gone with the cows, takin the bells off of the calves—we had bells on the calves so if they'd get out we could locate 'em—put it [the bells] in the, in the manure where we done piled it up for garden fertilizer, done buried it in that. And turned the calves out where they got with the cows. I don't know whether we had dinner—we came home, Papa said, "Lord, have mercy," he said, "Sweetheart!" She said, "What?" Then she said, "Those devilish boys done been here and turned the calves out." He says, "And don't hear no bells." He said, "And Lord look that!" What happened—accidentally happened—one of the little straps on the bell, you know that go around the neck. Happened that one of these was hangin out of the fertilizer, and that's the way my daddy knew it was in the fertilizer! [Laughs] And he said, "Sweetheart." Mama said, "What is it, Mr. Aaron?" He said, "I don't know nobody that'd do that but J. C. That's Fanny's boys did that." He said, "And I'm goin over to her house right now."

So, he had to go across—when you went 'cross our field, he'd come out right at her house, and he went over and talked to her and told her. She said, "I imagine they did, Aaron," she said, "I wouldn't put nothin by 'em." She say, "OK, which one of ya'll do it?" [Laughs] And the youngest boy that was with 'em said, "J. C. did it." J. C. said, "No, Mutt did it. Mutt did—you know you was with me!" And his [Mutt's] twin didn't go. His name was Willis—it was Wilford and Willis. Willis didn't go. Willis said, "Mama, J. C. and Mutt went. I did stayed here with Teresa." That was the baby girl, and the only girl, they was three boys. He said, "I stayed here with her. So they was the ones gone, Mama," he said, "and if anything's wrong, they the ones did it, not me, Mama."

So Papa takin them and brought 'em back over to the house and made 'em dig out. [Laughs] Then, he takin 'em back to her house. And she told him, she said, "And bring your switch when you come back, Aaron. And I want you to whip 'em for me," she said, "because I don't want somebody to kill my children." Said, "They do it to somebody else, they may kill 'em." So Papa got him a little switch, came on back.

Lead 'em on back to the house. He didn't do anything to 'em. He was just waitin for 'em and carry 'em back to the house.

She said, "Now Aaron, *I* want you to whip those boys until I tell you to stop." She said, "I'm tired and I don't want 'em killed. Somebody gonna kill 'em if they don't stop." Papa whipped Mutt. When he got through with Mutt, the other one's gonna break and run, and Papa got him. And Papa whipped J. C., and while he was whippin J. C., she had a brother that lived not too far, and he heard J. C. holler, and J. C. called his name. And he came up there with his gun. And loaded it on my papa and said, "If you hit him another lick, I'll blow your so-and-so-and-so brains out." And his [J. C.'s] mother went and told him, said, "You go home. I told him to whip my son because the way they goin, they gonna turn up dead, and you won't be the one to kill 'em, be somebody else. So, I want Aaron to whip J. C. till *I* tell him to stop."

Now, ya'll gonna laugh. Papa gave him that whippin, that broke that boy. And do you know who my first boyfriend was, was that boy! Growed up, that was the best boy in the community! J. C. loved my dad to death. [Laughs] J. C. loved my dad to death. And we used to sit up and laugh and talk about that. He used to come and see me and he started to callin Papa, "Papa." He said, "Papa," he said, "do you remember when you gave me that whippin and my uncle came up there and loaded his gun down on you and said, 'If you hit him another lick, I'll blow your so-and-so brains out'?" Papa said, "Yes, and I was ready to blow his out." He said, "And Mama told him to go home." He said, "Papa, you know," he said, "that was the best thing you ever did for me." He said, "If you hadn't a did that," he said, "I may a not be livin today."

Chapter 4

MAMIE'S DEATH

I was the little nurse for the baby, and helpin mother when she was sick in bed, and the rest of 'em was in the field helpin my dad, see. So I cooked the dinner. Mama'd lay in bed, and I'd take the pan and she'd say, "Bring me the meal," to cook the cornbread, "Bring me the meal." She'd tell me how many cups to put in this pan. "Bring me the flour, bring me the bakin powder, and then the salt." And she always put a little sugar in it. And she learnt me how to cook. She'd tell me, "Like this. Now put so much in." Sometimes she'd say, "Now get you a big spoon." Well they didn't have measurin spoons. I didn't know anything about a measurin spoon till I was workin in the city. And we had to go by if this is enough. Mama said, "Now, hold your hand." And now my hand was my measurin spoon. And she'd have me to put so many hands of this and so many hands of that and like that. And my hand was small—you see it's small. Then it was smaller.

And that's the way I learned: listenin and obeyin. And that's what I did. And by me bein the youngest girl, and she [Mama] was sick. The rest was helpin my daddy in the field. I cooked the dinner.

Mama raised one garden after she had my baby brother, and then she take me back down, and she said that was the best garden she had ever raised. And she said, "I'll never raise another garden in there." And she'd tell me to go out in the garden and pick this and that, and I'd come in and she'd help me pick the greens. She'd let me snap the beans. And she loved butter beans, and we had butter beans and she'd help me shell them. But she taught *me*. She wasn't *able* to do all of this because she wasn't strong from that last baby. That was what carried her away.

And she would have me to do the things that *she* would usually been doin, but she taught me *how* to do it. And no measurin cup—we had tea cup—that was the only cup we had, and so she just taught me that way. And she said, "You have to use your head and think, now, I'm gonna put so much of this," she said. "Remember, now, how much you put there." So I was puttin it in my head as I was learnin it. And I can't come in here and measure you up some flour, and measure you up some biscuits by *measurin*. You won't have no good biscuits. I can come in here and get this flour and everything and put it together, and I don't measure. I'll take me a spoon and I'll dip bakin powder and what not. Now *that* I learned afterwards. But before then, mother had me doin' this [motions with hands as if scooping], so, she said, "Now you see how much you got in there, now remember that." You had to look and observe what you're doin. And that's the way my mother taught me how to cook, layin in her sick bed.

∽

I look back over all of that now, and I say, "Oh, she had patience." Because I had a brother under me, Oliver, and the baby was two years apart. And there Oliver was, and there was the baby. I was havin to wash the baby diapers, and I had to pack water from a well, and Mama'd say, "OK, the baby's asleep now. You take the baby's diapers and go up to the next house"—we was on a farm at that time—"and you wash the baby's diapers, and bring 'em back to the house, and we'll put 'em on the fence here and dry 'em." The rest of 'em's in the field. I'm doin what she's tellin me to do. I'm followin her instruction. And they . . . they started callin me "Little Mamie."

∽

So, my mother was my grandmother's oldest child, and I guess by her bein her oldest child, she clinged to Mama a lot. Then when my mama got sick, she [Grandmother] wanted Mother to be in her house—and I don't see how in the world she wanted *Mother* there with all the children. She had two boys and one of her other daughter's kids there, and I'm tellin you, I ain't never seen a house so crowded! But it was peace and happiness there. I don't think kids could live like we did there and bein as happy, and agreein, and doin together.

And sometimes Mother would be feelin pretty good, and she'd say, "I want ya'll to get up and sing me some songs." And she had special songs that she liked to hear. Grandmother say, "You feelin up to it, Mamie?" "Yeah, Mama, I want to hear 'em sing." And my oldest brother was a basser, and my next oldest brother was a lead singer. And she would have us all together and we'd sing. Sometimes they'd have other young mens come in, young boys then, would come in and sing with my two brothers—a quartet. They had a quartet. They'd get together and *sing* for my mother while she was sick. And when she got to where she couldn't be goin to church, that's what would happen. Different times, different ones would come in and sing and give her whatever she wanted to hear. They would sing for her. So, I was just raised up in that, in that bond, of givin and reachin out.

❦

When Mama got real sick, Margie used to rub my mother and rub the pains! Margie got so she could not go and rub my mother, and Mother realized it. She was just that afraid. And then Mama had to take to me 'cause I was just the little nurse. I was that little nurse. And Mother said looked like my rubbin soothed her, because she said, looked like I was tryin. I didn't want Mama to have no pain. And I'd be rubbin Mama, and I'd just be sayin, "God, let Mama hurt no more." I'd just be talkin [whispers]. I didn't want her to be hurtin. And she said that was soothin to her. But Margie, she said Margie could rub her and the pains would go away. But Margie was afraid! So she stopped callin [her].

❦

My oldest sister had came home and been with Mother durin the time she was sick until she died. She gave up two years with her married life—she quit her husband to come home and be with Mother, because when she told him she was comin, he didn't want her to come. Because she told him, she said, "Well, if you don't agree, I'm goin anyway." She said, "I can get another husband, but I can't get another mother."

And when she came, Mother picked up on that. After she was there so long, she would write letters, she'd get letters, then the letters stopped. And Mother [thought] it was somethin had happened, so she asked her one day, she said, "Ruth," she says, "what about Austin?" That was his name. And she said, "It's OK, Mama." She said, "But, Ruth, I don't want you to leave your husband." She said, "Mama, you're my mama." She said, "You gave me life," and she said, "I can get another husband, but I can't get another mother." Mother didn't say another [word]. She said, "I'm through." And she didn't say another word to her about it.

And Sister went outside, and she cried and cried and cried. And I went out, "Sister, what's the matter? Sister, what's the matter?" She said, "I'll be alright, I'll be alright." And I didn't know what was happenin until I overheard Mama tellin somebody else what she told to Sister. She didn't want her to leave her husband. She [sister] said, "Mama, I can get another husband, I can't get another mother." And she told him if she couldn't go to her mother, if he didn't agree, she was goin anyway. And so she came and stayed until mother passed away, and then she stayed with Papa until she thought she had him settled with the children.

∞

My mother's funeral was hard on me. I sit where they put the casket in the church, right in front of the little table in front of the altar. And she left a baby, two [years old] and one four [years old], and me [ten years old]. My father, I think, or one of the sisters had the baby. The casket was sittin like this, and my little brother and I was sittin behind that casket, with our back to the pulpit and our face to the congregation. And there's mother's casket here, and Oliver and I was sittin behind it. And that's where we sit through that funeral. And all I could do was sit there and look. There was nobody to pacify me. See, the other sisters and brothers was with the rest of the family. They had some on one side and some on the other, as close up as they could [get] 'em in the front.

We was the smallest, and that was where they could find a little seat to put there, and that's where they sit, that's where Grandma put us. And I think today that if she hadn't a did that, I coulda taken it better. Because it looked like every time I closed my eyes at night, looked like I seen my mother for a long, long time.

I used to tell Papa, "Papa, I seen Mama last night." He said, "Oh, Baby." I said, "Yes, I did, Papa, time I went to bed, I seen Mama." He said, "You went to bed." I said, "Well, Papa, I saw Mother." And when Mother was sick, she used to tell us, when she knew she wasn't gonna make it. She said, "I'm gonna have to leave ya'll one day." I said, "Mama, will you come back and visit with me?" She said, "I'll only come back if you be doin somethin that you don't have any business. You be bad," she said, "I'm gonna come back. I'm gonna get you." And that stayed with me 'cause I thought Mother—see when Mother said, "I'm gonna get you," she meant she was gonna get you if you did somethin that you didn't have any business. So I just knew Mama was gonna come back. If I did somethin wrong, she was gonna come back and get me. And so [laughs] I got to where night come, I would be one of the first ones that would go to bed, so I could go to sleep so I wouldn't see Mama. But, I've seen her a lot of times.

∾

People would separate the kids [when the mother died]. She'd [Mamie] told 'em, "I don't want you to separate my kids." 'Cause, one auntie said she wanted me, another said she wanted me. One said she wanted my sister, Mary. One said she wanted Margie. And Papa says, "I'm not gonna separate them 'cause Sweetheart"—he called my mother Sweetheart—"Sweetheart told me not to separate the kids." So, I was the youngest girl, and I was there home with my dad the longest, with my two brothers that were under me. But when my oldest sisters was ready to go to school, [my relatives] taken 'em. The next oldest sister—the one had fixed all my school clothes—she went to my dad's ... one of my dad's sisters. And she [Dad's sister] had a son and a daughter, and she went and stayed with her to go to school.

So, I was the one left at home with my dad and *both brothers!* And I had learned how to wash those clothes. And I used to cry, but I was glad that I learned a lot before that happened.

Because a lot of times I was really lonely, and I used to go to my dad cryin, and he'd say, "What's the matter?" I said, "Papa, I feel so alone." I was the only girl at home then with my dad and brothers, and I had to wash their clothes and mine, the bedclothes. And he had relatives there that sometimes some of 'em would come and help me. Most times I was by myself. And my dad and my [older] brother would be gone to work.

Chapter 4

My two little brothers was too small to help me wash, but they kept to the wood around the wash pot—we had those black wash pots, that was what we'd boil the clothes in. And my baby shirts. When I'd get through washin, I'd be wet from here all the way down. I'd have to go and put on more clothes. 'Cause, rubbin the clothes, I was just pickin 'em up and splashin, and I was reachin and hangin 'em on the barbed wire fence and all that.

So it was my life comin up after Mama died—it was a hectic one, yet it was a good one. Because it was the experience that I had went through with her, the experience that I went through with her death, that gave me the courage and the strength to keep doin what she and my dad had taught me.

Chapter 5

OTHER MOTHERS

I'll tell ya, I was somethin else. I'd ask a question—I'd ask 'em in a minute—anything I wanna know. And Mama taught me that, before she died! She said, "All you don't know, then you know somebody that knows, you ask!" She said, "How are they gonna know you don't know if you don't ask?" And so she said, "Whatever you wanna know, don't feel [bad] about askin questions!" And so I asked a lot of 'em, I'll tell ya! [Laughs] I asked a lot of questions. Lord have mercy! Some of them questions I asked!

After she [Mamie] died, I went to my dad. And the things I asked my dad, he'd say, "I'll get back to you." So when he came back, it was from the mothers in the community, or some of my relatives, he would bring me. And I had a cousin, and she didn't have any kids, Cousin Rena didn't, but her mother was a midwife, and she learned a lot from her mother comin up. And her mother had passed away, but Cousin Rena, she was up on raisin girls. She knowed all that because of her mother, I guess. She was grown when her mother passed, so she knew everything, you see. [Laughs]

So something I had asked my dad one day, he said, "I'll get back to you." I said, "OK," so Cousin Rena came to the house. She said, "Baby?" I said, "Yes, Ma'am." She said, "What was that you asked your daddy?" And so I told her. She said, "Well, now when you want to know things like that, you don't go to no man!" [Laughs] I don't know what it was—it was something I asked my dad. She said, "You go ask a *woman*. Now you come ask me, and you know your godmother, Carrie?" I said, "Yes, ma'am." "You go to her. But don't go to Martie up there!" [Laughs] That was my dad's auntie, where we stayed when the house burnt down. 'Cause Aunt [laughs] . . . Aunt Martie would tell you, she'd use some nasty words [laughs]—she'd get the devil—I don't know, that's the way she'd turn you off. If she didn't want to tell you something, she'd just flip like that, and say, "I don't know." So she said, "Don't go to Aunt Martie. Now you go to your aunt, you come to me, and you go to your godmother, Carrie."

And so those were the three that I went to. After I was home with my dad and brothers for a while, I went to those three. My Cousin Rena, that was my dad's first cousin, Papa's father's sister, Mary. That was Cousin Rena's mother. It was Daddy's sister. So, I'd go to her, and he had a sister I'd go to. Then I had a cousin [Carrie]. I called her cousin, but Papa said there wasn't any relation, but I think they were, somewhere off. But I'd go to her 'cause she was my godmother. And I didn't know that until after mother died, and she came and told me, she said, "I am your godmother, and anything you want to know—"

She had one daughter, Mary. Oh, I loved her! When I started gettin up, like twelve or thirteen, I'd go, "Mary . . . so-and-so and so-and-so and so, and what's so-and-so?" "OK, I'll tell you. Now don't you tell nobody!" [Laughs] And then she would tell me things. Her baby son was Harvey. That was her baby, Harvey. I'd go to Harvey and say "Harvey, I heard Purcell say so and so and so, and brother sayin so and so and so, what was they talkin about? What does that mean?" "Now I'm gonna tell you this—don't you tell 'em I told ya." So, I got it all! [Laughs]

When I ended up at home without my older sisters, and it was just my dad and my two little brothers, Harvey was my backbone. I'd go to Harvey in a minute. "Harvey, so-and so-and so-and—." And some things I would ask him, he would laugh. "Girl, you crazy! You don't ask me those kinda things." Then he'd go tell his mama, "Mama, you got to talk to my little sister." "What, what's wrong, Harvey?" "Mama, she—" And he didn't bite his tongue. He'd tell her, "Mama, she asked me so-and so-and so-and so, now you know you got to tell her that!" And she would come and talk to me, and then she started tellin me, "Now you don't ask the boys those kinda things! You come to me about this, or you come to—anything you wanna know, come to me!" So I said, "OK." So that was my godmother, Carrie Griffith. [Laughs] But Harvey, he was my brother, though, that was my brother. He'd tell 'em in a minute, "Don't you mess with my sister."

And so it happened when she [Carrie] died, I was there in Texas, and they got in touch with me. And at that funeral, I had to sit with the family. And the family had enlarged then. It was one girl, she didn't have any children, but the boys gave her a lot of grandkids, and her funeral was pretty large. But they got in touch with me and let me know my godmother had passed, and I was at her funeral.

Chapter 6

COMMUNITY

When that first house burnt down, I was home and we was gettin ready to go to church. And I had gotten all of my school clothes ready. That was before I ever went to Houston to go to school. And my brother [Purcell] smoked cigarettes. And we was gettin ready to go to church, and Papa said, "Well, I'm not goin. I'll stay here with the little boys." That was right after mother had passed.

I had all my school clothes—we didn't have no closet. We had hooks in this corner, across here, and you hung them on a hanger. You put a curtain over it, that was the closet where you hung your clothes. And my sister had made me some cute little dresses. I had bolts that you could get two and a half yards for 25 cents. So I could take two and a half yards and make me a dress, 10 cents a yard. But you could get some good cotton material—it was cotton—you could get cotton material. You'd get cotton material for 15 cents and 20 cents and 25 cents a yard. Honey, you had some good cotton material. So, my sister had made up my school clothes, and I had them on hangers, and my oldest sister had sent me some.

And my brother came in my room. I said, "Purcell don't go there." And he would look in there anyway, and he had a cigarette.

Well, when I got through dressin, this cousin of mine—we would meet, they'd come by my house and we'd all get together in the mornin and we had to walk three miles [to church]. So, they came along and I said, "OK." I left. Well he [Purcell] was still dressin.

And before we got to the church, we met some cars and people comin that way. Well it was more houses up that area, but they said, "Somebody's house is on fire." We looked back, and I said, "Sure is." We kept goin. When they came back, they said, "Your daddy's house burnt down, everything."

My daddy was in it. He had went to the garden—we had a garden right out from the house—he went out to the garden and my brother run out and said, "Papa, the house is on fire in the corner." And that's where my clothes was. And I told Purcell, I said, "Purcell, you lit a cigarette." He swore by God he didn't set that house on fire, but I'll always have within me—bless his heart, he's dead and gone. But I know Purcell was the cause of my house, all my school clothes, every piece [getting burnt].

But the funniest thing about it, it was a warm day. School started the next week. I had on a summer dress. And everything of mine got burnt up. Everything. It was a four room. It was a hall, like I was tellin you, a hall. Well, on the other side was a big room, this was the big room, and mine was in that corner, and it was another room over here where my two brothers was sleepin. He got some of the things out the window. Pulled it out the window. But that house bein old, that house went up just like paper.

Well, the next day, I went to pick cotton. The cotton wash just about out. And I thinks about these people all the time, and I want to try to get in touch with 'em and thank 'em again. We was pickin cotton for a man by the name of Vic Dickerson. His brother, Pete, used to come and pick us up. He'd come in a wagon, and we'd get up early in the mornin, and they'd bring us, come and pick us up and take us to the field. He came that mornin, and that mornin he came—it got to the wind—everybody got the wind that the house burnt down.

So he came that mornin, and before he got to the house, he had to pass by my dad's auntie's house. She had a two-room house, and that Sunday, I went back to that house. She had her three daughters and her son and her stayin in that house. Her son, he was grown and everything, but he had been married because he was back there with Mom because sister had died and he was helpin Mama raise the kids.

So me and my two little brothers was there at Aunt Mollie's. We spent the night there. She put us all up in that room, bless her heart.

Chapter 6

And that Monday mornin, when Pete came to pick up the kids to go pick cotton, I was the one that was there. My two brothers had went to my godmother's house, so they left. So when he takin us to the cotton patch, the little dress I had on was a summer dress, and I had two slips on to keep childrens from seein through when you walked. That's what I went to the cotton field [in]. When he taken us, he went and told his brother. And his sister-in-law was named Erma. And Erma came down in that field, she measured me and she went back and she went to other people and she taken some of her clothes and cut 'em down for me. From when I came out of the cotton field that evenin, she had a pack a clothes for me.

I love those people today. I have lost connection with them, but I told Everett [Edith's son], I said, "When I go back home, I'm gonna try to find them again." Now I don't know—my brother in Houston said he see Pete there once and a while. It was only two sons in that family, and so Pete's brother Vic had got married, and I think Erma was pregnant at that time. She taken some a her clothes and cut 'em down for me. And when I came out of the field, she had a bundle a clothes. And then she went to some of the neighbors that they knew around and got things. And she come in the field and measured me up and went back, and when I came out of that field that evening: blisters. I was blistered from the cotton sack because I had on thin clothes, and the sun was hot. But, it had just parched me. And she had me a sack of clothes.

∽

After mother passed away, it was a lot of work that my dad got for the childrens to do—I look back over it now—and I used to think Papa was a little hard on us. But it wasn't that he was hard on us. He was teachin us to the best of his ability to know how to accept and how to do and how to appreciate. And that was one thing they taught us. You learn to appreciate what others do for you and what you can do for yourself. And that, and that's what it taught us. You could teach me, she could teach me, any elder person could teach me, regardless of what color.

Now, we used to go and work for white people that knew my mother while she was livin, and after my mother died, we could go and work for them, and they'd deal with us just like it was my mother. See, they looked after you like your mother. "I knew Mamie, now, Mamie was a good woman. And now, you can do thus and so for me, and I'm gonna give you so much and so much. But now, you have to do it good." That was it. But, just to say we're gonna lollybod around and gonna half do something—no, no, no, no, no—that was a no-no.

So, it was, I think, it was a unity. Community unity. But when I hear them say that it takes a village to raise a child now, I think that's what they had then. Everybody in the community looked about after everybody else's children.

It was a man named—I was tryin to think of him—it's Mirandy. Now that Mr. Mirandy and them used to raise a lot of peanuts. And he love for Mama and us to pick off those peanuts. They said we picked off clean peanuts. [Laughs] And I remember when, I think Mother was pregnant with one of my brothers too, and Mr. Mirandy came and he wanted us to pick off peanuts. We went into his field and brought over—Spanish peanuts was the best tastin. They are the best tastin there is. They were small peanuts. And we'd go and pick off his peanuts for him.

And Miss Mirandy could do the best cookin. Oh that woman could cook! And she and Mama would get to talkin. Mama used to make what they call a jelly roll—I never learned how. And she used to make what they call a butter roll. Now Miss Mirandy told my mother, she said, "I can't make that dough like you, Mamie." Now Mama would make up the dough and she'd be makin all the other ingredients together, and they'd make that together. And we'd be pickin the peanuts off, and then she'd fix dinner. She had two daughters, and one of her daughters, her oldest daughter, was older than I was, and the youngest daughter was a little bit younger than I am, so if she's livin, her youngest daughter would be about seventy-five or seventy-six, somewhere like that. But we was like stair steps, and we used to play, play, play. And then Miss Mirandy would tell us, "Now ya'll have played, now get in there and pick off the peanuts." And we'd get in there and pick peanuts. But it was fun. Everybody seemed to have cared about each other then. Cared more.

Chapter 6

Brother had an appendix—he had went on a cotton pick, and he came back with a bad case of appendix. And when he was in pain, two womens couldn't hold him down in the bed. And it was one of the ladies that went to school with him—young lady, Ella Palmer—I think she weighed around three hundred and somethin pounds, maybe four. She walked about seven miles 'cause I think they was three miles further in one direction than we were. And she heard about brother. They used to be in the same class when they was in school. And she heard about how sick brother was and all, and how it was that we was there takin care of him. She walked up there to our house from their house. And she came there, and she stayed I think it was two or three nights, day and night. And that woman could hold my brother almost by herself. When that pain would hit him, he's just in misery that bad. Brother would just start jerkin like that, and the doctor said we had to keep him quiet. She would just take his arms, put 'em down like that, and she would get over him, and she'd say, "Andrew, be quiet, be quiet." She'd just be talkin to him. But she had him where he couldn't wiggle. She held him *by herself*.

The doctor told Papa, he said, "You're just gonna have to work with him" 'cause that winter was a bad winter. After he come back off the cotton pick, he said, "That was a bad winter," and the roads was rough, and you couldn't get him the sixteen miles to no hospital to get the appendix removed.

So, one gentleman in the neighborhood, he had one son, white fellow that we knew. They had one son, and that son had his appendix bursted. They went on in with the town carryin him so they could put him in the hospital, and they had that sixteen miles to drive. I think they had a pickup truck was takin him. And his son's appendix bursted, and they lost that son, and that was the only child. And the doctor said if they hadn't a moved him, they may have coulda saved him. But his appendix was so bad that they said they don't know if they coulda saved him or not. Because it had ruptured up so. But the mother and father thought that they could get him to the hospital. They could operate on him after they found out it was really appendix.

So, that was before brother come down with it, so everybody knew, don't move this child if he has the appendix. Keep him just quiet, and that's what everybody would tell everybody, if they child has somethin, they let it go to the next person, regardless they're white, black, or what, we would tell it. "My child done had this, and if your child come down with this, you know what to do." You know, they'd pass the word around.

Chapter 7

RACISM AND RESISTANCE

OK, this man was a Patton. He was a Patton. You heard of General Patton, in the service? Well, now my daddy's family, the Pattons, was a off[shoot] to them. That's some of our generation. That's where some of my generation come in, of the white Pattons. They came from the slave side of the Pattons, but these were born, I think, after the slaves was free. And they knew where the Patton history was. So every time he'd see Papa, he hollers, "Hey, Cous!" He wasn't really his cousin. But we was all Pattons. And he said that it come from the slave time.

So, Papa and I was in town once at the same time. I was gonna do some shoppin, I think, that time. And Papa showed him me, and told him, "This is my daughter." He said, "Well, hi little cous." He said, "That's my cous." And I'm lookin at him, you know, I'm wonderin how this is happenin [laughs]. And he say, "Aaron, look at these eyes, won't ya?" Says, "She's lookin me over." He said, "You gonna know me the next time you see me?" I say, "Yes, sir!" He said, "OK." And this was durin the time I was at home with my dad. I was about fourteen or fifteen when I left my daddy to go to Houston to go to school. And [laughs] when Papa introduced me to him, and he said, "Now, anytime you see me in town and you're here in town," he says, "now if there's anything I can do for you, you just let me know, OK?" I said, "Yes, sir!" And so Papa say, "He means that now, Baby." I say, "Yes, sir." Well, I was the only girl at home with my dad and four brothers at that time.

So, this particular time when I went to town to get me some shoes [laughs]—it wasn't nothin but a square block—you done went all over Crockett. So, I done went to all the stores lookin at shoes in the window. Didn't see nothin I liked there. So I had done passed this store, and I saw a pair of shoes in there I liked.

So, he [Patton] was comin down that same street, on that sidewalk where I was. And I was standin up lookin in the showcase, and he come up. He said, "You see somethin you like?" Now Papa had done showed me to him, to name me to him, but I didn't pay him no attention this day. And he say, "You see somethin you like?" I say, "Yes, I'm lookin at that pair of shoes in there." He say, "You like 'em?" I say, "Yes," I say, "I come up here to get me some shoes, and I done walked and walked," and I said, "These are the ones I like." He said, "Well have you been in to see if you can try 'em on?" I said, "No." He said, "Well, go in!"

So, I went in the store. There was some more people in there buyin, but they was all white, and so, they was buyin shoes and tryin 'em on. And I was standin up there, and I had got me some stockings. I was supposed to dress up. I gonna get some shoes and a dress, but I wanted to get my shoes first. So, I went to stand up there and the man said, "What you want, Girl?" I said, "Could you come out here, I wanted to show you some shoes in the showcase?"

Well, he [Patton] was still standin outside. Now that man know what was happenin. He knew that this man didn't wait on no black folks, but I didn't. So he [the shopkeeper] came out there. I said, "This pair of shoes here, I would like to try 'em on." He said, "Try 'em on. Do you know what size you wear?" I said, "Yes, sir." He said, "Come on." So this man [Patton] walked in behind me. And he heard him talkin to me. So when he walked in behind me, and I sit down and I was gonna put on these stockings, to try on the shoes—he said, "What size you wear?" And so I told him. He went and got the shoes. And he said, "Let's put 'em in the box." I said, "I wanna try 'em on." "If you know what size you wear, don't need to try 'em on." I said, "But, I need to try 'em on."

So he [Patton] said, "Let her try the shoes on." So, he looked at him. He said, "Well, if you know what—" I says, "Well, I like to get 'em a little bit longer," I said, "but this is the size I had before, and now my daddy told me to get *this* size," which was a little size larger. So the man says, "Let her try on the shoes. She has some stockings." "Well, we usually don't wait on [whispers] niggers in this store." And I was the only one in there, and I didn't know it. And so he said, "Well, let her try these shoes on. If she can wear 'em, she'll tell you." So, he looked at him, and he was stalkin, look like a soldier. And he let me try those shoes on. I put my stockings on, and then I put both shoes on, and I stood up. My daddy told me how to work my foot to see. And he said, "You want those?" And I said, "Yes, sir." He said, "OK." And so he told me how much, I think it was $2.98.

And I went to get my money, he [Patton] said, "That's all right." He said, "Tell your dad I said hello." He paid for those shoes. He carried me in that store. Now I'd a never gotten those shoes in that store if that man hadn't a come by there.

See, we was all Pattons. And he knew—it was a huge family of the black Pattons—that's where we all come from. But, see they knew my mother had passed away and Papa was raisin' us, and he knew Papa's family. And he really did chew this man out about those shoes that day. He [the shopkeeper] didn't want me to try them on. He said, "How can she tell that she can wear those shoes if she don't try 'em on?" He [the shopkeeper] said, "Well, she knows the size." He said, "Look, try 'em on. She got some new stockings here." He said, "Put your foot in the stocking," and "let her try 'em on." And so, that started breakin that barrier down. Other shoe stores you could go in and try on shoes, but this particular store wasn't, and this particular store carried the better grade of shoes. And this was the type of shoe that I wanted.

And after I got home and told Papa, Papa said, "Oh!" He said, "You never see no black person in there." And I said, "Well, this is where I got my shoes." He said, "Well, OK. You like 'em?" I said, "Yes, sir." And I told him, and I said, "Cous said to tell you 'hello.'" He said, "Cous?" And I said, "Papa, I can't think of his name, but he's that white cous." [Laughs] I had forgotten his name when I got home. And then Papa looked at me. He said, "Oh, I know who you're talkin about, OK, OK." I said, "He told me to tell you 'hello.'" I said, "And he's the cause of me gettin my shoes here, Daddy!" I said, "That man wasn't gonna wait on me, and he told him to wait on me and let me have those shoes." I said, "Papa, he paid for those shoes, $2.98." I had my little $5.00 up there to get my shoes, and I was so thrilled. I found me a little dress for $1.98. And I said, "Papa, he paid for the shoes." He said, "Bless his heart." He said, "Well, I'll have to tell him when I see him."

And that was one thing that made me feel good that day. I hadn't seen no shoes I liked but these—they was little heels—that was the first little heels I was gonna have, and that's what I wanted, and I got it. And so, this man [Patton], he told me when I came on out, he said, "Now," he said, "I'm gonna tell you. Don't go back in there no more by yourself." He said, "He don't wait on you." I said, "Oh." He said, "No," he said, "now I'm glad I came along," he said, "and saw you, and you got your shoes." He said, "But don't go in that store no more." I said, "OK."

But he was sweet—and then they was another man had a store, his name was Patton—Papa could go over there and get anything he needed out of that grocery store. And if he didn't have the money—sometime Papa would run out through the winter time—and he needed some flour or sugar, or somethin like that, that man would let him have it, and if he didn't get the payment until he made a crop, he would let him go like that. So it was hard with big families, makin it.

Anywhere those white Pattons seen Papa, they'd holler, "Hey Cous, how Cous?" That helped the childrens of us. Because it was so much racism then, and by them sayin "Cous," it helped us to overcome that racism. And it kilt out where we would have been havin hard feelins. And he told Papa, he said, "You know," he said, "I know the blood is there."

And I had a brother had gray eyes, just like 'em, my brother Purcell. Had gray eyes like 'em. He had that fair complexion. And I used to be a red girl. And Papa said, he say [laughs], "When you were first born," he said, "people was sayin I wasn't your daddy!" I said, "Why Papa?" He say, "You were so red and yellow." [Laughs] But on mother's side, it was Irish. Her father's relatives was from the Irish side. So mother had that Irish, and my daddy had this Patton. So this blood mixed up. [Laughs]

It was some white blood in that generation. *I* used to be the lightest one—I changed a lots—I used to be a *red* girl. My sisters and them used to call me, "You ole red thing." My brother Purcell, he was almost as light as you, my brother Purcell—we was the two lightest in the family until my brother Oliver was born. Now they was three kids in Mama's family had different colors than any of them. And then there

CHAPTER 7

was my sister and my oldest brother and another brother, come in with that, with my mother's side of the family features and their complexion. Mama had a baby she lost looked like any white baby you ever seen.

∾

There was this white man, he liked her [Auntie]. I don't know if he said he was a doctor or what. But, she was *married*. Now she was from a slave side family, she was. But this man that saw her, that liked her, he come to her house and he raped her at her house and got her pregnant. And when it time for this baby to be born, he dared her husband to raise up about it. "If you want to keep livin," that was the word he gave.

Well, Uncle Shade, he was scared to say anything. And that was his wife. And the picture on her wall of her, she looked like a white woman herself. She had a very fair complexion, but her husband had a dark complexion. So, they had childrens with fair complexion and children with dark complexion.

But when this man got this baby by her, he dared her husband. When her baby was born, he had a doctor, and he [Uncle Shade] had been havin midwives for his wife when they was havin babies 'cause they couldn't afford a doctor. When this child was born, he [the white man] had a doctor there and *he* was there with her when that baby was born. He was gonna *see* that that baby got the best. He came out just as white as you are. They raised that baby, and when that baby got up older, that man seen that he went to school and went to college, and he was a doctor. He took my sister's tonsils out when she was in the school. That's the one I was tellin you about.

She was scared when that man raped her and she found out she was pregnant. She told her husband, and they was lynchin and everything. Whatever they said went. If you went through life, you shut up, and that's the way that was. They had to take it, or fight and die.

And that's the one [the child fathered by the white man] I used to dodge on the church ground [laughs]. He had came home, and one third Sunday in August, that was homecomin day. And I saw this man and Papa walkin across the church ground and talkin and "ha ha ha ha," and every once in a while they'd hold hands, then they'd hit each other, and stop and talk. I seen 'em, so, every time I see 'em, they was headed towards me, I would turn and go a different way. And I was sayin, "Who's that white man Papa with?" I said, "They sure is talkin." Well I hadn't seen him, and I didn't know who he was. So finally they was tryin to catch me. 'Cause Mother had passed on, and everybody had told him I looked like Mother. [Laughs] So, finally Papa caught up with me, "Baby Rae!" I said, "Yes, sir." And he said, "Come here." And I went over and that man looked at me and started laughin. He said, "Lord, this is just little Mamie over and over!" And Papa said, "That's what everybody says." He said, "And she got a lot of her ways, too." Said, "She's determined, just like Mamie was."

And I'm a lookin at him, all sarcastin, you know, cuttin my eyes at him, and I looked down. And he said, "Aaron, I think you need to tell her, it's time to tell her." He said, "You don't know me, do you?" I said, "No, sir." He said, "Aaron, tell her." He said, "This is my cousin," he said, "you remember them talkin about Aunt Sarah?" I said, "Yes, sir." He said, "That was my mother." And, he said, "Your dad and I is first cousins." He said, "You know when your sister was in Dennison?" I say, "Yes, sir." And he said, "When she was in Dallas?" I say, "Yes, sir." "She went to Dennison and her tonsils was taken out?" He said, "Well, I'm the one that did it." I'm lookin at him and so [laughs] he said, "Aaron, she still don't understand. You gonna have to explain everything when she get home." He said, "Now I'm one of hers, from your Sarah. I'm your cousin." Said, "Your daddy's my first cousin."

Well, his mother and my father's father were sister and brother, and see that made them close. So, when this happened, you had to keep your mouth shut and let it go. Or you'd be fightin and maybe get killed. So, when he [the white man] knowed that she was pregnant, he said, he was gonna be it. So *he* was there when the baby was born. He was gonna be sure that nothin happened to his child. So he [Sarah's child] was a doctor. He ended up bein a doctor. But it was good in a way, but it was sad in a way that it had to happen like that.

He [the white man] seen my daddy's auntie, and I think Papa said she had Irish blood or something in her. But she was from the slave

Chapter 7

time, and that's mixed up. And he [Papa] said, "Baby Rae, she was a pretty woman." And it was my daddy's mother's sister. And he say she had gray eyes, we used to call 'em blue eyes, but they was gray eyes, and he said, "You talk about a beautiful head of hair," said, "she had a beautiful head of hair." She didn't have to do anything to her hair but shampoo it. But she had the sandy hair, somethin like you.

But this man saw her and he wanted her, and he dared Uncle Shade to say anything when he knowed that she was pregnant. When he raped her, he told her, "If he [Uncle Shade] come after me, he won't be livin." And everybody went to tellin him, "Don't bother, don't bother." But they didn't know about this abortion and all that then, so they got pregnant. They brought those babies on. And when that baby was born, *he* [the rapist] kept watch, and *he* put a doctor to watch her.

They loved that baby. And when her husband knew about it, he told her, he said, "Well, Baby, that's not gonna stop me from lovin you." She worried about it at first. Papa said she liked to worry herself to death, and her husband told her, said, "Now look. You stop worryin about that. You wasn't the cause of it," he said, "we gonna still be husband and wife." And that's what happened. They stayed together, they raised it, and *this* [white] man seen that he went to college and was a doctor.

Chapter 8

THE DEAD RETURN

I used to see my grandmother, my dad's mother. And I didn't know who she was, and that was when my mother was livin. And the first house that my daddy built that was off in the woods. We had a picket fence around the house, and Papa had ... he had dug a well off in the corner. And I loved to feed the chickens.

And one evenin I had fed the chickens, and I was sittin on the steps, and here came a lady down the fence row. She had looked like [she wore] a white blouse with a long black skirt. You know how those old fashioned ... the way they used to have those collars. I sat there and I was doin like this [turning her head], and I was watchin. She would go down to the corner where the well was, and then I wouldn't see her no more. And then after while I'd see her walkin back up. And every time she'd get even with me, looked like she'd stop and look at me. So, I kept sittin there. I was watchin and watchin.

So, I would go *every evenin* to watch and see if this lady gonna come again. And I did it about three evenings before I said anything to my mother. I'm gonna try to see who that woman is. I just know that was a woman. But I didn't know this woman. So, finally, mother saw me, and I was sittin there that evening, and I'd go and sit there on the steps, and I'd be watchin.

So, this particular evenin when [laughs] she came down, mother saw me lookin, and she saw me watchin, saw my head turnin. So she said, "Valerie?" I said, "Ma'am." She said, "What is you doin turnin your head?" I said, "Mama, there is a lady, goin down—" I said, "Don't you see her Mama, she's goin down. She's right in front of us now, she's goin out—" Mama said, "Where?" I says, "She's down by the well now." That well was in the corner in the yard. I said, "Mama, she's past it, but I can't see her no more." Mama said, "A woman?" I said, "Yeah." I say,

CHAPTER 8

"She's sorta tall and—" Mama said, "What's she got on?" I said, "Mama, she got on a white blouse, and look like it's a little black bow tie." I say, "And she got on a long skirt." And I described what she was buried in, and I was the baby when she died. Mama said, "Can you tell me what that skirt looked like?" I said, "Mama," I said, "that skirt got some little stripes in it," I said, "they's sorta shiney." I said, "Mama, it a little bit looks sorta like there white or somethin in that material."

I heard Mama tellin my dad. She said, "Mr. Aaron," she said, "Valerie has seen your mother. She goes and sit in that hall every evenin, on those steps," and she say, "I wish you could watch her. She followed her up and down," and she says, "she described her to me," she said, "it has to be your mother."

So next time Papa and Mother both were sittin out there. And I would like to feed the chickens, and I had been feedin the chicken, so it was gettin dark. After while, there she come walkin down. And I saw it, and I was just followin her like, just to see how far she's goin, and I turned, and she come back by. And every time she come she was lookin at me. She'd pass by and look at me. And so, Papa said, "Baby Rae, whatcha doin?" I said, "Papa, don't ya'll see that woman passin by?" And he said, "What has that woman got on?" And I told him. He said, "What's she got on her feet?" I said, "I can't see her feet." I said, "She got on a dark skirt, long and"—they wore their dresses long then—I said, "I can't see her feet but she got on a dark long skirt." I said, "Look like it's got some shiny streaks in it, silver lookin' stripes in it." I say, "And she got on a white blouse," I say, "And it's up tight around her neck," and I say, "She got a little black bow tie, Dad," I said, "Now, don't ya'll see it?"

Now they's tryin to see it. They didn't see. So when they couldn't see it, I got upset. And Papa said, "Oh, well, that's OK, Baby." I said, "But Papa, ya'll ask me and I was tryin to show you that woman." I said, "Here she come again, Daddy!" I said, "See! See!" And when she got right in front of me, she stopped and looked at me. And then she went on. But when she come back by that time, goin, I watched her and she passed the henhouse, and that's when she disappeared. And I didn't see her no more.

The Dead Return

My mother came back time [when] my brother was sick. Brother had an appendix. He had went on a cotton pick and he came back with a bad case of appendix. When my brother was sick, I got up one night and Papa was remodelin the house, and he had this one room that was gonna be the kitchen, but he hadn't got it for the kitchen, so he had two beds in there. Our bed, my two sisters' beds, we had across this way, and my two brothers' bed was near the door. And it was hot in the summer, so we slept with that door open so that air could come through and we had a window. So I'd say, "I'm not carryin out no chamber pot now." Everybody wanted to use it. If I'd a brought it in at night, in the mornin, I was gonna have to be the one [to empty it], so I had tired of bein the chamber pot carrier. [Laughs]

So I said, I'm gonna go out to the outhouse. And this particular night [laughs] the moon was shinin so pretty and bright. Well, I had to go to the bathroom. I got up to go out, and Brother was comin down with this. We didn't know how bad it was. And I got up to go out to the outhouse, and just as I passed by their bed—I had to pass by my brother and them's bed as I go out by the door. So I just start to go to the bathroom [laughs], and my mother was just as plain. She was sittin there with her arm over brother like this and lookin in his face. And I walked out that door, that I went to go out—her feet was in the aisle across like—she drawed her feets back. I went to step over 'em, and she drawed 'em back. And I looked! And I said, "That's mother!" And I didn't get scared. I went on out to the toilet. I came back in. Mother was still sittin there, and she was lookin in brother's face. And I went to step across her foot again—they were stretched out—and she drawed 'em back, and I didn't step across her foot.

I got into the bed [laughs] and my sisters Mary and Margie was in the bed. We three were sleepin in one bed. I said, "Mary, Margie, Mary, Margie!" I said, Mama's sittin up there and lookin down at brother's face!" [Laughs] When I said that, my sister Margie pulled all the cover out and wrapped up in the cover. [Laughs]

It didn't frighten me. When I came back she was still there, and she had her hand over brother, like this, and was lookin in his face.

The *first* night I saw her, she was at the *door* of the room, and I went out to the toilet. I didn't pay that no attention. I knew that was

Chapter 8

Mama, and I was passin by, and I didn't think nothin of it. But the next day it sort of dawned on me [quietly as if talking to self], "Did you know that was your Mama you saw? No, that wasn't Mama." You know, just like that, I pushed it off. But the *next* time I saw her, Mama was comin in the door and I was goin out the door. And she did like this with me [stepping aside], to pass her. I didn't touch her. I was goin out the door and she was comin in that same door.

And the third night was when she was sittin, with her legs crossed like this, and her arm was over brother, and she was lookin in his face. And that was the time that he came down [with appendix]. And when I told Papa about it, I said, "Papa," I said, "that's the third time in a row!" He said, "What?" I said, "Papa, that's the third time," I said, "I seen Mama." And I went to tellin him all the times that I saw her. Papa said, "Well, I don't know what that is."

Well, he went and told my godmother about it. And *she* came over, and she said, "Baby, are you feelin alright?" I say, "Yes, Ma'am." She say, "Well, I'm gonna talk to you. Your daddy's upset about you." She says, "Now he come and told me about what you told him about," she said, "now you understand?" I said, "Mama Carrie," I said, "I done saw Mother three times." And when I told her how I seen my mother in the positions and where she was, she said, "Hmm." And when I told her, I said, "And the last time," I said, "she was sittin on the side of brother's bed with her arm over him, like this, and she was lookin in brother's face and brother was asleep. She said, "Well, she sees something." She says, "must be your brother gonna be sick."

And sure enough, my brother, he come down with that appendix. He had been out west pickin cotton, and his appendix was gettin bad. Brother got down with those appendix, and I'm tellin you, we thought we was gonna lose him. Mother saw this, and before she died, Mother would tell us somethings. She say, "I may not be with ya'll forever." I say, "Well, Mama, if you leave us," I said, "they say the dead knows what the livin are doin." I said, "Will you come back?" She said, "Not on this earth, I can warn you or somethin," she said, "that's the only time I'll come back." So, when that happened, that run back through my mind, and I was sayin, "Well, what's wrong with Brother?"

The Dead Return

༄

She was watchin over us. Mother was watchin over us. And she used to tell me, she used to tell me sometime when she was sick—mother never got over the last baby—and she said, "I'm gonna have to leave ya'll someday." I said, "Mama, if you do, will you come back and check on us?" She said, "Oh, yeah," she said, "if you be doin anything wrong, I'll come back, and you'll see me." But I wasn't doin anything wrong when I saw that.

But when I told Papa, Papa tried to figure it out. He couldn't figure it out, so he talked to Aunt Ann, his older sister. And he was tellin her, and then he was tellin my godmother about it. And my godmother told him, she said, "Well, Aaron, you know Mamie is gonna watch over those kids." She says, "If it's anyway Mamie can watch over those childrens," says, "she gonna do it." See. And I said, well, I say, "You know Mama told us, before she died, don't worry about her, she'll be watchin over you." And Papa said, "There's nobody been seein her but this child." But I was the one was at home with her more with the babies, when they was small. The other ones was workin in the field and all, and I was the one, the little cook that was bakin all with her and all this. And I think that's the reason I was the one seen her.

Interlude 1

RELIGION AND SPIRITUALITY

In these opening chapters of Edith Hudley's life story, religious faith and openness to the spiritual dimensions of life are strikingly apparent. This is the legacy to which she was born, and these commitments will continue to animate the chapters that follow. This legacy, nurtured by her family and church, is not only the source of many of her stories but shapes her narrative style. Notice, for example, that she often brackets her stories with supplications to God: "Lord, please forgive me for sayin that, but they [her parents] just went to soon. I didn't get to give 'em what I could." Mrs. Hudley's religious heritage is also apparent in the way in which she orients important life events in time. Religious rituals—family prayer, church services, funerals, homecoming day—form the grid on which other events are located. The family was going to church when their house caught fire. She met her white cousin on homecoming day.

These opening chapters also demonstrate that, from the beginning, Edith Hudley has lived and breathed a set of ethical guidelines rooted in Christianity. Experienced first within the family, Christian values also unified the community, motivating acts of caring and generosity. At times these values even bridged the racial divide.

Equally prominent in Mrs. Hudley's account of her early years is the example of religious faith as a source of joy and of strength and consolation. When her mother, Mamie, was too weak to attend church service, she still delighted in hearing her favorite hymns. When Edith was puzzled and distressed about the quiet stillness of her dead baby sister, Mamie explained, "Well, the baby won't be sayin anything. The baby's goin back to Jesus...." Young children were allowed to participate in these and other spiritual events in meaningful ways, and their own spiritual experiences were taken seriously. Edith's belief that the dead remain available to the living was introduced and reinforced by her parents and other adults, but it was she, not they, who actually witnessed the spirits of the dead.

What can one make of these mystical experiences? The developmental literature contains nothing like this. Accounts of African-American experience are another matter, however. Early African-American autobiographers recall direct communications with God and angels and describe visions of heaven and hell experienced during conversion, (for example, Foote, 1886/1988; Sobel, 1989), and Toni Morrison's (1987) novel *Beloved* is suffused with the spirits of the dead.

Contrasting Literatures

This curious disjuncture between the literatures most relevant to understanding Mrs. Hudley's life is not confined to religious and spiritual matters, as later interludes will demonstrate, but it is perhaps most dramatic here. The literature on African-American experience takes for granted that religion and spirituality have played an important role in the lives of many black Americans.[1] Although the terms *spirituality* and *religion* are sometimes used interchangeably, Randolph Potts (1996, 1998), and others see the two as related but distinguishable. Potts defines spirituality as "the direct, personal experience of the sacred; the awareness of a higher power, a causal force beyond the material or rational, that operates in all aspects of existence" (1998, p. 496). Spirituality has to do with the search for life's ultimate significance. Religion on the other hand, is a system of symbols, beliefs, rituals, and texts shared by a community of believers. Although religion provides a collective framework for expressing spirituality, individuals' search for meaning may lead them to embrace spiritual precepts and practices that are not specifically religious.

---

1. This is apparent in compendiums of African-American oral narratives (e.g., Goss & Barnes, 1989) and in scholoarship pertaining to history and culture (e.g., Franklin, 1980; Smitherman, 1977) and to religious experience per se (e.g., Fitts, 1985; Frazier, 1988; Freedman, 1993; Fulop & Raboteau, 1997; Lincoln & Mamiya, 1990; Moss, 1988; Wingfield, 1988).

INTERLUDE 1

Many African Americans say that their spirituality is an important source of comfort and strength, and there are several studies in which African Americans attest to the value of spirituality in coping with illness (Moore, 1991; Krause & Tran, 1989; Potts, 1996; Watson, 1984). However, much more has been written about the role of religion in the lives of African Americans. The black Christian church has been described as the oldest and the most influential African-American institution (Smitherman, 1977; Moss, 1988). In many African-American communities the church is the only institution that is owned, controlled, and patronized by African Americans (McAdoo & Crawford, 1991). Throughout its history, the church has nourished religious faith, promoted ethical conduct, and contributed to the social and material well-being of its members (Franklin, 1980; McAdoo & Crawford, 1991; Moore, 1991; Moss, 1992; Williams, Griffith, Young, Collins, & Dodson, 1999). Many African Americans consider the church to be second in importance only to the family (Moore, 1991).

Edith Hudley's spirituality found expression in conventional religious practices, such as prayer, hymn singing, and church going, but also in less widespread practices such as visitations from the dead and faith healing. When she gave a presentation in Haight's developmental psychology class, Mrs. Hudley described several miraculous healings that she had experienced. In one case, recalled from childhood, her "burst lung" was healed when she recited scripture while a neighbor dropped keys down her back.

These testimonies to faith healing continue a tradition that dates from the nineteenth century. For example, the African-American missionary Virginia W. Broughton (1907/1988) devoted an entire chapter of her autobiography to divine healing, describing numerous examples of miraculous recovery from accident and illness attributed to prayer. In recounting her life as a midwife, Onnie Lee Logan (1989) recalled appealing to and receiving help from God when confronted with medical emergencies beyond her experience.

In sum, when Mrs. Hudley's spiritual and religious life is approached from the perspective of African-American studies, she emerges as a familiar kind of person, one who is anchored in the church and unsurprised by the mysterious workings of the divine in ordinary life. But within the mainstream study of human development, many of the most deeply meaningful experiences of her early years are what Jacqueline Goodnow (1990) has called "homeless phenomena." There is literally no place for them within existing theories of development or even within conventional ways of carving out the domains of human development.[2]

A survey of textbooks bears this out. The terms *religion* and *spirituality* do not appear in the indexes or tables of contents of any of the leading textbooks in child development (for example, Bornstein & Lamb, 1988; Cole & Cole, 2001; Hetherington, Parke & Locke, 2003). This holds true even for textbooks that are written from a sociocultural perspective (Cole & Cole, 2001) or that contain major sections devoted to moral development (Bornstein & Lamb, 1988). The same applies to the authoritative and comprehensive *Handbook of Child Psychology* (Damon, 1998), the preeminent reference volume in the field. Even collections and reviews pertaining to African-American children per se—including the special issue on minority children published by *Child Development*, the flagship journal of the Society for Research in Child Development—do not address religious or spiritual development. Thus, students of human development who go on to become parents, social workers, teachers, doctors, therapists, and scholars receive at best minimal exposure to children's religious and spiritual development.

Similarly, the applied fields of social work and education contain little information about the role of spirituality and religion in human development. Only in the last few years have the leading textbooks for the Council on Social Work Education (CSWE) required course in human development in the social environment contained references to "religion" or "spirituality" in the index or the table of contents. Social work has had an abiding concern with ethnic and cultural diversity, but this concern has only recently extended into the realms of religion and spirituality (Bullis, 1996; Sheridan, Bullis, Adcock, Berlin, & Miller, 1992;

---

2. It should be noted that within the field of moral reasoning there are a few studies of age-related changes in understanding within particular religious traditions (e.g., Oser, 1991).

Canda, 1997), and rarely into children's experiences. Yet, understanding children's religious and spiritual experiences can open up opportunities for effective social work intervention. For example, church members can provide social support and mentoring to adolescents during times of stress, and understanding a family's religious beliefs can lead to the development of interventions for children that are consistent with other socialization messages (Haight, 2002).

Edith Hudley's life thus poses a significant challenge to those of us who study child development or work in professions that promote the welfare of children. Why have we been so slow to study children's religious and spiritual experiences? Are we afraid that attention to these dimensions of life will undermine our claim to rationality, our legitimacy as social scientists, or our professionalism as social workers and clinicians?

Finding Room for Children's Religious and Spiritual Experience

There are some exceptions to this picture. In *Stages of Faith,* James Fowler (1981) starts from the premise that nascent capacities for faith are present at birth and draws upon classic developmental theories to imagine how faith unfolds across the lifespan. Robert Coles (1990), in *The Spiritual Life of Children,* explores how children from around the world "sift and sort spiritual matters." Cindy Clark (1995) in *Flights of Fancy, Leaps of Faith,* provides a powerful argument that children's beliefs in childhood myths, such as Santa Claus and Easter Bunny, form the developmental foundation for religious faith. These remarkable works exist at the margins: they are rarely cited in the literatures on child development, educational psychology, or social work. There are some hints that this situation may be changing, however. For example, a new collection of papers, *Imagining the Impossible* (Rosengren, Johnson, & Harris, 2000), attempts to bring a fuller appreciation of children's religious experience into developmental psychology.

In addition, there is a growing awareness that religion and spirituality may illuminate the mysterious quality of "resilience" (Garmezy, 1985; Maston, Best, & Garmezy, 1990). People who are resilient are able to find meaning in their lives even in the face of extraordinary hardship—just as Edith did when her mother died. Robert Coles provides a memorable example, quoting the words of an eight-year-old girl who helped to desegregate a North Carolina school in 1962:

> I was all alone, and those people [segregationists] were screaming, and suddenly I saw God smiling, and I smiled. . . . A woman was standing there [near the school door], and she shouted at me, "Hey, you little nigger, what are you smiling at?" I looked right at her face and I said, "At God." Then she looked up at the sky, and then she looked at me, and she didn't call me any more names. (Coles, 1990, pp. 19-20)

These examples suggest that spiritual beliefs can be sustaining to children at a surprisingly early age.

The African-American church provides a variety of other benefits to children as well. For example, Kimberly Williams (1994) found that middle-class African-American children in Chicago were motivated by their Sunday School experiences to practice a variety of literacy and school-related activities at home. C. Eric Lincoln and Lawrence Mamiya (1990) emphasize the importance of the church as a place where young people can meet older adults who serve as role models—a point that is illustrated in the following chapters of Mrs. Hudley's life story. In still other studies, parents described the personal comfort and guidance that their families experienced from participating in church-related activities (Hurd, Moore, & Rogers, 1995; Arnold, 1995).

An Alternative Worldview

According to many scholars of African-American Christianity, the church embodies an alternative system of belief, one that is not a simple imitation or derivation of European versions of Christianity (for example, Becker, 1997). This characteristic may be especially important in nurturing children's strengths and competencies, because it offers a critical vantage point from which to view the realities of a racist society and a set of resources for maintaining a positive identity. It is the church, more than any other institution, that has kept this steadying vantage point alive. Scholars of African-American history and culture have argued that this alternative system of belief not only has allowed African Americans to resist oppression and maintain their humanity but also has been a great source of creativity (Long, 1997). Hudley's father's truth telling about racial oppression and his repeated exhortations not to take hate into one's heart exemplify this perspective, a perspective that bell hooks (2001) calls "love-oriented."

Each of the key features of this alternative belief system are discernible in Hudley's early years and echo throughout her life. For example, African-American theology has been described as a pragmatic intertwining of the sacred and the material (Smitherman, 1997). Drawing upon African traditions and shaped by the experiences of slavery and oppression in the Americas, the church evolved a set of practices that promoted the day-by-day survival of its members (Brown, 1991; Lincoln & Mamiya, 1990; Moore, 1991; Williams et al., 1999). In addition to the spiritually nurturing practices of prayer, hymn singing, and Bible study, the church provided social support and concrete aid in times of crisis. When Hudley's family lost everything in the fire, a neighbor came forward to sew clothes for her. When Hudley's mother was dying, members of the church came to her house to sing hymns for her mother. The African-American church also provided a safe context in which people could develop valued competencies, such as reading and writing (for example, Stack, 1974; Young, 1969). Although religious institutions may serve similar functions across the United States, for many black Americans the church has been the only institution in town that offers them a refuge.

A second feature of African-American religious beliefs is an emphasis on community. Many scholars have commented upon the centrality of community to African-American culture. The religious underpinnings of this orientation have been articulated by Janice Hale-Benson (1987) in her discussion of spirituals. "The spirituals lamented the loss of community and felt that this constituted the major burden [of slavery]. They felt that the suffering was not too much to bear if you had brothers and sisters to go down in the valley and pray with you" (p.15).

Throughout African-American history, the community of faith has nourished children's development. Ella Mitchell (1986) describes relationships that extended from the nuclear family throughout the entire slave community, allowing children to survive under inhumane conditions. In Edith Hudley's early life, the whole community took responsibility for disciplining errant children and for mothering those whose mothers had died.

Finally, the belief in the inherent dignity and worth of each individual is regarded by many as a cornerstone of African-American theology (see Mitchell, 1986; Hale-Benson, 1987). According to historian Leroy Fitts, (1985), the black Baptist church in America emerged, in part, in response to the theologically inconsistent policies of white Baptists. Christian slave owners, attempting to control and pacify blacks, imposed their religion, a religion that ironically affirms the values of charity and equality. The slaves heard the Gospels while sitting in the back or the balcony of the church. Disavowing this context of subordination, "Black Baptist preachers ... discovered in the Fatherhood of God and brotherhood of man, a ... concept of human freedom and dignity" (p. 44). The belief that God recognizes African Americans as equal to European Americans and that He recognizes each of them personally as His child has given many the inner resolve to persist in the face of harsh realities (Hale-Benson, 1987). Ella Mitchell (1986) notes that this "lesson was learned so well that despite the ravages of dehumanization, very few slaves ever gave up and fully accepted the servile image thrust upon them" (p. 101).

The Socialization of Religious Beliefs

Mrs. Hudley's account of her early life allows us to begin to imagine how a young child might come to imbibe the tenets of African-American Christian belief that were available in her family, church, and community. However, we know very little about how such beliefs are passed on to children in the twenty-first century. Wendy Haight's (2002) ethnographic study of the Baptist church that Mrs. Hudley attends in Salt Lake City is an exception. In this rare glimpse into the workings of an African-American Sunday School, adults and children elaborated a system of religious beliefs through narrative, discussion, conflict, and play. This belief system directly parallels the features of African-American theology just described.

For example, Sunday School teachers expressed and put into practice their belief in the utility of spiritual beliefs in everyday life. Freedom, justice, and forgiveness were not just appealing ideas. They were viewed as a lifeline to healthy spiritual development and essential components in coping with the challenges of everyday life. Teachers wanted such beliefs to be so readily at hand that they could be reached for in times of need. One Sunday School teacher said that children must know how to "put on the armor of God." This protection can be carried inside of each child to school, work, and the mall.

The importance of community was also evident at First Baptist Church. Children were treated as valued members of a cultural community stretching back in time and including members of the church who were highly esteemed for their wisdom and spirituality. Each child could participate in meaningful ways alongside esteemed community members. They could usher worship services, lead devotions, sing in the choir, or provide service to families in need. Children also learned in Sunday School and Vacation Bible School about powerful role models from earlier times, such as Dr. George Washington Carver and Rosa Parks, who faced great challenges and prevailed.

A third hallmark of the belief systems elaborated with children at First Baptist Church was the inherent worth of each individual. Each person is valuable, regardless of material success and social status. In the words of a popular hymn, each individual is a "child of the King" with unique, God-given gifts. As such, each child is entitled to love and respect, and with opportunity and effort will go far. However, the journey will be difficult. Just as many were blind to Jesus, many will not see black children's inner resources and strengths. Just as the Egyptians enslaved and oppressed Moses' people, some will attempt to oppress black children. The stories told with children also stress that through faith, effort, and community, they too, like the Hebrew people, can prevail. The challenge is to remain a loving and moral person throughout the journey and to maintain a deep optimism in its ultimate rewards.

References

Arnold, M.S. (1995). Exploding the myths: African-American families at promise. In B. B. Swadener & S. Lubeck (Eds.), *Children and families "at promise": Deconstructing the discourse of risk*. Albany: State University of New York Press.

Becker, W.H. (1997). The black church: Manhood and mission. In T. Fulop & Raboteau (Eds.) *African American religion: Interpretive essays in history and culture.* New York: Routledge.

Bornstein, M.H. & Lamb, M.E. (Eds.). (1988). *Development psychology: An advanced textbook.* (2nd ed.). Hillsdage, NJ: Erlbaum.

Broughton, V.W. (1907/1988). *Twenty year's experience of a missionary.* Reprinted in H. Gates, Jr. (General Editor), *Spiritual narratives.* New York: Oxford University Press.

Brown, D.R. (1991). Religious socialization and educational attainment among African Americans: An empirical assessment. *Journal of Negro Education,* 60(2), 411-426.

Bullis, R.K. (1996). *Spirituality in social work practice.* Washington, DC: Taylor & Francis.

Canda, E.R. (1997). Spirituality. In R.L. Edwards (Editor in Chief), *Encyclopedia of social work. (19th ed., 1997 supplement).* Washington, DC: NASW Press.

Clark, C.D. (1995). *Flights of fancy, leaps of faith: Children's myths in contemporary America.* Chicago: University of Chicago Press.

Cole, M. & Cole, S.R. (2001). *The development of children.* (4th ed.). New York: W.H. Freeman & Company.

Coles, R. (1990). *The spiritual life of children.* Boston: Houghton Mifflin.

Damon, W. (Editor in Chief). (1998). *Handbook of child psychology.* (5th ed.). New York: Wiley.

Fitts, L. (1985). *A history of black Baptists.* Tennessee: Broadman Press.

Foote, J.A.J. (1886/1988). A brand plucked from the fire. An autobiographical sketch. Reprinted in H. Gates, Jr. (General Editor), *Spiritual narratives.* New York: Oxford University Press.

Fowler, J.W. (1981). *Stages of faith: The psychology of human development and the quest for meaning.* San Francisco: HarperCollins.

Franklin, J. (1980). *From slavery to freedom: A history of Negro Americans* (5th ed.). New York: Alfred A. Knopf.

Frazier, E.F. (1988). *The Negro church in America.* New York: Schocken Books.

Freedman, S. (1993). *Upon this rock: The miracles of a black church.* New York: Harper Perennial.

Fulop, T.E., & Raboteau, A.J. (Eds.). (1997). *African American religion: Interpretive essays in history and culture.* New York: Routledge.

Garmezy, N. (1985). Stress-resistant children: The search for protective factors. In J.E. Stevenson (Ed.), *Recent research in developmental psychopathology.* Oxford: Pergamon Press.

Goodnow, J.J. (1990). The socialization of cognition: What's involved? In J.W. Stigler, R.A. Shweder, & G. Herdt (Eds.), *Cultural psychology: Essays on comparative human development.* (pp. 259-286). New York: Cambridge University Press.

Goos, L. & Barnes, M.E. (1989). *Talk that talk: An anthology of African-American storytelling.* New York: Simon and Schuster/Touchstone.

Haight, W. (2002). *The socialization of African American children at church: A sociocultural perspective*. Cambridge: Cambridge University Press.

Hale-Benson, J. (1987). The transmission of faith to young black children. Paper presented at the Conference on Faith Development in Early Childhood, Henderson, NC, December 8-11.

Hetherington, E.M., Parke, R.D. & Locke, V.O. (2003). *Child psychology: A contemporary viewpoint*. (6th ed.). New York: McGraw-Hill.

hooks, b. (2001). *Salvation: Black people and love*. New York: William Morrow.

Hurd, E.P., Moore, C., & Rogers, R. (1995). Quiet success: Parenting strengths among African-Americans. *Families in Society, 76*(7), 434-443.

Krause, N., & Tran, T.V. (1989). Stress and religious involvement among older blacks. *Journals of Gerontology, 44*(1), S4-S13.

Lincoln C.E., and Mamiya, L.H. (1990). *The black church in the African American experience*. Durham: Duke University Press.

Logan, O.L. (1989). *Motherwit*. New York: Penguin.

Long, C.H. (1997). Perspectives for a study of African-American religion in the United States. In E. Fulop & Raboteau (Eds.), *African-American religion: Interpretive essays in history and culture*. New York: Routledge.

Maston, A.S., Best, K.M., & Garmezy, N. (1990). Resilience and development: Contributions from the study of children who overcome adversity. *Development and Psychopathology, 2*, 425-444.

McAdoo, H., & Crawford, V. (1991). The black church and family support programs. *Prevention in Human Services, 9*, 193-203.

Mitchell, E.P. (1986). Oral tradition: Legacy of faith for the black church. *Religious Education, 81*, 93-112.

Moore, T. (1991). The African-American Church: A source of empowerment, mutual help, and social change. *Religion and Prevention in Mental Health, 10*, 147-167.

Morrison, T. (1987). *Beloved*. New York: Plume.

Moss, B. (1988). *The black sermon as a literacy event*. Unpublished doctoral dissertation, University of Illinois, Chicago.

Oser, F. (1991). The development of religious judgment. In G. Scarlett & F. Oser (Eds.), Religious development in childhood and adolescence. *New Directions in Child Development, 52*, 5-26.

Potts, R. (1996). Spirituality and the experience of cancer in an African-American community: Implications for psychosocial oncology. *Journal of Psychosocial Oncology, 14*(1), 1-19.

Potts, R. (1998). Spirituality, religion, and the experience of illness. In P.M. Camic & S.J. Knight (Eds.), *Clinical handbook of health psychology: A practical guide to effective interventions*. (pp. 495-521). Seattle, WA: Hogrefe & Huber.

Rosengren, K., Johnson, C., & Harris, P. (Eds.) (2000). *Imagining the impossible: The development of magical, scientific, and religious thinking in contemporary society*. New York: Cambridge University Press.

Sheridan, M.J., Bullis, R.K., Adcock, C.R., Berlin, S.D., & Miller, P.C. (1992). Practitioners' personal and professional attitudes and behaviors toward religion and spirituality: Issues for education and practice. *Journal of Social Work in Education, 28*(2), 190-203.

Smitherman, G. (1977). *Talkin and testifyin: The language of black America.* Boston: Houghton Mifflin.

Sobel, M. (1979). *Trabelin' on: The slave journey to an Afro-Baptist faith.* Princeton, NJ: Princeton University Press.

Stack, C.B. (1974). *All our kin: Strategies for survival in a Black community.* New York: Harper & Row.

Watson, W.H. (1984). Introduction. In W.E. Watson (Ed.), *Black folk medicine: The therapeutic significance of faith and trust* (pp. 1-15). New Brunswick, NJ: Transaction Books.

Williams, D., Griffith, E., Young, J.L., Collins, C., & Dodson, J. (1999). Structure and provision of services in black churches in New Haven, Connecticut. *Cultural Diversity and Ethnic Minority Psychology, 5*(2), 118-133.

Williams, K. (1994). *The socialization of literacy in black middle-class families.* Unpublished doctoral dissertation, University of Chicago, Illinois.

Wingfield, H. (1988). The historical and changing role of the Black church: The social and political implications. *The Western Journal of Black Studies, 12*(3).

Young, V.H. (1969). Family and childhood in a southern negro community. *American Anthropologist, 72,* 269-288.

PART 2

Youth

Part 2 of Mrs. Hudley's oral history encompasses her youth from the time she left the family farm to pursue her high school education in Houston in 1935 until she married in 1938. Houston, Texas, is roughly 150 miles south of Edith's home. At the time of Edith's arrival, Houston was a southern metropolis. The deepening of the Buffalo Bayou around 1914 had made it possible for ocean-going ships to come up from the Gulf of Mexico and established Houston as a major seaport. Houston's first skyscrapers were built shortly thereafter in the 1920s. During Edith's stay, Houston had a population of approximately 300,000, second only to New Orleans in the south (Johnson, 1997), approximately 41 percent of which was African American (U.S. Department of Commerce).

During her youth, Edith and her family continued to face the obstacles of segregation and discrimination. In Houston, Edith attended a segregated high school, used separate public facilities, and experienced both the kindness and the hatred of individual whites.

Edith Hudley's childhood and youth took place during the Great Depression. At a time when employment opportunities were limited,

Edith's opportunities were further restricted by virtue of her status as an African-American woman. In Houston, many African-American women like Edith worked as domestics: cooking, cleaning, doing laundry, and baby sitting for white families. As late as 1960, more than 30 percent of employed black women were domestics in contrast to less than 6 percent of employed white women. In 1935, the typical wage for black women who did housework and laundry was only $3.00 a week (Lerner, 1972). Economic hardship eventually forced Edith to leave school, give up her cherished ambition to become a nurse, and return home to help her father.

When you read part 2 of the oral history, it may be helpful to refer to Appendix A, which lists several key events in Mrs. Hudley's youth. In 1935, Edith moved in with her oldest sister to attend eighth grade at Jack Yates High School. While in Houston, Edith worked as a domestic (housecleaner, cook, laundress, and babysitter) for a white family. In 1936, Edith returned home to Kennard. During her brief stay in Houston, Edith experienced the kindness and support of some teachers at Jack Yates, racism in the home of her trusted employers, attempted assault by a family acquaintance, and dancing in the clubs. Through all of these life-shaping experiences, the advice and example of her parents remained an important touchstone.

Appendix B lists a few of the important people in Mrs. Hudley's youth, including her teachers, Miz Cavanaugh and Mr. Goodwin; her employer, Miz A., and her family; and her older sister and brother-in-law, Ruth and Thello.

For students and teachers, Appendix C raises topics for thought, discussion, and further study. These issues are designed to complement coursework in social work, education, human development, and developmental psychology.

References

Johnson, P. (1997). *A history of the American people.* New York: Harper Perennial.

Lerner, G. (1972). Doing domestic work. In G. Lerner (Ed.) *Black women in white America.* New York: Random House.

U.S. Department of Commerce. Bureau of the Census. *Fifteenth Census of the United States Population.* http://www.doc.gov.

Chapter 9

EIGHTH GRADE

Mr. Goodwin was my history teacher. Miz Cavanaugh, she was my math. And then, I had another one. I can see that woman now, but I can't call her name! Those two women and that man, they were a buildin block to me. And it seemed like they taken an interest in me, more than they did the other kids. When you registered, you had to tell if you mother and father was livin. And see, they knew my mother was passed. Then I had to tell them my mother had passed when I was ten years old. My dad was tryin to help me get an education. Out of eight children, my older sister was the only one who was really grown and married then. And it seemed to me they [teachers] was my guardian angel. And I appreciate that.

Mr. Goodwin was my history teacher. And, Lord, I didn't like history. This [referring to this life story project] is like history to me. And he explained it to me too. And that's what made me start to lovin' history. He said, "Now, you tell me about your mother." He lined it out for me, so I could see what history was. See, just to be readin that history book, "Why I have to know *this* old stuff?" Then he brought it down to my mother, to my father, to my grandmother, and he told me, he said now, "*This* is history." He said, "That's history." He said, "Your mother passed away. You tell me about that. You tell me about your grandmother helpin. You tell me about your dad and how he made cake." He lined it all out to me. And my dad helped me learn to cook. My mother helped me learn to cook and all that. So, I have others. I have a godmother, she was good. So he told me, he said, "This is history." And that is what started makin me to like history. I love to read history books after that.

Chapter 9

It seemed like they took an interest in me because I was tryin. I wanted! And every time you go to a school then, they want you to know they are with you if you are willin. And they want to know what you want to be. And that was one of the first things. After you got all signed up into the class and everything, always the principal would go over this with the teacher. He [the principal] listened. He would come in and listen and want to know what all the children want to be. That was they main interest. You tell what you want to be. So he knew each teacher's room: what boy, what girl, and what they want to be. And if they's failin because of the work, had to go through him. Then he would conference with the teacher. And I thought that was good. He was workin with the teacher and the children.

And when he come to me, he asked me, "Why you want to be a nurse?" I said, 'Cause my mama was sick, and we could have no nurse, and she was home sick. And I was her little nurse. 'Cause I was the youngest one, and the others was in the field workin, or somewhere else. And I had to help her. Mother laid in the bed and taught me how to cook. And Papa and them was in the field. She wasn't feelin good, the baby was so little, and so I had to be the little nursemaid and the baby sitter." And when I was tellin him, it just came back to me. I said, "Oh! That's the reason why." I said, "Mama used to help me helpin her."

ᑫᕙ

Well, you know what, Baby, let me tell you something. When I was goin to school, in Houston, I had a teacher as white as you, but her family wasn't. You see what I'm sayin? And that woman told us in class that she "didn't care for no black young'ns." Now, that was a teacher teachin her own race of people. She didn't like black people. And she went on to tell what her background was and explained it to us. But you know, she wasn't there too long. She was a good teacher, but she didn't like no black kids. Now, if they was brown skinned like that or light skinned, they was her pick. That was hers. But if you had the skin of mine, she didn't have no time for you.

And one day she made that remark in the classroom and I started to cryin. She made a slur remark to me about something. There I was tryin to get all I could, comin from a stressed-out family, where my mama had passed and my daddy was doin the best he could, and she was downin me. And I started cryin. This one girl said, "Go tell Professor Rhime [principal] on her." And I can't think of that child's name. I wished I could. I can see her face. She would talk up, but she was light complected. The teacher asked her, "What you got to do about it?" She [the other child] said, "I'm tired of you doin people like that. Why don't you talk to me like that?" So, she said [to Edith], "C'mon, I'll go with you now. Leave this class alone." I said—now I was scared—I said, "No, I got to stay in the class."

And when we come out of the class, she said, "You goin to Professor Rhime." She said, "You goin to Professor Rhime, now!" She took me by the hand and she said, "I'm gonna stand with you. We gonna break her up from that." So, we went on down to Professor Rhime's office. And I was still cryin, and she went in there tellin Professor Rhime what this woman said, and how she did. And he said, "What?" Well, he was the same color she was, and he wasn't like that toward us. So, he said, "I'll see about her tomorrow." And I never did go to that woman's class no more. He changed that around. He took me out and put me in another class.

I would know my lesson good when I would go in there, but the way she'd treat me, I would go in there and I'd forget everything. And she would start to talkin ugly to me and I just would start cryin. He [Professor Rhime] told her she [the teacher] had to straighten up. But then the next year, she wasn't there.

Chapter 10

WORKING FOR MIZ A.

So when I got up in my womanhood—I thought I was a woman, I wasn't. [I was] in my teens [fifteen years old], and I went to Houston to go to work. I was tryin to go to school, and I wanted to go to school. I wanted to be a nurse, and I had to help myself. My older sister had just got married. I had two more sisters was workin. My older sister never had any kids, but the other two sisters had childrens, so they didn't have nothin to help me with. So there I was tryin to work. I went to school the first year, and then, nobody could help me. My dad was tryin, but farmin work wasn't good. So, I said, "Well, if I can, [I'll] work and go to school." So, they had opened up a night school, and *that's* where I said, "Now I can go!"

I was workin for some people. I'd be nursin their babies and doin for the child what the mother couldn't do. I thought this would be great, if I told them what my plan was. I wanted to work and go to school at night. And they had just put on this night school, so I thought, "I want to be a nurse." And I was already nursin her baby. The head wasn't formed right and we had to use sandbags the doctor had. And every so often, I had to go in and change those bags, massage the head, and lay 'em a certain way. Baby come out as a beautiful baby. She had a *bad*-shaped head when I started with her.

Her father [the baby's grandfather] was an ex-minister. Now this is what hurt me. And she [Miz A.] told another lady, one of her friends, I'll never forget. I overheard them. They would have meetings at each other's house, and in that meetin I overheard them. Now, I'm servin them, and it was my day off, Thursday. And she was tellin this lady what I had told her. She said, "Well, if that happen, you're gonna lose your good maid." And she said, "No, you don't want *that* to happen because you won't have no maid." And, I'm *tryin* my best! I wanted to be that nurse.

And so, then they fixed it. I said if I could get off at six thirty or seven thirty—I *had* to be in that classroom no later than seven thirty. If I could have got off at seven o'clock, I coulda got to the school. And I talked to the teacher and everything. I had tried to make all the plans. He's [the teacher's] tryin to help me.

That old man, her father, was the ex-minister, and he said, "No!" He didn't want to have his dinner till six o'clock. He would sit at that table, and I couldn't take everything off that table until *he* moved. And one night, I guess the devil got in me too, that was in him. I says, "I'm gonna pull those dishes off this table and wash 'em, and I'm gonna *walk* out the door! If I come back tomorrow and don't have a job, I'll just go look for me another one." So when I left, he was sittin at the table. I washed up all the dishes and everything, and always had to mop the kitchen and everything before I leave. I did all that. He's still sittin at the table, in the dining area. I went out, closed the door.

Next day, when I got to work, Miz A. said, "Valerie," she saw I was hurt. I showed the expression in my face. I wasn't angry, I was just hurt. 'Cause I loved those kids so much, and she knew I love those kids too. And she say, "Valerie," she said, "What's wrong?" She said, "I come in and the dishes were on the table." Instead of him just leavin his, he got some more and put them on the table! Yes, he'd done put some more! She said, "You left all them dishes." I said, "No." I said, "I just left Mr. S. settin at the table with his plate, playin with Elizabeth, and I was tryin to get out and go. And he didn't want me to take the plates off until he got up from the table," and, I said, "I went out. I asked him was he finished and he told me he'd let me know." So, I said, "I finished everything else, and I mopped the kitchen." She said, "What?" She said, "There was milk on the floor in the kitchen." I said, "Oh, Miz A., no!" I said, "I mopped the kitchen before I left!" I said, "Now, he coulda come in here and wasted some on the floor," I said, "but I left the floor clean."

That hurt me so bad, for him to be a ex-minister of a church that she [Miz A.] was brought up in! And I couldn't understand that, and it

Chapter 10

puzzled me. So, I called the lady that had worked for them a long time before me, and I says, "You know what?" I says, "Something wrong with Mr. S." She said, "What?" And I told her what happened. She said, "Well, that's the one reason I left because he started actin different," she said, "I don't know what it is," she said, "but something's wrong." She said, "'cause he used to wasn't like that." And she had worked for 'em for years, and then he started actin like that with her, not cooperatin. And so I said, "Well, you know what, Berta?" I said, "I don't know if I'm gonna be there much longer," I said, "'cause I wants to go to night school." She said, "Don't tell them!" I said, "Well, I've already." She said, "Oh, you did the wrong thing." She said, "You shouldn't a never tell them." She said, "I told 'em about some things I wanted to do," she said, "and that's when he got like that with me." She said, "And that's why I had to leave."

So, that stopped me from my night school. After I left them I finally got another job. But, it didn't pay enough. And my dad was in the country with two little brothers under me, and I had to try to help him. And when I left my dad, I told him, I said, "Pop, I'm gonna try to help you." In the country then, pickin cotton you got 50 cents a hundred [pounds], and it was hard! And so my dad said, "Well, you work and try to put yourself through school." He says, "If you can help me, get somebody to wash the clothes." So every week when I would work for these people I got $6.00. And I had to pay a dollar for car fare, I had to send my dad a dollar so he could get the clothes washed, and I had to help my sister where I was stayin. So that's what I had left, to try to save. And if I needed a pair of shoes, a $1.98 pair of shoes, I couldn't go to the store and buy me a $1.98 pair of shoes. I put them on layaway, and paid 50 cents a week till I'd get them out. For, say, Easter, if I wanted me a dress for Easter, I had to start in January to put that in the layaway. And I never bought one over $2.98. *That* I thought was a *dress* dress [laughs]—$2.98!

Before the poor man [Mr. S.] passed away, I had done stopped workin for 'em a long time. And I didn't get a chance to go back to school. But, when it happened [Mr. S.'s illness], Berta was the one that called and told me. She said, "Have you been down to Miz A.'s lately?" I said, "No, Berta, I don't go anymore... I say, "You know I quit and I'm doin day work." So, she says, "Well, Mr. S. is askin for you. All the maids. He wants you to come down there." I said, "Berta, I don't want to go there." And she said, "Well, I'm gonna tell you," she said, "it's horrible." She said, "I'm gonna let you know—I went," she said, "but I wished I'd a known the condition he was in," she said, "I never would've went." She said, "It's real hard for you to see it, if you have sympathy for anybody." I said, "I can't go see him then." She told me what was goin on. They had to change him in the bed, now. An ex-minister! And I told Berta, I said, "Berta, I can't go see him." She said, "He's askin for you," she said, "he's askin for all the maids. He want to apologize to them." I said, "Well, he can apologize to God and I'll forgive him," I said, "because I can't go," I said, "I just can't go." And I didn't go, I didn't go.

∞

But that man was so nice with the kids when I started workin there. Where he started gettin off is we had to keep the front door locked, because the oldest little girl was about two-and-a-half or three years old, and she liked to go out, and she'd run. And he knew this. And one day I was busy in the kitchen. I had dressed her and everything and she wanted to go outside. I said, "Wait, Elizabeth." I said, "We gonna go outside today. We need to get through now in the kitchen." I said, "We goin outside." She said, "I want to go for a walk." I said, "We'll go for a walk," 'cause I'd usually take them for a walk.

That man got evil in him. You could lock the door, and she didn't know how to unlock the screen door, and I had the screen door locked. I looked around, and that child was goin through the door! And I had to come from the kitchen down through the dining room, the living room. And time I got to the door, she was runnin right down the street. She'd run right out the door, and the house was right on the street. She was goin down the street and it was a busy street. And, I started runnin behind her. That little girl could run, and I was runnin sayin, "Wait, Elizabeth! Wait, Elizabeth! Wait! Wait!" And a train was comin. She went down the street, went up a block, and then come down, and she turned again—she knowed where she was goin—and when she turned again, it [the train] was goin down a railroad track. And I looked up and here's a switch engine freight train comin down the track, and it said, "Whoo, whoo, whoo, whoo, whoo!" And she was runnin and laughin! Lord have mercy! I was runnin, sayin, "Elizabeth, stop! The train's gonna hit you! Elizabeth, look!" And I finally run and caught her, and I just grabbed her like, just picked her up. I almost fell with her. If I'd a fell on her we'd a both been hurt. And I was almost out of breath. And when the man [engineer] came by on that switch engine, he looked at me and shook his head. He said, "Give her this!" [indicates spanking] I didn't though. He saw her, and they was slowin that switch engine down, because they saw her runnin on that track. And I was scared nearly to death. When I picked her up and got off the track there was a trail right where you could pass goin down by the track. She was up in the middle of the track like, and laughin. She didn't know what she was doin. It scared me so bad, I was just tremblin. I'm holdin her like this [indicates cuddling] and sayin, "Don't you know, the train would run over you!" And I'm tellin what all would happen. "And Mama wouldn't have her little girl anymore, and I would be to blame for this! Don't do this, Elizabeth, to me!" I was almost in tears.

So I went on in, takin her back home. And I went in, and Mr. S. was sittin on the porch with his leg crossed and had his Bible. Readin his Bible! And he had let that little girl out of the house! When I walked up on the porch and saw that, I got so angry that I didn't know what to do! I always been with children. I love children. And I was just thinkin: what if that child would've got killed on that railroad track. And he was the cause of it. But I was the one takin care of her. I'd a been the one to blame. I looked at him, and he's sittin there, and I walked in with her. Mr. S. said, "Where you been?" I said, "I've been chasin Elizabeth, where you left the front door open." I said, "I chased her all around." And I said, "A freight train was comin," and I said, "I just got her off the track in time!" I didn't tell him it was a switch engine. I said freight train. I said, "Mr. S., Elizabeth cannot unlock that screen door. How did she get out?" He looked at me and turned his head and went to readin his paper like he didn't see anything. And he knew I knew he opened that door. I said, "Mr. S., will you please don't open the door for Elizabeth. I locks the doors when I'm workin." I said, "And I can't keep my eye on her and do the work in here." I says, "I try to do my work fast enough so I can take her out."

Chapter 11

PROTECTION AGAINST PREDATORS

My dad set me down one day. He said, "Baby Rae"—I was twelve goin on thirteen. He said, "Baby Rae," he says, "I want to talk to you," he says, "I am your father." I said, "Yes, sir." "Papa loves you." I said, "Yes, sir." He said, "Now I want to tell you *this*." He said, "I am your father, but I want you to remember this till the day you die." I said to myself, "Ooooooh, Lord! What's this?" And I said, "Yes, sir." He said, "All men have dog in 'em." He said, "I'm your father, and I want you to hold your head up and be a lady." And that's the way he was tellin me that men can rape you. And he says now, "Men, young men and boys," he said, "old mens too, will try and overpower you." He didn't say rape. He says, "When they do that," he says, "they're gonna try to pull your clothes off." And he said, "take that ding-a-ling"—he didn't say his "privates"—"and then insert it into you." He said, "Now, that's bein a dog." That's what he would say. He didn't know how to say "rape" and all that. He didn't know. He said, "But now I want you to do this one thing." I said, "What's that, Papa?" He said, "You too little to fight it off," he said, "but I want you to say, 'Wait a minute, let me do it.'" He said, "And you get that hand in there and you twist it, and you turn it, and you jerk it, and push it, and jerk it, and," he said, "They'll leave you alone."

∾

One time, I was in Houston workin, this young man was goin with a little friend [Bernice] of mine. We was from the same county. She was with her sister—her mother had passed—and she was with her older sister goin to school. I was workin. We had been singin in the country. I sung in a quartet, and we had been at this church, and this man had been at this church, and he used to sing in a quartet. So, he

Chapter 11

ended up in Houston too. And Bernice said, "Oh, Valarie," she said, "you know that quartet that used to sing together?" I said, "Yes." She said, "One of 'em is here in Houston." [She] said he'd been comin to see her and wanted to take her out. And her sister told her, "No," she wasn't gonna let her go by herself. So she said, "I want to go to the movie, and he said he would take me, but my sister said I couldn't go." She said, "Will you go with me, on your day off?" I said, "Sure, Bernice." So we talked with her sister, and her sister said, "Yeah." She said, "Now, you two, I don't mind her goin with two of ya'll." She said, "But two of ya'll can master one." I said, "Oh, yeah!" So [laughter] this particular Thursday, she [Bernice] said, "OK. He gonna come and pick you up. He's drivin his car, and he gonna come pick me up and we goin to a show." There was some particular show she wanted to go see. I thought, "OK." I got off from work and I raced home and I dressed. It was my day off, on a Thursday. So I got off early.

He came by to pick me up, and I knew him because I had been singin in a quartet. We got in the car and he said, "Well, I got to go by my cousin's house." I didn't know he had no cousin, and I said, "OK." He said, "And then we gonna go to Bernice, and then we'll go to the show." I said, "OK." Went to this house. It wasn't no cousin's house. It was a rooming house where everything went on there. And he said, "I'm gonna run up, and I'll be right back." I said, "OK." He went upstairs, he went to his room. He came back down, and he said, "My sister's gone to the store, and she said for me to wait here, and told for us to wait." I said, "OK." He said, "Come up—she said for us to wait. She's gonna go with us." I went. I was little stupid, innocent. I went up. So I'm sittin up there with him. "When is your sister comin back?" "She'll be back."

And finally, I guess what he said [to himself] was, "I can't do it no other way, I'm gonna overpower her." And, honey, he did the wrong thing! [Laughter] He did the wrong thing. When he tried to overpower me! I did just like my daddy told me. My daddy said, "Now you have to play it cool." He said, "Make him think he gonna get what he want, but you get that and you twist it, and you jerk it, and you pull it, and you twist it." Honey, I sent him to the doctor! [Laughter] I take my coat, and I had my purse, and I made him lead me to the door. And they had some stairs I had to go down. I got to those stairs to the door and, and

I kept twistin and jerkin, twist and twist and jerk and that man fallin back. [Laughter] Down the stairs I went.

I went back to my sister's house, and I cut cross. The way we drove, if I'd a went that way, he'd a probably caught up with me. But I cut through, and I knew a shortcut to get from there. And there was a school there where they had been findin bodies—people had been gettin killed, and they'd been findin people dead around this school. And his house was right close to this school.

But Honey, when I got to my sister's house, I ran up in there [indicates knocking], "Hello! Open the door! Open the door!" They was gone to bed. Thello [brother-in-law] come right to the door. "What's the matter?" I said, "Open the door, open the door!" Just as he opened the door, the guy drove by the house. And I went in. He said, "I thought you's goin to the show!" I said, "Thello, sit down." [Laughs] I said, "Ya'll, I got to *tell* you about this." And when I told him, he got so angry, he said, "I ought to go find him now. And kill—" I said, "No, Thello." I said, "He gonna have to go to the doctor." He say, "What?" I say, "Oh, yeah. He gonna *have* to go to the doctor."

So, Bernice was sittin at home over at her sister's house waitin for us to come pick her up, 'cause she told him to come pick me up and come pick her up and we'd go to the show. We didn't get to the show. *I* was the show.

So the next day I went to work. Her sister called me on the job. She said, "Valerie?" I said, "Yes." She said, "This is Shirley." I said, "Yeah, Shirley." She said, "What happened?" I said, "Shirley," I said [laughs] I said, "I have to tell you." [Laughs] I said, "I ain't got time to tell you now," I said. "When I come from work, I'll come by your house." 'Cause I could ride the bus and streetcar and get off in about half a block to their house. But, I said, "Now, somebody'll have to—" She said, "Oh, I'll get you home. I'll get you home." She said, "Honey, I want to *hear* of this!" [Laughs]

When I got off from work and I went by her house, Bernice said, "How come you?" And I said, "Bernice, Honey, you sure's did me wrong." And she said, "What did I do?" Shirley put her hands on her hips and she said, "Wait a minute. Is it what I think it is?" I said, "I think it is." [Laughs] She sat. So I said, "Y'all sit down." And I said, "Let me tell you about it." So when I told 'em, Shirley said [claps], "I *knew* it was something!" [Laughs] She said, "Now, Bernice, you wouldn't a had sense enough to do what she did!" [Laughter] But by my dad tellin me these things, and he told me, he said, "Now, this'll stop him," he said, "'cause it will hurt." He said, "And there ain't no man," he says, "gonna force himself on you if you can do it." He says, "'Cause this gonna be hurtin so bad that they gonna try and take care of themselves." And he had to go to the doctor. They sent him to the doctor. He was off work for a week.

Chapter 12

KEEPING TO THE RIGHT PATH

I can look back over my life [and] see from whence I came and guidance that I had from my dad [and] the ten years mother had with me. She instilled life in me. She started me in piecin a quilt. I was nine years old. But when mother died, I had a quilt piece. I didn't know how to quilt then. So, I went back over it, the little bit that I was learnin here and there, all of this put together, and it kept *me* doin the right thing instead of the wrong thing.

I made some bad mistakes! Yes, I did. [Laughter] I used to go from the church to the dancin house. I loved to dance! Sunday night when church was over, I'd get the streetcar and the bus and here I'd go to Oak Grove. And one night, I look back and say, "God, what saved me? You're good to me." It was way out and the streetcar would go so far, and then you had to get out and walk about four blocks. One Sunday night I'm goin to Oak Grove. Got out of church [giggle], caught the bus, went to Oak Grove. I *loved* to dance.

Got out there and everything was goin fine, and two guys got started and they pulled a gun! And I said, "Lord, if I get killed here my daddy'll never get over it!" I didn't think of *myself* gettin *killed*. But, I thought about what my *daddy* would say, 'cause he didn't raise me up that way. And [laughs] so I said, "Lord, let me get outta this place." And people started gettin out. I got my little self together and I started easin and easin and I got to the door, and I told the man, I said, "Mister, let me outta here!" [Laughs] And he was tryin to get out, too! And, so he said, "I'm goin out like I'm with you." He was scared. We went through that door and I started runnin. I had to go 'bout a block and a half to where the *bus* come. Remember, I rode the bus out there. And I didn't know if there was gonna be no bus at the bus stop or not. I was gettin away from there because they had had some shootins out there. I ran and I got to the bus stop. I was so tired, and I stood there huffin and blowin, look like no bus gonna never come. I said, "Lord, it's outta my hand and I'm gonna have to start walkin. But I could walk so far, and I could catch another bus. I could catch that Dawlin bus and go to town, then I could catch the Lawns bus, and it would take me on out to where my sister were, and I could get off and just cross. Run a whole block from where she lived. Well, I finally made up my mind to start walkin. I looked up there and here comes the bus! Lord, Jesus! I was so *glad* I saw that bus, I didn't know what to do! My heart was in and out of my mouth, and it looked like it said, "Boom, boom, boom, boom, boom." I said, "Thank you, Lord! Thank you, Lord!" Then I thought back. Now Pop didn't raise me like that, and Mama didn't go for nothin like that. Now, somethin just talkin to me! "Now, you know you wasn't raised like that, now why you wanna keep on doin that?" I just wanted to dance! I just wanted to go dancin!

So, when I got on the bus [laughs], my heart looked like it was sayin, "Scoopta, scoopta, scoopta, scoopta, scoopta, scoopta." I say, "Lord, stop my heart!" And the bus driver looked at me, he say, "Are you all right?" I say, "Mmmm hmmm." [Laughs]. He say, "What's goin on out there?" He knew it was somethin was goin on there. And I said, "Two guys was fixin to start fightin." He said, "And you ran, didn't ya?" I said, "Yes, sir, I did." He said, "You did the right thing," he said, "because they don't care who they shoot when they start shootin." And he was tellin me about two weeks before that, how some guys got killed. They started shootin, and guys started to runnin, and stray bullets hit 'em.

So, that taught me a lesson. And that's why I try to talk to young people today. I tell 'em like my dad say, "Don't think you can do somethin and get by, and nobody know about it. It's gonna be somebody gonna see ya." And every time I thought I was gonna be gettin by, and I'm gonna slip out to this dancin place, and nobody see me, if I don't see 'em. If I didn't see 'em when I got there, I'd see 'em before I leave. Somebody that knows me. And so I stopped. But, I loved to *dance!*

But, it would hurt my dad to know that's where I died, in a dancin place. He didn't raise me that way. So I stopped. It made me stop and look back from whence I come. And my dad used to say, "Help 'em, Lord, to look from whence they come." He would pray for us. And he'd say, "Lord, help 'em. Keep 'em on the right path."

Chapter 13

SEGREGATION AND INTEGRATION

Segregation—bad, bad, bad. But it was still some good, good, good white people, that was good to you. You see what I'm sayin? So everybody wasn't the bad ones and didn't treat you bad. I had some that treated me bad, but I had lots that treated us good. And like my mother and daddy used to say, "The good can overcome the bad." So that's the way we was brought up. And, regardless of what we went through, we was taught not to hate. Hate will destroy you. That was one thing my dad and mother instilled in us. They said, "Regardless of who, don't hate them. Because if you start hatin, hate will destroy you." [God] didn't say just because a you color and my color, you stick with your color. God give us all an opportunity to spread that love that we have with one another. So, if I take care of your baby and you take care of my baby, what's the difference?

∾

Well, durin this same time, when I got those shoes—it was a store that blacks couldn't go in there and try on a dress if they wanted to buy a dressy-dress. That's why most black people was makin their clothes. They was finding seamstresses that would make their clothes. They would get the catalogs so they could see what styles was goin on. My mother, before she passed away, and before she got too sick, she used to make all of our clothes. Mama could take a catalog and look at it and she could—didn't have paper to cut out no pattern—she'd measure how far she have to go and cut and everything. And she measured on that cloth and mark it and that's the way she did. She had one of those treadle kinds of Singer sewing machines. And I used to have to get down there and push. Her legs would get tired of peddlin and she'd say, "C'mon." And I'd have to get down there and peddle that machine with my hands to help.

So, it was just at that day and time—the way segregation and everything was—parents wasn't keepin it all from the kids, but they were tryin to raise the kids where they could accept it. And they was tellin them what they could and could not do, and what to look out for. "Well, why they do that?" "Well, they don't know no better." That's what they would say. "Well, Mama, Mama how come we have to—?" "But, they don't know no better, Baby."

And I looked back over it after that and after I got older and I said, "Well, poor Mama and Papa had a time with they kids." But they taught us all of the time, "Don't hate nobody." Now, that was one thing I praise God for, that they brought that to us, "Don't hate people, regardless to what they do to you. Don't hate them. Leave it to God and He'll fix it." I used to wonder, "Why do they tell us to leave it to God? How come God haven't fixed it already? How come He hasn't fixed it already?" Yeah! I used to be, "If He let it go this far, why ain't He done fixed it then?" [Papa said], "Leave it to God, He'll fix it." "Well, Papa, how come He haven't already fixed it?" He said, "He'll fix it in his own dear time. He have a time set to do all things." And that's the way he would leave it. He say, "You can't fix it. God have to fix it. It takes time." Yeah. And he'd say, "It's gonna come a day—the Bible don't lie—when everybody is gonna be as sisters and brothers, before the end of time." And say, "He's comin again. It's gonna be for all the good. It's gonna be just like sisters and brothers."

We are all His children and we are all brothers and sisters. So, how come we can't live here together and be as brother and sister? That was the hardest thing for me, and I used to tell Mother, "Mama, why is it we can't sit here and they can sit there?" But, in the field, we could pick cotton together, we could work in the field and hoe together. We could do all of these workin things together. But, you know, thank God we start to breakin that [segregation].

༄

In our church, we had a quartet group. I think I told you about that. We had a quartet group, and we used to go to white folks' church singin, and when we'd go to they church, we'd have to sit in the back of the church. We'd sit in the back until they want us to perform, and then we'd go up. And in our church, we'd put them on the front seat, and we did that so much until that broke it down. We would put them in the front. It would just be a group of them from their church and the preacher wouldn't be with 'em. We'd hand them choir programs and things like that. And they loved to hear Negro spirituals and they'd come to our church and we'd give them our front seats, next to the front of the pulpit. But they would invite us to come and sing, but when we got there, they had our seats lined up to when you enter the door, you start sittin down. So, we started puttin them in the front.

Finally, one time we invited them, Honey, they was gonna be there, they loved the singin. And the preacher came to our church, and our pastor invited him up in the pulpit. The man didn't know whether to come up in the pulpit or sit with his people. And the pastor told him, "Brother, come on up here with us." And them people looked at us! Some of them got red, red, red! That blood boiled up and he said, "Brother." And this young preacher, he was sorta young there, he got up there and he said, "I just wanna say this before our young people starts to singin. I invite my brother. This is my brother in Christ. We different colors, but he's still doin the same thing I'm doin, tryin to save souls." He said, "So, God is with him, and God is with me." That meant a lot right there. So, they started coolin down, but you saw that face! If you could have seen they faces when he said, "Brother, come on up." And he [white preacher] didn't know whether to come up or stay down. When our pastor got up, he told 'em, he said, "Well, I know that my people has been sittin at the back. We don't mind that, but we are all God's children and we love one another." After that, we didn't have no more trouble. Whenever they invited us to come to their church and sing, they'd have our seats with theirs or in the front. If we got there early, wherever we want to go and pick our seat, that was our seat. We didn't have no special place. And that started breakin it down, breakin it down. And that's what had been a thing in our lifetime that we had to respect and had to work towards it, and we had to break it down.

I wasn't taught to hate whenever things like that would happen. When I bought these shoes, I asked him [my dad] why they was like that and he said, "Baby, this God works in mysterious ways, His wonders to perform. He plants his footsteps on the seeds and rises from the storm." He said, "Just keep on doin good and good will overtake evil." Now, that was my daddy's way of talkin to us and teachin us not to hate. He said, "Regardless if somebody do you bad, you do them good." He said, "That's the best way to whup 'em." He said, "If they do you bad, you turn back and do them good, and God'll bless you for that." He said, "They gonna have to give an account of their act and you got to give an account of yours. So, if they gonna do you bad and you do them bad, then both of you got to suffer for it."

 распр

My daddy sat down and started explainin to me about it [racism] and he told me, he said, "Baby, you might live here 'til you die, and you still won't be considered as a regular person." He said, "But don't forget that the man above, God, sees and knows all things and you be good to those that be bad to you and you'll get repaid for it." He said, "It may not be here, but it's after you're gone." And that's what he say, "You might live here in Hell, but you don't want to die and go to Hell." He said, "If you live here and do good and you die, God's gonna take you with Him." And that was one thing that made me feel better, 'cause I was gettin that little hate feelin—"How come I have to be good to them and they're not good to me?" You know, that kind of thing, but my daddy stopped that and before Mother died, she used to lay in her bed and get different scriptures in the Bible and call us around her bed and say, "I want y'all to listen to this." And she would read to us and explain to us. My daddy always told me, "If you do bad, bad gonna come back to you, and if you do good, good is gonna come back to you." He said, "It may not come when you expect it, but it will come." So, that made me have more courage and more determination to overcome that bad.

распр

Now, a thing that I learned, that my daddy taught me and my mama, till she died—after that I had cousins and aunts and whatnot to teach me—and some things that they taught me and told me about, I couldn't dare at that day and time to talk about it. You see what I'm sayin? Like I can talk about it now. Then you'd talk about it, somebody was goin to come up missin. If it got out, they'd come to your house and say, "I want so-and-so-and-so out of that house. Send them out now!" Some of them would shoot 'em down in front of the parents! You see what I'm sayin? So, now I think it's time for that healin to come. If I can help you heal from something, you are helpin me to heal from somethin, because we are bondin more together to one another, which God wants us to do.

Now, in that day and time, we had relatives that was murdered. Some was hung, but it was those people's time that they was doin that. But as the times changed, why hold that against the new ones that's comin along, those that didn't have anything to do with it? You see what I'm sayin? You understand? Those that did that, they have to give an account of what they did, and they have to meet God for it. But those that didn't and reached out and said, "I love you"?

He created us all, and why can't we live here on earth together? If we want to see His face again, we gonna have to do that, and that is why I feel like whatever I can say, whatever I can do to cause a togetherness, I'm willin to do so. I believe the Bible, and I know that He is been good to me. He's been my all and all ever since I've been here. And what I lost in my mother and my father, He picked it up and He guided me through shady streets, dangerous places, saved my life when I just knew I was gone, and it wasn't nothin but God that did it. Now why would I turn against Him? And He teaches me in the Bible, "Love ye one another." Now, He didn't say the color of your skin. And I have relatives that was white! So, it wasn't none of our faults to be like that. Why should I turn against them? I don't see it, I just don't see it. If I can be close to you and we can learn from one another, why can't we? I think that's what God wants us to do.

Interlude 2

OPPRESSION AND RESISTANCE

Although Edith Hudley's life story is first and foremost a story of religious faith, it is also a narrative of resistance to oppression. During the first eighteen years of her life, she experienced profound social inequities linked to race, gender, and social class. With the guidance of supportive adults, she resisted oppression through religiously based belief in her own worth. Mrs. Hudley's account is part of a long history of first person reports of oppression and resistance in the U.S., a tradition that is traceable to the classic slave narratives (Gates, 1987; for modern examples, see Featherson, 1994). Yet, like religion and spirituality, the role of oppression in the lives of children and youth has received little attention from developmental researchers (Fisher, Jackson, & Villarruel, 1998).[1]

However, scholars of child development increasingly recognize the importance of context in human development, and oppression remains a formative context for many children. Researchers and practitioners alike use the concepts of risk and protective factors to understand how individuals like Edith Hudley have developed well despite intense, ongoing stress (Frazier, 1997). Risk factors, such as poverty, increase the probability that psychological problems will develop, progress, and become chronic. Protective factors, such as positive relationships with adults, can moderate the effects of risk factors so that more positive developmental outcomes may occur.

---

1. See also Leadbeater and Way (1996). This collection of papers directly addresses, through a combination of quantitative and qualitative methodologies, the role of racism, sexism, and classism in the lives of adolescent women of color including identity development, peer relationships, sexuality, health, and career development.

Risk and protective factors vary, depending on where children are positioned in the sociopolitical world. For African-American children and many other children of color, racism is a very significant risk factor that can limit opportunities for development and undermine motivation, confidence, and self-esteem. It is interesting that in Comer and Poussaint's (1992) popular book on raising black children, the vast majority of questions from parents, teachers, and others involved with African-American children center on issues of race, including how to prepare children to resist racism. For European-American children, who do not carry the burden of membership in a devalued group, racism operates differently as a risk factor. It can limit opportunities for cultural enrichment, for self-understanding, and for awareness of the detrimental effects of privilege on their own lives.

As a child and teenager, Edith had to contend with the intertwined oppressions of race, gender, and class, but these conditions were mitigated by a variety of protective factors: excellent health and intelligence, competent parents, a loving family, and a caring community of relatives and neighbors. A great deal can be learned about oppression and resistance from a careful analysis of Edith's varied experiences, particularly when viewed in conjunction with other first-person accounts and research reports. Mrs. Hudley's life story is especially relevant to the complex issue of how adults can help children to respond to oppression in a manner that supports their psychological development.

Oppression in Edith's Development

As defined by sociologist Louis Kushnick (1998), racism is the distribution of resources in favor of particular groups at the expense of others. One of the earliest and most far-reaching ways in which Edith's development was affected by racism was the death of her mother. The absence of basic medical care to poor, rural blacks surely contributed to Mamie's death from anemia at the age of forty-two when Edith was only ten years old. Mamie died at home, without the benefit of medical care, including the iron supplements available at the time. Had Mamie received medical care, it would have been within a segregated medical system.

Edith's development was shaped as well by the quality of education available to her. A highly motivated and competent student, she attended for eight short years schools that were segregated and lacking in the basic resources available to white schools in the area. Even the textbooks that Edith and her classmates used were castoffs from the white school, and Edith recalls that many had pages missing. These race-based restrictions interlocked with poverty to curtail educational advancement. Despite her repeated attempts to obtain training as a nurse and despite her hard-working and highly resourceful father, economic hardship ultimately foreclosed on Edith's ambitions.

The combined forces of racism and poverty constrained Edith's life in systematic ways that would be hard for any child to comprehend. But, like others of her time and place, Edith also encountered racism in less abstract form as deliberate acts of cruelty aimed at her and her family. While walking home from school, she and her relatives were taunted, called hateful names, and even beaten by white children. When the violence escalated, the response from the school board was to dismiss the black children from school half an hour early each day, further limiting an already strained educational program. As a teenager, Edith endured Mr. S.'s provocative and spiteful behavior. Throughout her childhood and youth, Edith was aware that racist beliefs could be expressed through violent acts, including murder, perpetrated by the Ku Klux Klan on black people, including members of her extended family. The toxicity of this everyday environment has been described in numerous first-person accounts, essays, and works of fiction and occasioned Mamie's and Aaron's urgent advice to not "take hate" into oneself. (For first-person accounts, see Lee, 1994; for an essay, see hooks, 1995; for a fictional account, see Morrison, 1970.)

Edith also experienced oppression within her African-American community. Virginia Harris (1994) defines *colorism* as: "... prejudicial or preferential treatment of same-race people based solely on their color.... [T]o ascribe value and privilege to a same-race person based on lightness of skin" (p. 9). While attending a segregated high school—an outwardly safe place for children of color—one of Edith's African-American teachers explicitly favored light-skinned children and degraded Edith and other children because of their dark skin. Racist ideologies internalized and socialized by people of color have been described by a variety of authors as a particularly insidious form of oppression. For example, Virginia Harris (1994) describes the challenges to a child's self-esteem when racist ideologies are internalized and acted upon by those family members closest to the child. Tony Morrison's novel *The Bluest Eye* portrays the devastating effects of pervasive European ideals of beauty on the psyche of young black girls (Morrison, 1970). France Davis (1997) describes how divisive colorism has been within African-American communities including churches where dark- and light-skinned blacks once were assigned to sit in separate sections.

Although sexism was not as apparent in Edith Hudley's early years, it was clearly at work in her youth and, as later chapters reveal, it was responsible for some of the most wrenching challenges in her adult life. When she was a teenager, a member of a church singing group attempted to rape her. The complex issue of gender-based oppression and violence within black communities has been much discussed (hooks, 1995; West, 1993). bell hooks (1995) and others have observed that no individual or group of people is immune to oppressive behavior. Just as the African-American man may be oppressed at work, he may oppress his wife at home, and she may oppress her children. Consistent with Edith's beliefs, Cornel West (1993) calls for us to recognize the responsibility of all individuals to eliminate their own oppressive behavior. In addition, adults must work on behalf of children toward the elimination of societal and cultural forms of oppression.

Resistance

Students in Wendy Haight's developmental psychology classes consistently commented in their journals on Mrs. Hudley's inner strength, determination, and perseverance. Many middle-class, European-American students expressed surprise that she had remained motivated, loving, and focused on the basic goodness of people. Many resolved to put into practice in their own lives her advice passed down from her father: "If first you don't succeed, try, try, try, and then try again," and "All that you do, do with your might. Things done by half are never done right."

Like Edith in her youth, a significant number of girls who are growing up with racism, sexism, and poverty do not fit popular stereotypes of the teenaged welfare mother, school dropout, or drug addict. Indeed, the majority of young women of color live meaningful and productive lives (Leadbeater & Way, 1996). Many have resisted what Cornel West (1991) identifies as an important threat to African-Americans today: nihilism, that is, the loss of hope, the absence of meaning, and feelings of depression, personal worthlessness, and despair. An important issue for research and practice is to identify, understand, and support alternative, positive pathways to healthy development taken by many children and youth who experience oppression.

Clearly, strategies for resisting oppression are multiple and complex. Adults have a range of options available to them from simply living a personally meaningful life to organized political resistance. But, what are the options for active resistance available to children, and how can adults such as parents, social workers, and educators help? Some insight into these issues can be gleaned from Janie Victoria Ward's (1996) interviews with African-American parents. These adults described a variety of internal, psychological processes that they felt facilitated their children's ability to resist oppression as well as their own socialization strategies to support children's resistance. These antidotes to oppression included pride in their black heritage, self-esteem, and a critical consciousness of oppression. These and a variety of other related psychological and socialization processes are illuminated in Edith's account of her childhood and youth.

Truth Telling

Edith seemed to benefit especially from her father's honest, critical assessments of oppression. She was her daddy's "Baby Rae," an obviously competent individual entitled to love and respect. Furthermore, Aaron was honest about gender- and race-based hatred. In his discussions with her, he conveyed that she was capable of meeting these challenges, however difficult, and equipped her with strategies that would allow her to succeed. For example, when she was twelve years old, Aaron warned her that "all men have dog in 'em" and then explained how she could protect herself, small as she was.

When Edith was growing up, white neighbors, store clerks and others directed dismissive, and sometimes overtly hateful, behavior towards her. Aaron described the harsh reality: "Baby, you might live here till you die, and you still won't be considered a regular person." Then he linked this truth to advice based on religious faith: "But don't forget that the man above, God, sees and knows all things . . . you be good to those that be bad to you and you'll get repaid for it. . . . you might live here in Hell, but you don't want to die and go to Hell."

Aaron's practice of truth telling is similar to that described by African-American parents in Ward's study. These parents stated that they had an obligation to tell their children the truth about racism and articulated the negative consequences of silence. These parents were aware of subtle forms of racism and feared damage to a naïve child's self-concept. They felt that it was their responsibility to tell their children the truth about the sociopolitical environment as a first step to resistance.

Not Stereotyping Others

Edith Hudley's stories about her youth suggest that she and her family not only resisted the hurtful stereotypes that were imposed on them but also resisted reducing others to stereotypes. Very early in life, Edith learned that social status—for example, as white or black, male or female—may predict but does not determine whether an *individual* will behave with kindness and fairness or hate and exploitation. In Edith's world, it was dangerous to fall back on simplistic stereotypes based on race, gender, or class. Such stereotyping could delude one into thinking that there was no need to size up the individual and the situation. Edith's naïve assumption that Mr. S. was benevolent, by virtue of his status as a retired minister, resulted in her disclosing her plans to attend nursing school and his subsequent moves to block those plans. Neglecting to assess the individual also could lead to missed opportunities. As a child attempting to buy shoes, Edith benefited from the kindness of a white man, and a situation that could have ended in disappointment instead ended in triumph.

Critical Consciousness

Throughout the early chapters of her life story, Mrs. Hudley describes active rejection of the notion that she is not as capable or entitled as others. For example, after Mr. S. attempted to block her education plans, Edith quit a relatively well-paying job and, eventually, even refused him the comfort of providing her with a deathbed apology. A number of authors have identified active, psychological resistance to racist and sexist practices as an adaptive coping strategy for maintaining a healthy self-concept (for example, hooks, 1990; Leadbeater & Way, 1996; Lykes, 1985). For example, Pastor, McCormick, & Fine (1996) conducted ethnographic fieldwork and discussion groups with young women of color in urban middle and high schools. These authors describe how racism, sexism, and urban poverty challenged the development of adolescent girls of color. Many girls, however, displayed considerable strengths. They had developed a critical consciousness, questioning various educational practices and expressing an awareness that schools often are not designed to protect them or promote their interests. Furthermore, many girls described well-developed strategies for resisting oppression and asserting themselves.

Less developed in these girls was a sense of the potential power of their collective resistance. A critical awareness of oppression, if not combined with the development of strategies for effective social change, can lead to despair (Tatum, 1992, 1994). In later chapters, Edith provides stories about her involvement in organized group resistance in the pre-Civil Rights era. For example, she helped to expose and ameliorate funding practices that left her eldest son's segregated elementary school inadequately supported.

In conclusion, two points are important to emphasize. First, when oppression goes underground, resistance can become more difficult. The elimination of the overt, explicit forms of oppression common in Edith's childhood and youth results, in some respects, in a more complex developmental task for children and youth today as racism, sexism, and class prejudice take increasingly nuanced and subtle forms (for example, Lamar, 1999). In the words of a sixteen-year-old urban girl interviewed by Kozol (1995):

> It's not like, "Well, those babies aren't dying fast enough, ... Let's figure out a way to kill some more." It's not like that at all. It's like ... if you weave enough bad things into the fibers of a person's life—sickness and filth, old mattresses and other junk thrown in the streets and other ugly ruined things, and ruined people over there, then give us the very worst schools anyone could think of, hospitals that keep you waiting for ten hours, police that don't show up when someone's dying, take the train that's underneath the street in the good neighborhoods and put it up above where it shuts out the sun, you can guess that life will not be very nice and children will not have much sense of being glad of who they are (pp. 39-40).

Second, although it is tempting to read Edith Hudley's life story as simply inspirational, it is important to remember that oppression does exact a price even in the most resilient. Like many other African-American seniors, Mrs. Hudley has suffered from serious health problems directly linked to stress. Edith developed as a loving, productive individual despite a series of childhood losses and disappointments that might have been crippling. However, these consequences of oppression also left her with a profound and lasting sadness.

Thus far, Edith's account is of experiences predating the Civil Rights movement in the segregated South. Despite the great achievements of the Civil Rights movement, the continuing effects of racism are still chillingly apparent in modern U.S. society. The descriptions of educators, ethnographers, and journalists of the conditions of inner-city schools, medical facilities, and neighborhoods inhabited primarily by people of color leave little doubt of the continuing effects of racism on the lives of children (see, for example, Heath, 1995; Kotlowitz, 1991). Furthermore, recent statistics indicate that rates of poverty are substantially higher among children of color than among white children. In 1991, Puerto Rican, African-American, and Mexican-American children under eighteen years of age had poverty rates of 57 percent, 44 percent, and 36 percent, respectively, compared to a rate of 15 percent for white children (McLoyd, 1998). Clearly, there is a continuing need for adults to help children and one another to resist oppression in a manner that allows for healthy development.

References

Comer, J.C., & Poussaint, A.F. (1992). *Raising black children*. New York: Plume.

Davis, F. (1997). *Light in the midst of Zion: A history of black Baptists in Utah, 1892-1996*. Salt Lake City, UT: University Publishing, LLC.

Featherston, E. (Ed.). (1994) *Skin deep: Women writing on color, culture and identity*. Freedom, CA: Crossing Press.

Fisher, C., Jackson, J., & Villarruel, F. (1998). The study of African American and Latin American children and youth. In W. Damon (Editor in Chief), *Handbook of Child Psychology* (5th ed., vol. 4). New York: Wiley.

Fraser, M.W. (Ed.). (1997). *Risk and resilience in childhood: An ecological perspective*. Washington DC: NASW Press.

Gates, H.L., Jr. (Ed.). (1987). *The classic slave narratives*. New York: Mentor.

Harris, V. (1994). Prison of color. In E. Featherston (Ed.), *Skin deep: Women writing on color, culture and identity*. Freedom, CA: The Crossing Press.

Heath, S.B. (1995). Ethnography in communities: Learning the everyday life of America's subordinated youth. In J.A. Banks & C.M. Banks (Eds.), *Handbook of research on multicultural education*. New York: Macmillan.

hooks, b. (1990). *Yearning: Race, gender, and cultural politics*. Boston: South End Press.

hooks, b. (1995). *Killing rage: Ending racism*. New York: Holt.

Kotlowitz, A. (1991). *There are no children here: The story of two boys growing up in the other America*. New York: Anchor Books.

Kozol, J. (1992). *Savage Inequalities: Children in America's schools*. New York: Harper Perennial.

Kozol, J. (1995). *Amazing grace: The lives of children and the conscious of a nation*. New York: Crown.

Kushnick, L. (1998). *Race, class and struggle: Essays on racism and inequality in Britain, the U.S. and Western Europe*. New York: Rivers Oram Press.

Lamar, J. (1999). *Close to the bone: A novel*. New York: Crown.

Leadbeater, B.J., & Way N. (Eds.) (1996). *Urban girls: Resisting stereotypes, creating identities*. New York: New York University Press.

Lee, J. (1994). Racism doesn't grow up. In E. Featherston (Ed.), *Skin Deep: Women writing on color, culture and identity*. Freedom, CA: Crossing Press.

Lykes, M.B. (1985). Gender and individualistic versus collectivist bases for notions about the self. *Journal of Personality*, 53, 356-383.

Maston, A.S., Best, K.M., & Garmezy, N. (1990). Resilience and development: Contributions from the study of children who overcome adversity. *Development and Psychopathology*, 2, 425-444.

McLoyd, V. (1998). Children in poverty: Development, public policy, and practice. In W. Damon (Ed.), *Handbook of child psychology*. (5th ed., Vol. 4) New York: Wiley.

Morrison, T. (1970). *The bluest eye*. New York: Holt, Rinehart and Winston.

Pastor, J., McCormick, J., & Fine, M. (1996). Makin' homes: An urban girl thing. In B. J. Leadbeater & N. Way (Eds.), *Urban girls: Resisting stereotypes, creating identities*. New York: New York University Press.

Tatum, B.D. (1992). Talking about race, learning about racism: The application of racial identity development theory in the classroom. *Harvard Educational Review, 62*, 1-24.

Tatum, B.D. (1994). Teaching white students about racism: The search for white allies and the restoration of hope. *Teachers College Record, 95*, 462-476.

Ward, J.V. (1996). Raising resisters: The role of truth telling in the psychological development of African American girls. In B.J. Leadbeater & N. Way (Eds.), *Urban girls: Resisting stereotypes, creating identities*. New York: New York University Press.

West, C. (1993). *Race matters*. Boston: Beacon Press.

PART 3

Married Life

Part 3 of Edith Hudley's oral history encompasses her courtship and marriage to her first husband, Eugene, from 1938 to 1961. It takes place in Oakland, California, and in rural Texas. U.S. census data from 1940 indicate that during Mrs. Hudley's stay, Oakland had a population of about 300,000. From 1940 to 1950, the black population in the bay area increased from 16,500 to 147,000 as a result of labor demand in the Oakland and San Francisco shipyards (Mendelsohn, 2002).

Edith's work in the shipyards during World War Two reflected a continuing trend of African Americans leaving the rural South for the urban North. This movement, known as the Great Migration, resulted from a quest for higher wages and an attempt to escape economic setbacks and racial discrimination in the South. From 1916 to the end of the 1960s, over 6 million blacks moved north. With World War Two, expanding defense-related jobs in California encouraged even more African Americans like Edith and Eugene to migrate north, (Dublin, 1991). Although there were more job opportunities, the North was not a haven from racial discrimination. Blacks in Oakland, for example, experienced discrimination in housing, education, and employment. Even in the 1960s, most Bay Area African Americans still lived in substandard housing in virtually segregated communities.

Mrs. Hudley's work in the shipyards also reflected new opportunities for women to enter into skilled occupations. During the Depression, the high rate of unemployment led to demands that all women, especially women who were married, give up their jobs to men. World War Two brought an economic recovery (Bailey, 1991). In addition, it briefly transformed demands for exclusion of women into an insistence that women take jobs in war industries. Black women like Edith especially benefited from a brief respite in job segregation and moved into higher paying, skilled jobs (Kessler-Harris, 1991). Edith's participation in the shipyards, however, meant more to her than relative economic comfort. It provided an opportunity to excel at challenging and meaningful work. To this day, Edith takes great pride and satisfaction in her work as a burner.

When reading part 3 of the oral history, it may be helpful to refer to Appendix A which lists several key events. These include Edith's marriage to Eugene H. in 1938. Four years afterwards, Eugene and Edith moved to Oakland in search of better employment. They stayed for four years during which time Edith worked in the shipyards. After Aaron's death in 1946, Edith and Eugene returned to rural Texas where they built and operated a general store outside of Houston. Their sons were born in 1948 and 1951. They returned to Oakland in 1956 in search of better schools and opportunities for their children. In 1960, Edith was injured when the car she was driving to work was hit by a train. Shortly afterwards, in 1961, Edith and Eugene divorced.

Appendix B lists a number of people, along with their names and nicknames, important to this segment of the oral history. Eugene's father and mother, Eugene, Sr., and Mary, played important roles. Edna was an adolescent girl whom Edith employed in the store and befriended. Her baby was Kathareen. Mother Pearl Ewing was a deaconess at Edith's church with whom Edith formed a close relationship and whom Edith credits with pulling her back from the brink more than once.

Students and teachers may wish to refer to Appendix C for a set of issues designed to complement coursework in social work, education, human development, and developmental psychology.

References

Bailey, B. (1991). Marriage. In E. Foner & J. Garraty (Eds.), *The readers companion to American history*. Boston: Houghton-Mifflin.

Dublin, T. (1991). Internal Migration. In E. Foner & J. Garraty (Eds.), *The readers companion to American history*. Boston: Houghton-Mifflin.

Kessler-Harris, A. (1991). Women and the workforce. In E. Foner & J. Garraty (Eds.), *The readers companion to American history*. Boston: Houghton-Mifflin.

Mendelsohn, J. (2002). African American history of San Francisco and Oakland, California. http://www.Africana.com

Chapter 14

COURTSHIP

We met in Houston. I was workin. He [Eugene] was workin. And I was workin for some people that his grandmother had worked for. And he was deliverin for a drugstore. And he used to deliver medicine there [house where Edith worked], and that's where we met.

So, then I got to meet his parents. Brookshire, Texas, was his home and it wasn't far from Houston. So he asked me one time, said, "Would you like to go out and meet my mother and father?" I said, "Yeah." He said, "My grandma, and I have an uncle." I said, "Oh yeah. Out in the country." I said, "You know I'm a country girl." So we went out and I met his mother. I met his father, his grandma and his uncle and aunt. And Uncle Ernest didn't have any children, so they called him "Big Boy." They called him [Eugene] "Sonny Boy" 'cause he was named after his daddy. Yes sir. His uncle said, "Now well, Sonny Boy, you done brought this young lady out here. I know she's a good lady because I can tell her a country person." I said, "Yes, I was born and raised in the country, just like everybody else." I said, "And I had a wonderful mother and a father." I said, "I had a lot of other mothers after my mother passed away." And I told them about my mother passed when I was ten and how good my daddy was, and I had all these other mothers that helped my dad with me. "Now Sonny Boy," his dad told him, "Now Sonny Boy, next time I see you, you have that Miz. H." I said, "Well, there's got to be a meetin before you can say that." So I had to test him out. I said, "Well, he got to go and meet my dad." [Laughs]

So, after I was in Houston workin, I told him, "Well, they have a homecomin at my home on the third Sunday in August." I said, "And I would like you to go up and meet my daddy." So, I wrote and told my dad. I said "Well Dad, I have met a young man." I said, "He was raised in the country just like I am." And I says, "I met his family and they was very nice people." I says, "I would like for him to come up and meet you." I says, and, "in case we get married, he'll have to come and ask you for me." [Laughs] And my daddy, he wrote me a letter, laughed about it, he said, "Mmm, I didn't think you would say that." So, sure enough, on the third Sunday in August, we went up. And he met my dad. And my dad thought very much of him. He was a country boy, and then, his father and mother was Christian people. And he was from a big family. I was from a big family. So my dad thought, "Hey, well that might be the right thing." And sure enough, we was in courtship about two years, or maybe more, then we got married. When we went up, I told him, I said, "You got to ask my *daddy* for me." [Laughs] I say, "*You* got to ask my daddy for me. I'm not gonna consent and say I'll marry you. And you just go meet my dad. My daddy got to give me to you." And my daddy gave him a good talkin. He said, "Now this is my baby daughter. And if I give you consent to marry my baby daughter, I want you to treat her like you *love* her. Now if you really love her, you're gonna treat her good, right?" "Yes sir." [Laughs] But, I was glad my daddy wasn't livin when we separated. My daddy had passed on before we separated.

Chapter 15

OUTSMARTING MR. BILL AND COUSIN OSCAR

I had been married. I went home to get my birth certificate. Now Mr. Bill knew me from a child up. And he was a [white] postman. And he used to pass our house every day, put mail out. But I had been livin away. My husband and I were gettin ready to go to California, and I was livin in Houston. And I had to go home and get my birth certificate. I didn't have my birth certificate. And so, you changed states, you had to have everything. Gene had gone to California. He was workin durin the war time. He said, "Be sure, and go and get your birth certificate. You have to have your birth certificate." I said, "OK." So, I went home from Houston to Crockett. And I went to my dad's and I told him what I had to do, and I told him when I had to get back and everything. So he says, "OK." I said, "Now Papa, I got to go to Crockett." He said, "Well Baby Rae, I'll tell you what," he says—Bill had mail on our route for years. He knew every one of Papa's people—He said, "Bill is runnin mail now, from Kennard to Crockett." He said, "And you can go up there with him. He goes and carries after all the routes come in to the town of Kennard. He picks it up and carries it to Crockett, so it can get the trains and things outward." So he said, "I'll get him to take you, and you can come back with him." He said, "If not," he said, "There's lots a mens now that you know that drives the log trucks, and they in and out of Crockett." I says, "OK." He said, "But, Bill will bring you back." I said "Alright." Papa told him [Mr. Bill]. "Yeah, Aaron, I'll take her." So, I had a cousin and another friend of his was sittin there listenin. He had done told them they could go to town with him. Now, he really wasn't supposed to be lettin no one ride with that mail, but he would do that. So he told the boys. He said, "Well boys, I promise ya'll that you could go with me at the time." He said, "But, this is Aaron's daughter and she got to get her birth certificate, and I'm gonna take her." One of the boys looked at me, and he knew the man [Mr. Bill].

And so, he got all ready and everything, got all his mail in the car and here we go. Along the way, [he said] "Well you know it's been a long time." And I said, "Yes, sir." The man started conversation, and I said, "Oh no, this can't be this man that knowed me when I was a tot!" You know? So he went to tell me about the highways, and the tree market roads, and all this that's been built since I was a livin there. I said to myself now, I got to play this to get to town. I said, "Well you know what, I don't like to be in no hurry." [Laughs] "But, I'll tell you what. Let me get to town," I said, "'cause I got to get there 'fore the courthouse close to get my birth certificate." I said, "And then we can take all the time you want." I smarted him, oh yes I did. So, I said, "I'll tell you what." I said, "We'll go, and you put off the mail. I'll go and get my birth certificate, and I'll meet you at Duke's and Airy's store." He said, "OK." [Laughs] But first, he went off the main highway. I don't know *where* I am now. And he was gonna stop anyway. I said "No, no, no!" I said, "We gonna wait," I said, "'cause I don't like to be in no hurry." So he said, "OK." Then he take me on to town. We drove up to that post office where he put that mail up. I got out of that car and never looked back! [Laughs]

Went to the court house, got my birth certificate. Then I said, "Lord, I got to find my way back home!" Sixteen miles! So, my dad had told me some of the boys was drivin these log trucks. I walked around the block and I saw one, and it was the boy I used to go to school with. And I said, "Ed, Ed!" He saw me, and he didn't know I was there. He got a brake on. I said, "Ed, how soon you gonna be goin back?" He said, "I'll be goin back in a little bit." I said, "Wait a minute." I said, "Let me tell ya, I got to go with you if I have to ride on your couplin post withers!" [Laughter] He said, "What's the matter?" I said, "Ed, let me get in here and tell you." So he opened his cab and I got in. He said, "Oh my God." He said, "Your dad didn't have no better sense than send you—" I said, "Ed, you know Papa don't know." He said, "Honey, that man is somethin else." I said, "He was even gonna stop, but I topped him. I said I'd meet him." Ed just died laughin when I was tellin him all how I did. I said, "But Ed, he went off the road!" I said, "He went onto some kind of tree market road." And we just died laughin. I said, "I had never been on that road before, and he was gonna stop anyway. I told him, 'No, let me get to town, and get the birth certificate.' I said, 'If I get to town and it's closed' I said, 'Papa would know that I didn't go straight on to town.' I say, 'He knows when the office closed.'"

I had a cousin—you wouldn't believe it—that was his *job*, gettin womens for the men. And he was my *dad's* blood! I got out of there, and I saw Oscar. I said, "Ed," I said, "oh, here's Cousin Oscar." I said, "I can get him to run me up to Papa's." He said, "OK." He didn't know. I didn't know either. So I got out and I said, "Cousin Oscar?" He said, "Yes." I said, "How are you?" He said, "Fine, Baby, how you doin?" I said, "Fine." He said, "When you come in?" I said, "Oh I haven't been here long, Oscar. I had to come and get my birth certificate 'cause I got to go to California where my husband is." He said, "Oh." I said, "Can I get you to take me up to Papa's?" He said, "Yeah." And I said, "Well, I'm sort of in a hurry 'cause I got to leave out tomorrow—goin back to Houston." I says, "I have a train that I have to take out, right away," I said, "and I have to come right back." He said, "OK." He said, "Let me go round here." What happened, Bill had done got back to Kennard. He'd done got Oscar, and I guess he'd done told him what he wanted me to do. And he was payin that man, and that man was takin money. So, he said, "OK, let me go around here, I'll be right back." So, he went, and he stayed awhile. I didn't know where he was goin, and I was in the car waitin.

He came back and we took off up to Papa's. We had about three miles to go. Cousin Oscar got close enough to the house that I coulda got out and hollered and Papa woulda heard. He kept drivin and lookin in his rearview mirror. Drivin and lookin at his rearview mirror. Then he went down the hill, and he's actin like his car stopped. He didn't know I could drive a car. [Laughs] So when his car stopped, he said "Oh, there's somethin matter with this car." He got out, raised the hood, and angled around, snappin it back down, tryin, tryin. I caught it. He was lookin back over the hill. So this man had to come over this hill, and now that's where that car was sittin. And somethin hit me, "Oh, you better see if you can't drive the car." And he didn't know I could drive a car. I got down by the steerin wheel, flipped the key in the switch, turned it, car cranked up. I said, "Cousin Oscar," I said, "I know what you doin." I said, "I'm gonna give you five minutes to get me to my Papa's house." We wasn't far. "And if you don't have me at my daddy's house in five minutes," I said, "I'm gonna tell Papa on you." I said "I'm gonna tell him either way," I said, "but I'm gonna *tell* him on you!" Now my dad's mother, I think, and his mother was sisters. He was close! And I said, "And you better come on and get me to my dad's." I said, "I'll just drive off." "No, wait, wait!" And what happened, he had a peg leg, and he was drivin with one leg. He got in that car, and I said, "I'm gonna give you five minutes to get me to my papa's house." You ought to see that man get me to my dad's house.

When I got to my dad's house, "Oh Cousin Aaron!" Oh, he was just talkin to Papa, settin on the porch. I'm burnin up. I want to tell Papa so bad! So, after awhile, Mr. Bill came. And he looked over there. And Cousin Oscar dropped his head. Papa didn't pick up on it at first. He [Mr. Bill] went past, and he went cross the bridge, down the hill past the house. "Boom," he hit that bridge. After while, he come back by, "Boom," goin across the bridge. He come by our house, looked up. Cousin Oscar was goin to carry me and drop me! That man passed twice. And Cousin Oscar stayed at our house till twelve o'clock that night, talkin to my dad. I think he was scared, 'cause, see, he [Mr. Bill] give his money [to Cousin Oscar]. So, he was talkin to Papa, "Cousin Aaron, I'm so glad to see you." I said, "Yeah, and I got to go in the mornin." I said, "I got to get ready." I was packin my clothes and everythin. I said, "'cause I got to go." "Want me to take you?" I said, "No, that's alright." I said, "I'm gonna get the bus in the mornin." I said, "Papa's gonna get me out." Papa said, "Baby?" I said, "No Papa." I said, "*You* gonna take me to the bus."

So, [laughs], after [Cousin Oscar] left it was around twelve o'clock or after. Papa said, "You know," he said, "that's the first time Oscar been up here in, I can't tell *when*." He says, "Why did he stay so *long*?" [Laughter] I said, "Papa you want me to tell you why?" He said, "Baby, do you—?" I said, "Papa let me *tell* you." And when I told Papa the whole story, Papa said, "Lord, have mercy!" He said, "I been hearin it but I didn't believe it, and now he did it to my child." I said, "Papa," and I told him what all happened. And he said, "Lord, I've been hearin this

Chapter 15

about Mr. Bill." He said, "But, he know'd you before you was *born*, before you come in this world!" [Laughs] I said, "Well Papa," I said, "that's what happened." I said, "I outsmarted him goin to town." And, I said, "I caught Ed Lams comin back and," I said, "Ed told me if I didn't get no way back he had to go down and get a load of logs." I said, "He told me when he come back if I was still down there, you know, he would bring me." I said, "But I saw Cousin Oscar." [Laughs] And I says, "No. You must bring me home!" He [Aaron] said, "You know what?" He says, "That hurts my heart to know my own blood is doin that to my child."

Papa was so mad at that man he went over to his sister's next morning. I had to leave and go back to Houston. So Papa takes out early, and he takes my suitcase and he tied it, and he told me I could ride the horse. I said, "Is there a way you can put the suitcase and tie it up?" He said, "Oh yeah." I had two [suitcases], so's I put one on each side. So he put a rope crossed and had it on the horse, and he and I walked. And I had to get down there time enough. They had a bus that would go one trip to Crockett and one trip back every day. So I got that bus that went into Crockett, and it would put me there time enough to get the train to Houston. So, that's what I did. And I told Papa, I said, "Papa be careful." I said, "Because if Oscar did that to me, ain't no tellin what he might do to you." I said, "You're by yourself." 'Cause my dad was livin by hisself then.

So when I got back to Houston, I wrote and told him the day that I was gonna be goin to California. I said, "As soon as I get there I'll send you my address and everything." So Papa said he ran into Oscar and they had a long talk. He said, "But, Baby Rae, I never was so hurt in my life as I was when I talked to Oscar." He said, "I wanted to kill him." I said, "Well, Papa." I wrote to him and I said, "He didn't get to do what he thought he was goin to do." I said, "He may have got some money, but the man didn't get what he wanted." [Laughs]

Chapter 16

WORKING IN THE SHIPYARDS

They had jobs in the shipyards. And I said, "I'm gonna go to the shipyards." And I was married then, and my husband told me, "You can't go! They ain't gonna hire you!" I say, "Yes, they are too." I say, "I saw it in the paper where they're wantin people." I went to the shipyard and I went with this friend of mine [May] and she said, "I'm goin to night school." So I said, "I'll go too, May." And, so we both went at night. We went to school at night. And that was a good thing. Oh Lord Jesus, I thank you! So, we went to night school to learn how to be a burner in the shipyard.

[Burners] cut out pieces to fit the ship where they weld things together. And when they want it taken apart, the burner has to blow that weld apart. You had to know how to use that torch, heat it and mash on it, and melt that weld from inside. And then, you had to learn how to do circle burnin. That's cuttin out, like the windows you see in the ships. I cut out some! The pipes they put in the double boiler room, and all through the ship. I did that. The windows on the ship. [Laughs] I did those. I think God was with me. I was so determined. I'd sit on a swing, and they had it hitched to the side of the ship, and it was marked. And I had to cut that window out. But, I had to start right on the line, and bring it on around. I did some dangerous things in the shipyards, but I didn't realize it.

So, May and I did those hours. They told us, "Ya'll got to stay here [burner school] because they need welders bad." And after you get so many hours in, they gonna test you. And when they tested me and her, we passed. And we went on in the shipyard to work. We didn't have to do so many hours in the school because they was short. May and I

Chapter 16

was good workers and we got apprenticed in the school. And when we come out and they told us we gonna have to go take the test. You had to have a special jacket. It was leather, lined with something. But anyhow, that was to keep the heat [away] and they taught you everything. They give you a slip with everythin you had to have. And there was a special store there in California where we would go to. They had these supplies. And everythin you needed you got there. And I told May, I said, "May, they sendin us to school to get these supplies, and then we got to go over to the yard and take the test. How do they know we gonna pass?" I said. "Well, May, I'm gonna tell you one thing. I'm gonna pass if I have to *walk* by!" May just died laughin. May said, "Girl you—!" I said, "They better not fail me. I'm gonna *walk* by!" And both of us passed. And both of us started workin at the shipyards at the same time. And I lost track of her, but I learned through some more friends of mine that she was doin fine the last time they heard. But, she had a family too. I didn't have any children at that time. Just my husband and I. [Laughs] But, I made a lot of friends in that shipyard!

And ended up, time we got there [shipyard], they separated me and May. We couldn't work together. But the same time, they put us through some of the worst tests on their ship. Now, when we first started, I was in the yard where they cut out the pieces and weld them together for the ship. I was good on that. They called it a torch burner. I would get that torch and just go with it. Like I just take somethin like this, and I burn it like this, bringin it, and then turn and I'd go. Anything you wanted cut out—"Hey! Get that little one over there!" One day they worked me so. I was so tired. I told 'em, I said, "What are ya'll gonna do, work me to death?" I say, "I see these others standin around here." And the foreman said, "Be quiet. That's all right. You're the best one we've got out here. And if you take up with him, we'll [have some problems]." And I said, "OK. I'll hush." And do you know, you had to be out there six months before maybe you could go to be a journeyman. You had to be good. I was out there three months! And, I got my check, May and I got our check, and I said, "May! Look. Look, May!" You start out at $1.05 an hour. I was gettin $1.20. That was journeyman pay. So you raised from $1.05 to $1.20. So I had got promoted!

So, Sanett and I walked together to work. She lived where I live. I come down by her house walkin through the shipyard. So I said, "Sanett." She said, "What?" I said, "Girl, I got journeyman pay." She said, "What?" I said, "They pay me journeyman pay. They pay me $1.20." She said, "Are you sure?" I said, "Yes." So she said, "Well, don't say nothin. See if they gonna do it again." [Laughter] Next week, I got it and sure enough, there it was. She said now, "Honey, if they are makin a mistake, you better see about it before it goes too far. Because they'll take it all out at one time."

So, I got to studyin then. "Must I tell them, or must I not?" So, I decided, "I'm gonna go ask Cal." That was our head man where we sign in every mornin. He'd sign us out to our job for the day. I went in that mornin. I said, "Cal." He said, "Yeah." I said, "I want to ask you somethin." He said, "What's that?" I said, "My last two checks I got, they payin me $1.20." He said, "Edith, you earned it." I said, "What? I'm a journeyman?" He said, "You journeyman brother now." He said, "And you's the best I got here in this group." I said, "Cal, no." He said, "Yeah!"

He said, "You know, when you went up there on that pole?" They had put it down wrong at the bottom and they wanted to take it all out at the bottom and turn it around, but the inspector said, "No, you can take it loose up here and put it around so you don't have to do all that." Because the bottom was a wider bottom. It was somethin like this table, the way it was shaped, but this was cut off like that. He said, "They need that ship to go out." And he said they could do it better if they could take it loose where the flag part was at the top. And they carried me up there, and I taken it loose. And, I didn't know it at the time, they had an inspector from Washington, D.C., that's over these ship people. He was there watchin. And I went up there, and I turned it around. I taken it loose where they could turn it around. And that's when I started gettin my journeyman pay." He signed it, and said, "She did journeyman work. Now she gets journeyman pay." That was the highest pay for that type of job. And I worked a year, and I said, "This is enough."

༄

And, I did a silly thing!! Couldn't swim a lick! [Laughter] That ship was in the water now, they was gettin it ready. They had to cut out the

CHAPTER 16

windows in the ship, you know. I was swingin over the water. [Laughter] And they put me right there! I couldn't swim! And, I didn't have sense enough to be scared. I was showin what I could do. That's what I was doin! Anybody else can do it, I can too. That was my way. And they had these portholes. The little windows in the ship. And they said, "Edith, we want you to work over here." I went and they told me, "You got to get out here." And I said, "Man! I can't swim." [Laughter] "Well. We gonna fix it." I said, "If I fall down there, I can't swim. I fall down there," I said, "I never come up no more!" He said, "We gonna fix it so you *will not* fall." They put me in that swing. They put me over and down and it was fastened on to the ship like this. But, I was in that swing before they put me there. They had this crane. After I got in that swing they had this crane to pick it up, put me over, and fasten it to the ship. And I sit there with that burner and cut this one out. [Then] they'd move me down to the next one. They had me there all day long!

I told them one day, "Why you all come to get me?" He said, "Well, you're the best little burner, and you can get into small little holes." He say, "You don't have no business bein so good and so small!" I was one of the smallest burners. Then, that wasn't enough. They was gettin this ship, they was gonna put it on trial. And when they put that ship on trial they discovered that in the double boiler room there was some holes where the pipes runnin through that wasn't cut out. I think back over that now! I was a big fool! 'Cause, you know, I crawled down through that hole, so I could lay on my stomach and cut this hole out. That was just how big it was that I had to lay on my stomach to cut it out. Then I had to crawl through it to cut that other hole. I was crazy! But, you know what, I was showin them I knew what I could do. By me doin that, I stayed on the ship. Now, some of them that got to be journeymen burners, they wasn't always on the ship. They was on the lay out and things like that. But, after I got to be that journeyman burner, when they take me off that field and carried me to that ship for the first time, I never went back out again. I was on the ship until I quit.

And when I finally quit, I looked back over it, and I shivered. I got cold sometimes. I couldn't swim a bit! And I was next to those ships sittin in that water. And I'm sittin out there. [Laughter] I was so determined to show them that if they could do it, I could too. Now, that was my daddy's motto teachin. I blame my daddy for that! 'Cause, Papa always told us, "Don't let nothin outdo you. You outdo it. If anybody else can do it, you can too!" Now, that was my daddy's motto. "If anybody else can do it, you can too. Just try, try, try, and try again." He didn't let you say you could not do somethin. Now, you had to keep on tryin. And he said, "Finally you will succeed." So that was in me. And I was thinkin about that. My daddy said, "Don't say you can't. Don't say you can't until you've tried. Have you tried?" That was my motto. Every job I went on, I succeeded in it. And I think that's the reason why, my daddy had that drilled in me. You don't say what you can't do until you try, you try, and you try again. Now them three tries. He didn't give up on that. If you do three and you don't succeed, then you try and you try and you try again. And finally, you will succeed, 'cause, he said, you'd get better every time. And that's what stayed with me.

Chapter 17

AARON'S DEATH

And my dad—oh Lord, he was a *wonderful* dad! Ooh, if I could make all of these daddies be like my daddy! We wouldn't *have* no trouble with our children 'cause he was a dutiful, devoted father. And my daddy taught me things that he told me, "This is something I want to tell *you*, and you keep this, and don't let it away from you, and it may come a time you have to use it." My dad was a dad that loved children. And it wasn't just his children. It was a lot of kids that called my daddy "Papa." "Hi Papa, how you doin Pop?" And then when he ended up by himself for awhile, before he got sick, my daddy was livin at home alone, 'cause the kids had all got grown and away. He had people used to come and was callin him "Papa." They'd come and see about Papa. They made special trips to go and see Papa. "Let's go see Papa. I haven't seen Papa." And he had relatives was alone, and they would want Papa to have dinner with them. And Papa was a good cook—oh yeah—now I wished I was the cook that he was!

And so, my dad was the dad to a lot of other boys. Now he wouldn't follow with any dad's little girls, unless they asked, "Can you be my dad?" Well, but the young men, my dad was a dad to them. And I think that was because my dad was the oldest son his dad had, and his dad died at a age where he had to step in and be just like the other father to his brothers and sisters, and it was a large family they had. So, I guess that made him to head to bein the expert father. He had it in him. He was just born to be that kind of father. He was a *grand* father, my dad was one. I told my oldest son and Andrew, I said, "I just hope ya'll can be a *half* the dad my dad was." My oldest son, he's strivin for that, he is *strivin* to be that.

Aaron's Death

He [Aaron] died just before Everett [was born]. And you know what? My dad could know things, and before he died, he said, "Baby Rae," he said, "I hates to leave you." I didn't have any children then. He said, "But you're gonna have some children." He said, "But your husband's not gonna be so well pleased." I didn't know what he meant, but I was tryin. My husband used to say, "I want a girl, I want a girl." And I told him, I'd said, "We can't do what we want. We thank God for what we have, and what we can get, what He gives us." And that's when, I guess, he decided he wasn't gonna be friendly. So all I had was boys, three boys, and I lost the middle one. And looks like that sort of put a tear, a sadness, a dividedness. Because, when I would give the attention to the babies, he'd say I didn't give attention to him. I think he got jealous of the babies. Everybody [that] would see the babies would talk about the babies.

Chapter 18

FAMILY TROUBLES

I was glad my daddy wasn't livin when we [Eugene and Edith] separated. My daddy had passed on before we separated. And he didn't know about all the trouble I had. And the thing about it was, he [Eugene] was from a big family. I was from a big family. He had a sister had gotten married, and she was havin babies. I have a sister that had gotten married, she was havin babies. Time we got married, just knowed we was gonna have a little baby. Next year, no baby. He just wondered why. And then he just started sayin, "I just can't understand why *we* can't have no baby. You from a big family, and I from a big family."

After he done kept doin that, I went to the doctor. Unbeknownst to him. And I asked the doctor, I said, "I want you to check me good, see why I am not pregnant." I said, "I'm married." He said, "Well, he could be over-reactin. And it could be a sperm of his." He said, "The men's sperm is what fertilizes ya'll egg." But I didn't know all that. So, when this doctor got through explainin everythin to me, I said, "Oh, OK." So I went home, and we was talkin about it. "I don't see why we not gettin no babies. My sister got babies." I said, "Well, maybe you ought to go to the doctor." I said, "The doctor told me, it's your sperm fertilizes my egg." He didn't know all of that. I didn't know all of that.

So I told him, I says, "You go to the doctor, and let the doctor talk to you and tell you." "Oh ain't nothin that's wrong with me!" [Laughs] I said, "Well, doctor says there's nothin wrong with me." I says, "Well, maybe someday we'll have a child, if God wants us to have one." I said, "I'm not gonna worry about it anymore." Sure enough, when I finally got pregnant, I think we had been married eight years. I was twenty-eight when my first child was born. I was thirty when the second was born. I was thirty-one when the third was born.

Family Troubles

∽

And he [Eugene] had got so, I don't know, I couldn't understand him. But the thing about it was, he had stayed in contact with his first girl. Now, we left and went to California workin in the shipyard and the man was gettin letters from her. And all this time when I was workin in the shipyard with him, tryin to save up to go back. And we went back to Houston. And we had some property. We built a home and everything. I had a little store. We was doin fine. That's when my kids was born. He was *still seein her*. He would go to town to bring stuff for the store sometimes. And he got to where he'd say, "I got to go, I'm goin early in the morning." I'd say "OK." I said, "Now, you hurry back." He used to go and come right back.

So, a man used to come in [to the store] and get a certain kind of cheese he'd like that we would get. It was *fine*. Big round cheese, they would have some good tastin cheese. So, he came in one day, and he said, "Where's my cheese?" He [Eugene] said, "I got to go tomorrow and get some." He said, "I got to go in early in the mornin." He [customer] said, "Oh, you go in early?" [Eugene] said, "Yeah." He [customer] said, "About what time you be back?" He said, "Oh, I should be back about nine thirty, ten o'clock." So, the man came back by the next day. It was about nine thirty. He said, "The man back?" I said, "No, he's not." He said, "Let me tell you somethin." I said, "What's that?" He said, "You know how to shop, don't you?" I said, "Yes sir." He said, "I want you to go and pick up one of these mornings. Don't tell him when you're gonna do it." He said, "You do it." He had a friend downtown. He had done seen him. But he didn't tell me. That was the way he was lettin me know it's something goin on you need to see for yourself. So I said, "OK." And he says, "Don't get him no leadway about when you goin, but you just tell him, 'No, I'm goin this mornin.'" Now, he said, "You know?" I said, "Yes." 'Cause I was makin out the list and everything, keepin everything, and I knowed.

So, sure enough, I did it one morning. I said, "I'm goin this mornin." "Oh you?" I said, "Yeah, I'm goin." But I waited until he'd gotten it ready, so he couldn't make no changes. If I'd a told him early, he'd a made a connection, so I didn't give him a chance to make no connection. So I goes down, and I do the shoppin. It was a farmers market where we'd pick up the fresh vegetables that we would bring in, onions and potatoes, and every time he'd go he'd bring some vegetables. Got downtown and parked the car. I had went to the market—the wholesale house for my meat and everything—and I was down there at the farmers market where I was pickin vegetables.

And I heard somebody say, "Here's his car, but I don't see him." I was talkin to a man about a pig, and he said, "Somebody's at your car." I said, "Yeah, I see." He said, "They lookin for somebody." I said, "Yeah, I see." He say, "Well?" I say, "No, don't tell 'em I'm over here." I said, "They not lookin for me." And he went to laughin. He said, "Oh! I pick up on it." He said, "We gonna have fun, and he [Eugene] ain't." I said, "Mmm hmm." I said, "I'm gonna move around." I say, "They may look up. They may recognize me." So, he said, "OK."

So, he said, "You go around there, and you may find so-and-so." I walked around where you couldn't see. I said "Keep your eye on it." So he said, "I'll hit on something so you know when they leave." I said, "OK." [Laughs] He did! I came back, he said, "They sure did look in that car, and they was just sayin, 'But he's here somewhere—this is his car.'" I say, "No they didn't!" And he say, "Yes." I got so choked up, I said, "Oh, I'd better get my vegetables and go now." I said, "I done seen what I wanted to see." He said, "You done seen—" I said, "Mmm hmm." I said, "This is why my husband's been takin so long comin." I said, "He used to leave home and be back in two hours, and he done got everything."

He stayed in contact with her the whole twenty-three years we lived together! And that store closed us out. And I went back to California. My oldest son had went to school one year in Houston. I told him [Eugene], "We're goin." Because it was gettin too bad, and I didn't want him to know everythin that I had done found out. Got to California. It didn't do any good. He still stayed in contact.

ଓ

You know what? I believe to my soul that a lot of it was from his [Eugene's] dad. One time when I was pregnant, his daddy—we had this little store, in Houston—and his daddy come down there one Sunday mornin, on his horse name Ole Joe, come down to the store, interferin. Couldn't get any of 'em [Eugene's family] to help him [Eugene] when he needed it. "Uh, now you know I raised you better than that! Now, you need to close that store and go to church." Well, everybody that was in that neighborhood, most of 'em worked. On Sunday mornin, they'd be rushin in, tryin to get something for their dinner. And we had a good market, meat and everything. People was comin in in the mornin and that was our livin in that store. "You know I didn't *raise* you like that." With his hands on the saddle horn, layin up like this, talkin to him. Here I am, way out here [pregnant].

I walked to that door, and I looked at him. I said, "You know what you do? You turn that horse around and you *get* away from here." He looked at me, "Daughter, I'm talkin to Son." I said, "I am your son's wife. And when we need anythin here, ya'll don't come to give us no hand." I said, "You turn that horse around and get away from here. Don't *come* down here no more, tellin him what he oughta do and what he shouldn't." He looked at me, and I said, "I mean go!" And he saw I was way out [pregnant]. He see he was upsettin me. But, look like that baby starts to doin this [motions]. And I caught my stomach like that and I turned around. That man turned that horse around, and he went home.

He went and told his wife, "Mary, I'm tellin you, that wife Sonny Boy got down there, she's a fiery little somethin. She told me to get from down there, don't *come* down there." She said, "Sonny, you must have said somethin that hurt Ree [Edith's nickname]." She said, "What did you say?" "Well, I just told Sonny Boy he should close that store and go to church. And the peoples comin in and out. And she told me to turn my horse around and get from down there." She said, "And that's what she shoulda told ya. And you shouldn't a been down there tellin in the first place." She said, "You know that woman is pregnant, and she can't do. And Sonny Boy sayin that's their livin."

He went and told her, "Well I guess I'll have to go to church and pray for 'em." [Laughter] Mama said, she told him, "Well, maybe that's what you shoulda done in the first place, before you went and talked

Chapter 18

to 'em." "Well that's my son." She said, "Yes, but you shouldn't a went down there interferin, and you didn't know what was goin on. You goin down there givin orders—you don't give orders. If you can't go down there and give 'em a helpin hand, if they need it, stay out and leave 'em alone." I stopped him, oh yeah, I did. I stopped him. He didn't come down there no more, sayin nothin to him [Eugene] about goin to church.

Chapter 19

NO MORE BABIES

Not any of his kids lived close around where Papa [Eugene's father] was. The oldest ones was movin away and gettin married and gettin to Houston. They [Eugene's parents] was livin 36 mile or more out in the country. They was in Butcher, Texas, where they was livin. And he got abusive to his wife. We went out there that Sunday, and she had done called, 'cause I had Bertha [Eugene's sister] down there with us then, and she was workin to help herself. And she had called Bertha and told her what had happened. I didn't know. And when we went out there, Mama had her suitcase packed. She was leavin. And she had two, three younger ones there. So he told her, "Mae, you ain't gonna leave me with these children." She had done packed her suitcase 'cause she was leavin.

She said she was tired of him abusin her *sexually*. Well, now she had done had all these kids, and she said, "Ree, I couldn't go to bed, he'd hang his hat on me." She said, "I was tired of havin babies, and I was tired of Sonny." And so she says, at night, he told her, "Yeah, you gonna satisfy me as long as you live." Now, she was goin through that menopause change at that time. She said, "Ree, I knowed I'd get another baby, and I wasn't gonna *get* no more babies!" So she had to fight him off when she was goin through her change, to keep from gettin pregnant again. Because she said she wasn't gonna get no baby in her change. She said that woulda been too much and he knew that if he could force her, she would get pregnant again.

And she said he would leave that house—and they was out on a lady's property, a good distance to the road—he would take the brush broom and sweep around that house to see if she'd come outside, or if somebody come to that house while he was gone. And she told me, she said, "That got me." She said, "Sonny, I have to go to the toilet." And

CHAPTER 19

the yard was clean, and rocky and sandy. She said, he said, "Well, if you go out to the toilet and back to the house, I know your tracks." Mama said, "Now you know, this is too much." So she said, "Well, I have to go to the toilet, I'm goin to the toilet." "Well you don't sweep your tracks, you just go out there and come back." Mama said, "Now do he think I'm that crazy?"

So she made it up in her mind that she was gonna talk to somebody else. And she knowed where he had to go to work, and when he's gonna get home. She went like she's goin to the toilet, left the broom out there. And then went on where she was goin. When she came back, she came back and come in the house and left the tracks, so he thought she went to the toilet and back. And she went to talk to some elder lady, and one that was a midwife. And they started tellin her what she had to do and what she couldn't do.

But when she finally told him she was gonna leave him, that's when we had to go out there. She had her suitcase packed. I had gotten Bertha with us, and she was workin in Houston and her mother would call her on the job. She could go and call Bertha on the job, and Bertha had told the lady she worked for about her mother. She told her she was sick, and she said, "Well Bertha"—she was very nice—she said, "Bertha, anytime your mother want to call you, you accept the call." And she called Bertha and told her to tell Sonny Boy to come get her. She wasn't stayin there no more. She was *leavin* this man. She wasn't goin to *stay* there no more! And when we got there, she had went to this midwife, and this midwife told her what would happen to her if she keep havin babies. She said, "You done had too many already." She said, "Now, if he's that way about it, let him do the next best thing. And you take care of *your health*."

And she was goin through that change, and so, she told Bertha, tell Sonny Boy to come get her. Well, we got there that Sunday, he [Sonny] said, "What ya'll doin out here? Mae ain't goin *nowhere!* Mae ain't goin *nowhere!*" She say, "Hmm hmm!" [Indicates nodding] And she just looked at him. So she said, "Sonny Boy, ya'll ready to go?" He said, "After while Mama." He said, "I'm gonna go talk to Daddy." So she said, "OK." She had her suitcase. She said, "Bertie, take my suitcase out there and put it in the car." She started out there. He's [Sonny's] goin, "You take

114

that suitcase back in there, 'cause your Mama ain't goin nowhere. And I mean you take it back 'cause, I'll kill you Bert, I'll kill you! If Mae leaves here Bert, I'll kill you!" 'Cause he felt like that Bert was helpin, because she was down there workin, and Mother could call her, and she was sendin a little change to Mama. And he was thinkin that Bert done get Mama the money to get away.

He went runnin up there, with the *gun!* "If you don't stop, Mae, I'll shoot you! I'll shoot you, Mae!" I say, "Oh Mama, turn around. Don't go no more, Mama!" He had that gun lever down. I said, "Papa!" I said, "Don't kill Mama!" I said, "*Please* don't kill her." And Gene, he was standin there, and I said, "Gene, go to your *Mama!*" He was scared to get between his mama and his daddy! I said, "Go to your *Mama!*" And he turned around and looked at me. I said, "Gene, go to your *Mama!*" His dad turned around and looked at me. I said, "Go to your *Mama!*" I said, "Mama, stop, stop, stop, stop Mama! He got the gun on ya, he got the gun on ya, Mama!"

She stopped, and she didn't turn around. She said, "Well, if he have to shoot me, he'll shoot me in my *back*. And I know he'll go to the penitentiary or the electric chair, so we'll *both be dead!*" He turned around and looked at me, as if to say, "You didn't have no business comin here." And he told Mama, I had put too much in her head. I was a little *town*. I done got too much town in me. And I was tellin her what to do. No! That was my mother-in-law! [Laughter]

And, so Gene talked to him, and Mama came up. I said, "Mama, come on back to the house." I said, "Mama, I tell you what." I said, "I'm gonna give Big Mama some money." I said, "We gonna leave enough money for you to leave. You can leave when he go to work." And it was a bus come through there. We told Mama how she could do, when he go to work. And Big Mama met us up down the road. And Mama could go by to her mother's house. And she says, "I ain't goin back to that house tonight." Big Mama's sayin, "He ain't gonna come here either," said now, "if he come here, he gonna be dead."

She [Mae] stayed with her mother. She came to Houston and stayed a few days, then she went back. And he *begged* her. And he went to her mother, and her mother told him, "If you hit her again—

if you do *anything* to her again—*you* goin to the graveyard." That was her only daughter. She only had two kids, it was a boy and a girl. She said, "That's my only daughter, and you done gave her a bunch a kids, and now you gonna abuse her?" She says, "Sonny, I have been on this hill and I haven't bothered you all's business." She said, "But she come to me and that's my *only* daughter." She said, "And if you do anything to her again," she say, "you gonna have to answer to me." She said, "And I'll get ya." She said, "I'll get ya. I'll have you dead." Mama say, "I'm goin to Houston to be with my children." She was gonna leave him, leave those youngest ones with him. And he had visited me, "I'll go by your place in Houston." That man got busy, and he came to Houston and bought a lot, built a house on it. She said, "I'm not gonna stay out here no more and live in the country. You to abuse me, away from my children."

And I told Gene, I said, "Gene, what *ever* you do," I said, "don't you ever dare to do to me what I saw your daddy doin to your mother." I said, "Now, I'm gonna tell you, my daddy'll hunt you like dog huntin a rabbit." I said, "My daddy will find you, and he'll kill you." I said, "My daddy never did talk to my mother like I seen your family." I say, "He never raised a hand." I said, "Mama has hollered things to my dad, but she never used no violence." And I says, "Now, I'll tell you somethin, Gene." I say, "If you get to where you want to hit me," I said, "You better be sure you kill me." I said, "Because if you don't," I said, "I'm gonna kill you." I said, "'Cause my daddy told me don't take no *hits* off no man!" I said, "I'm gonna tell you, *don't hit me.*" I guess he said, well, he'll go so long and then he'll see. And so, when I broke up with him, that was when it happened. He was gettin just like his daddy. He was tryin to follow right in his daddy's footstep.

Chapter 20

STOREKEEPING

And we had some of the best meat! We had good meat in that store. We ground our own hamburger and everything. I made pan sausage and sold my own pan sausage. Oh, we sold a lot of meat. And people would come there and buy meat. And they'd go to other stores and buy that same meat, and it didn't have the flavor. Then I had done cut me some guts to make sausage. And I stuffed and made sausage, and stuffed 'em. And then I got me some hickory chips, and I got me some liquid smoke—hickory liquid smoke—so I put some of it in the meat when I was fixin the sausage. Then I put it *on* the meat, on the sausage, and I'd let 'em sit a day in the box. Then I got some hickory chips, and I smoked it. I had a little pump house, over my pump. I could put the sausage in there and I smoked 'em, with that hickory. You talkin about some good sausage!

One man had me to make him *15 pounds* at one time! This man came there one day, and I was cookin some of this sausage in the back. I was makin it up, and I was, you know, tastin it. And so he asked my husband, he said, "What is that I smell? It smell like somethin my mama and them used to make?" And my husband said, "Well, my wife is makin the pan sausage." He said, "Pan sausage?" He said, "Yes." "Ya'll make your own pan sausage?" He said, "My wife makes the pan sausage," said, "she makes it." He said, "Well, is that what I smell?" He said, "Yes, she's cookin some." He said, "Could I taste some?" So he told him, "Yes." So he [Eugene] came back and he said, "Baby, you bring out one of those pan sausage. The man out here wants to taste some." Said, "He talkin about how it smelled. He was passin by and smelled it, and he come in." So I carried it out there in a saucer and a fork and everything, and he said, "Ooooh Lord! This is what my mama and them used to *make* in the country! Mmmm. How [much do] you sell it [for]?" At that time they was 49 cents a pound. So he said, "Can you make a batch of those pan sausages?" And so, he [Eugene] said, "Yes." He said, "These pan sausage, we makes 'em and smokes 'em too."

He [the man] said, "Ya'll got some of that river cane syrup in there too!" So, Gene told him, said, "Yes we have." [The man] said, "I want some of that river cane syrup, and I want me some of these pan sausage." And he looked around the store, he said, "I'm goin home, and my wife gonna cook me some biscuits. And I'm gonna have me a hometown cooked meal, like my mama used to fix." So he went home, and his wife fixed the biscuits and everything, fixed the meal. The man came *back*. They ate up those sausage. He came back! He said, "My wife wants 5 *pounds* of these sausage." I looked at Gene. [Laughs] Gene looked at me. I think we'd made up, like 10 pounds at that time. So he got the man the 5 pounds of sausage. I think he had a good size family why he wanted it. So he got the 5 pounds of sausage, and so Gene looked at me and I said, after he left, I said, "Gene, we got to make up some more sausage, 'cause people comin *in*, then." I said, "They gonna want their sausage." He had to go back to town 'cause we bought most of our lean parts from the market, from where we buy the meat. I say, "Gene, go back." And I said, "You better get about 20, 25 pounds of that meat," I said, "'cause once this gets known," I said, "people gonna be comin in here sayin, 'Sausage, sausage, sausage.'"

Just like I told him—that man went home and he passed everybody's house, "I want ya'll folks to know this. That little H. store over there got some of the best pan sausage you ever put in your mouth! If you want some good pan sausage, you go over to that there H.'s store over there and you'll *find* good ole pan sausage. That old fashion—mmmm! I'm tellin you. I went over there and I got some, and my wife fixed me some of them biscuits, and I got some of that syrup in there, and I'm tellin you, I'm *full!* But I went back and got me some more sausage!" [Laughter] He sold it, as he left goin home. And I told Gene, I said, "You better hurry up and go get some more meat." Before Gene got back, I had sold up *all the sausage* that was left in the store. And people was still comin, and I told 'em, I said, "My husband's gone to town to get some more meat, so we can make more sausage." I said, "So we'll have some more later this afternoon or early in the mornin." I said, "We may have to wait till we close the store to make it. We'll have some more for tomorrow." I said, "We'll have some more pan sausage tomorrow."

We didn't have time to make 'em that day. So we made 'em up that night when we closed the store. There we was, makin up sausage. We put sage in there. Sage gives it a good flavor. And we *sold* pan sausage! We could sell 15 pounds of pan sausage in the mornin, in a hour. That was one of our biggest *meat* sellers, those pan sausage. I made pan sausage and they bought pan sausage. And I had never seen people run for pan sausage. And the kids would say, "Miz H., do you have any pan sausage? Mother want this amount in pan sausage." She'd have the money tied up in a handkerchief or somethin, and they'd hand it to me. And they knew how much it was a pound. Sometimes some would want 3 pounds. One little boy came down and the mother told him she wanted 5 pounds. I said, "Baby, you can't carry no 5 pound pan sausage home." So when he came, and she wanted 5 pounds, we didn't have much more than 5 pounds left, so, we fixed it up for him. I said, "I'm gonna take this baby home." [Laughs] I say, "That mother send him for 5 pounds of sausage." I say, "If she let somebody know," I said, "some of them kids along the way could take it." I said, "I'm gonna take him home." I say, "You [Eugene] better get some meat cut so we can start makin some more." And that was around about eleven thirty. So that evenin time, people gettin off from work—the *word was out!*

We had the best hamburger meat there was. I didn't have no lot of fat and no gristles in it like they grind 'em up in the market where they make 'em. I had done worked and seen how they did all of this, goin in and out buyin, and I told Gene, I said, "Uh uh." I said, "We gonna make our own hamburger. We ain't gonna *buy* no hamburger." They would take *gristles*, and see their machine could cut that gristle up. And that little white stuff you was seein in that [meat] was *gristle*. You couldn't chew it. Whenever you ate the hamburger meat, it would just go down, because you didn't chew it. And so I told Gene, I said, "We not gonna do this. We gonna give out good stuff." And we did, we had good meat. That's where most of our money came from was through the meat that we sold.

Chapter 21

EDNA AND KATHAREEN

We had the little grocery store and Edna was workin for us there. Her mother kept her out of school. She couldn't spell "meal," big teenager. And so, we built this little store and everything. She wanted to work and I told her, "OK." We weren't able to pay her much. I had to start with her just like when I started to work, $5.00 and $6.00 a week, till we built up. Well, Edna was workin in this store, and *my* husband raped her. And she would not tell me.

And when she went pregnant with that baby, her mother come down to the store and she said, "Edna! I want so-and-so-and-so. Now, if you got any money you can get!" She kept that child out of *school* to help her with her other siblings under her. She had Edna helpin her, and she wasn't tryin to help Edna. Edna couldn't spell "flour," she couldn't spell "meal." I said, "Edna, go to the store, and bring me a small sack of flour, a 2-pound sack of flour." "Flour, flour—Mama, how you spell it?" I said, "F-L-O-U-R, F-L-O-U-R." And before she'd get a distance, she'd holler, "Mama, what'd you say?"

Now, I learned her in that store, once a week. Spellin and writin and arithmetic. I learned her that while she was workin. She got up to where she was takin care of sick peoples, callin doctors. And that was, you know, Baby, when they lay it out to you in orders, for sick people. Edna, she growed up. She got married, and she didn't have another child. When she had Kathareen, she didn't have another child.

☙

He [Eugene] was gonna try to put it on another young man that used to come up there, and Edna used to [go to] church with him. Edna wouldn't tell me. She was scared when it happened. So, when this all got to the point where the baby was comin, her mother told her, "You gonna have that baby at home, and I'm gonna bring that little baby in here." Edna was scared. I said, "Edna," I said, "every week, you put aside some of your money, Baby." I says, "Put your money aside," and I said, "when it's time for the baby to be born," I say, *you get Sheriff Fields to take you to the hospital."

So I got her in the county hospital. Carried her and got her in the county hospital. And she was goin out there takin her treatments and everything. Her mama didn't even *know* when we first got started. When she found out she got *mad* at me and started comin out, goin into our house. And I told her, I said, "That's your daughter." "Well she don't tell me!" Well, Edna wasn't tellin her who it really was. And she said it was another young man that liked her very much. Well it wasn't that. It was my husband, and Edna was scared. And when I finally found out, that was *after* the baby was born to her, and I said "Edna, why didn't you tell me?" She said, "Mama, Mr. Gene told me I'd better not tell you."

But what happened, I had went to the doctor with him [baby son, Everett]. And Edna was in the store with my husband. So I told her, I said, "Edna, when you get through with this," I give her somethin to do, "shampoo your hair good." And I said, "When I get back, I'll press your hair and fix it for you." She said, "OK, Mama." I was "Mama." But I got back, Edna was gone home. And my husband settin up in there [gestures as if blotting blood from face]. She had done gave him some claws. And I say, "What's the matter with you?" He say, "That ole Edna. I told her to do somethin, and she got mad. I coulda poked her rib, that's what I wanted to do. She just went *wild* on me!" I didn't know for a long time that she was prey. That's what I didn't know. He tried to get another young man—this young man was crazy about Edna—gonna try to work that on James.

I told Edna, I said, "Edna, I'm gonna get you where you can go to the hospital." Her mama come out where she was gonna do it, "I'm gonna jerk this little baby, whatever it is, the little *bastard!*" I didn't want Edna to get upset. I said [to Edna], "You can be with me." I said, "Mama's not gonna leave you." I said, "I'm gonna be right with ya, OK?"

Chapter 21

She said, "OK." So, sure enough, I was by her side with everything. I gone with her. I made sure she would go get her treatments and everything that she had there. *All this time,* now I'm not knowin!

So, after I got to know, I said "Edna!" I said, "Why?" That was after the child was a big girl. I said, *"Why* didn't you tell me?" She said, "Mama," she still calls me "Mama." She said, "Mama, I wanted to tell you, but Mr. Gene told me I better not tell ya if I want to live. And if I want that baby to live. She said, "I was afraid to tell you, Mama!" That hurt me to my heart, when she told me that. She was a good child. She was a wonderful mother. Her mother had four kids then that she was raisin without a husband. Now why she want to mess with her [Edna] like that, when she had done stepped through some of the same stitches? You see what I'm sayin? That hurt me so much.

ᘒ

[Edna] finally got her a job in town. She was takin care of a lady. And she was able to stay there with the lady, and with her baby comin, that wasn't a burden so bad. That's where she started takin care of sick people, and she started to learn. And she'd call me and ask me different things. And I'd always give her advice on the phone and everything. When Kathareen was born, little walkin girl, she was the cutest little thing. On her off day, she'd come out to visit me. And, so when she passed by her mother's house to get down there, and she'd say, "Anytime we get to Mama's house," said, "Mama say, 'How's Kathareen?'" "I ain't got time to stay 'cause I'm goin on over to my *mama's* [Edith's] house!" And, her mother got angry at me! Her mama got angry with me! And she came down to the store one day. She say, "Miz H." I say, "Yeah?" "I just want to know this one thing." I say, "What is it?" She was sittin there. "I just want to know what is it that you have done that Edna be comin by the house, and she won't stop to say hello to me or nothin." I say, "That's for *you* to find out. *I* don't know." I said, "Now you have to find that out for yourself." I say, "I treated Edna nice before Kathareen was born."

So, after it went so long, I asked Edna one day, I said, "Edna, I got to talk to you." So she said, "Yes'm, Mama." And so, I told her, I say, "Now I want you to tell me, the *truth.*" I say, "I been hearin this through the air, and it's through the grapevine." I said, "I want you to give it to me mouth to mouth." I say, "Now, I want you to tell me *who* is Kathareen's dad?"

Her eyes started fillin up with water. And she just grabbed me and started cryin. I said, "Did it happen that day when I come back and you had gone home?" She said, "Yeah." I said, "Well, Baby, why didn't you come and tell me?" "Mama, he told me, I better not tell ya. When I come in and she had done scratched him up so and he sat about puttin cotton, wipin his face, and I said, "What's wrong with you?" "That old Edna there. I told her to do somethin, and she said, 'Mama done told me what she wanted me to do, and I'm gonna do what Mama tells me to do, then I'll not do what you want.'" That's what he told me. But he raped her.

༄

Edna never had another child. And Kathareen got grandkids now. And now she calls me with her problems, just like if I was right there. And I'm *"Grandma."* I'm "Mama" to Edna, still. Edna call me this week I get home to Salt Lake. Don't you think my phone won't start ringin. "Mama, where have you been?" [Laughter] And I told 'em, I told 'em before I left that I was comin up to be with Everett, but I didn't say how *long*. And the kids' graduation. Now she'll be callin me, "Mama! Now you done been gone too long, and I ain't heard from you, now where you *been?*" She'll be wantin to know all this.

But the thing is, what hurt me so with her—he knew that that child was havin a hard time, and then he took advantage of her behind my back. I said, "Edna," I said, "If you'd a told me," I said, "You and I'd a had everything, and he'd a been gone." I said, "That wasn't right." I said, "Now, let me tell you somethin." I said, "Longest day you live, don't you take that off a nobody else." I said, "Anybody start's doin you and darin you," I said, "Now you get away." I said, "But you should a came to *me.*"

༄

I sat down and told my two sons, I said, "Now Everett and Andrew," I said, "I want to tell ya'll somethin." After I separated from their dad, I said, "I want to tell ya'll somethin. Ya'll do have a sister. I didn't give

ya'll a sister, your daddy gave you one." I said, "I want ya'll to know."
"Who?" I said, "Kathareen." I said, "I want ya'll to love her. I want ya'll to realize that Kathareen is your daddy's daughter." I said, "If he don't do it, I want ya'll to recognize her, and love her."

He [Eugene] recognized her as *his*. But for him to *do?* I think the only recognition that she got from him when she was growin up and I was there, and Edna was bringin her to the house. He'd have her sittin up in his lap. And Andrew, my son, he'd be sort of jealous.

But I went through it all. I stayed with him till I got my kids up. We could stand on our own. And I quit him in California after I was in that car and train accident.

Chapter 22

THE ACCIDENT

When I was in that car and train accident, I was goin to work. That switch engine hit me from the side. We had to cross both tracks, and when I went to cross that first track, the guard didn't come down. I was goin 'cross, the train was comin. It was a plant on this side of the street, and a plant on that side. And this side, it extended back where the train had to go 'round, and it made a bend comin 'round. That switch engine—they say it was seven mens on it—they was comin around. The guard didn't come down. Just as I hit that first track, that train hit me. That switch engine hit me. And they said they was seven mens on that. They was gettin offa work. They done come in and went to the yard and left, and they was on it. It hit that car, and carried that car down the track. I come out, went out that door and landed cross *all* those other three tracks, from the first through the forth, in a *sittin position!*

Doctor had made me a brace, and it come under my hip, and that keep my back straight. And I had that on workin [at the plant]. I was wearin that because I was standin a lot, and my back had been botherin me, and *I had that on* that night. I said, "I'm gonna wear this." I said, "This'll help my back, standin." Doctor said if I hadn't a had that on, I'd a been *crushed*. But that night, I was lucky that I had that back brace on. If I hadn't, the doctor said I wouldn't be here today. I wouldn't be here today. I just *know* I wouldn't.

And when I went to the hospital—they called an ambulance to carry me to the hospital—my husband was workin with carpenterin then, on the job. All his carpenter tools is in the back of the car, in the trunk. And that train scattered [them] all over [like] litter. I think he got a little of it, but he didn't get much. So when they call him, when he saw the car, he said he just knew I was dead. They said, "She's at the

Chapter 22

hospital." They called an ambulance and they carried me to a hospital close by from the plant. So when he came, he called my brother and told my brother. So my brother came by and picked him up from over where we was livin. And they both, my sister-in-law and my brother, and he came to the hospital.

When they put me in that hospital, they pulled the curtains around, and I'm layin up there sayin, "Well, what else? What is they gonna do?" I was *conscious*. I say, "I wonder what they got me here for, and not doin anything." Well, I didn't have much of a feelin, but I was *conscious*. And I was layin there, and everytime I see somebody comin, pull back and peek, and then they go back. So I lay there and looked, and I'm tryin to figure out why do people come in here lookin and nobody come in here and *do* anything? So finally one came, and I say, "Doctor?" And it wasn't a doctor, it was a orderly. I said, "Is somebody gonna come here and do *anything* for me?" I say, "Can you tell me something?" He come there, he said, "Oh, they got in touch with your husband, and your husband is on the way." I said, "Oh." He said, "They waitin till he come." And this was the county hospital. They had to wait till *my* husband come to sign some papers before they did *anything* to me. They had to get *my husband*, and then he had to get *my brother*, and then they had to come. And they told 'em where to come, and they had to find the hospital, and that's why I was layin there, until they got there and signed the papers. So, my brother said, "Well, all this length of time, and ya'll haven't did *anything?*" And my sister-in-law was sayin, "Ooh, look at the glass!" She said, "Ooh, look at your hair! Ooh, your hair!" I said, "Well get it out, Sis, get it out!" She said, "Oh my God!"

༄

It [the hospital] wasn't far from where I was roomin then, where we was livin. And my kids was in school. And Andrew was cryin, "My mama gonna die!" Everett was cryin, "My mama gonna die, ain't gonna have no mama!" And so I told 'em, I said, "Well I got to go home." I had the landlady bring the kids up to the hospital where I was. And I looked out the window. They was thinkin I was dead because I hadn't gotten to come back home. And so I had her to bring 'em up, and I waved out the window, and Everett went to cryin, "Mama! Mama, when you comin home? Mama, come home, come home!"Their daddy didn't have any patience with the boys. And so I told 'em, "I'll be home." I said, "Mama be home."

So when the doctor came—the doctor was comin every day, sometimes twice a day checkin on me—I said,"Doctor," I says,"my kids are worryin about me and they in school. I don't want them to get too upset." I said, "They want Mama to come home." I said, "Is there any way I can go home and be with my kids, so they'll be quiet and be OK?" I said, "I don't want them to get to where they can't cooperate with the teachers at school." He said, "Yes, but this is what you have to do." He gave me a list of what I had to do, and I went home. He said, "You got to get a three-quarter-inch plyboard and put it on your mattress. And that's what you have to sleep on." I said, "OK." He says, "And you have to keep your back as flat as you can, 'cause you have some vertebrae damaged." And he says, "You have to keep yourself in a position where it'll heal, so you won't have a crooked back, and you can't use your back." I promised everything. I followed his instructions.

~

But you know, that's where my husband and I separated. That's what caused us to separate. I was on my back. I had to sleep on that board. And he came to me one night, and talkin about, "When can you supply my needs?" I said, "Gene, I can't." I says, "I am still sore." I says, "And I have to sleep on this board." I said, "It's not a comfortable thing, and my back is still healin." He told me, he went about two nights, he came in and told me, "You's my wife, and you are supposed to supply my needs." Now listen at this. "And you gonna supply my needs." I'm on my back, that's the onliest way I could lay and sleep. I couldn't lay on my side, I just had to lay on my back. And that man screwed me on my back, with me layin on my back. And look he just went straight down, looked like it was just, through the *bones* on the board. Miserable! Now you talk about miserable. And I hate for this to go out, but it's the truth. It was *miserable!* And I *cried*, and I cried.

Then I told the landlady upstairs, Miz DeFrance. I said, "Miz DeFrance, I want to tell you somethin." I said, "I don't have no mother." And I said, "I don't have no sisters here." I said, "I only have a brother,

Chapter 22

and I want to tell you this." And I told her. She said, "Lord, Baby, hush your mouth." And well, she didn't have but two daughters, and both of her daughters was out there. So she said, "Baby, that is *rape*." I didn't know, I hadn't ever heard of rape, and she told me that was rape. She said, "I'm gonna have my daughter come talk to ya when she come in."

So, when her daughter came in for her work, Miz Nofleys came in, she worked at a laundry, and she came in. She told her and she came downstairs. And she came down there and she hugged me, she said, "Miz H., what can I do? Anything I can do?" I said, "I'm in pain, I hurtin," I said, "but I can't go through this no more." I say, "It felt like he was just goin through the *bones* in my back." She said, "Oh Miz H.," she said, "he raped you!" I said, "What is rape?" And so she went on and told me. She said, "Now when you go back to your doctor, you tell your doctor what happened."

So when I went back to the doctor for my treatment, I told the doctor what happened. That doctor looked at me, he said, "What did you say?" And I told him again. He said, "You want me to put him in jail? And he can go to the penitentiary?" He said, "You, on your back, in this condition, and this is what he did?" I said, "Yeah." I said, "He told me I had to supply his needs." I said, "And I'm hurtin." I said, "Doctor, I haven't stopped hurtin since." He said, "Well you tell him, *I* said come to my office. If he get in too late, he better come by my office before he go to work, or [if he] don't, I'll have him picked up."

So, when he came in, I told him. I said, "Gene," I said, "the doctor wants to talk to you." "What he want with me?" I said, "You have to go and let him tell you." I said, "He said come to his office, and be at his office tomorrow morning before you go to *work*. If you don't, he will have you brought there." "I don't know what—I got a long way to go, and I—" I said, "Well now that's what he says."

Then he got on the phone and started callin where he worked, to get them to know he would have to be late comin in. "I got to take my *wife* to the *doctor*," he said, "It's a *must*. She's been grumblin, and he wants *me* to come in with her." He lied to the people where he worked. So he went in, and the doctor explained to him what he had did and what could be done to *him* for this. And told him as long as I was sick, and as long as I say no, "You don't touch her no more. The woman is in pain all the time."

And when he got back from that doctor's office—he didn't go to work that day—he got mad at me! "So, you go tellin the doctor what we do at home! You tellin about *our* privacy!" I said, "Gene, I was hurtin, and I told you *no*." He shut up, because he knew the doctor had done told him what he did was rape.

Chapter 23

MOTHER EWING

I told Mother Ewing I wanted to kill him [Eugene]. And after I told her that, I said, "Mother Ewing, he doesn't deserve to live." But, Mother Ewing kept me from killin that man. I had made up in my mind, and I had looked back over my life with him, with my childrens, and how he was doin us then. He wasn't givin me the support for the kids [during the separation], what he was supposed to. And sayin what he *wasn't* gonna do. And I went to Mother Ewing cryin, I said "Mother Ewing," I said, "I'm gonna kill him." She said "What Baby?" I said "Yeah, he don't deserve to live." She said, "Baby!" Now, he had been takin over the kids, but now, he was gonna take all that time, and the weekends from me, to have the kids with him. And I said, "Mother Ewing," I said, "that's not right." I said, "The kids got to have me some." I said, "I'm workin, and I have to do for the kids through the week." I said, "He wants them on the weekend, and do for him." I said, "And you know what the kids was sayin, 'Papa have us cleanin up his house, then tell us to get us a hamburger and stuff like that.' He wasn't cookin at home." So I told her, I said, "Mother Ewing, I'm gonna kill him."

And I found out that this woman was out there in California. He had done sent for her. And she was out there, and the kids had seen her, but I hadn't. And they come, tellin me this woman lived there at his house, and described her, and called her name. And I knew that was that same woman. Ooh, I went to Mother Ewing cryin. I said, "Mother Ewing, he doesn't deserve to live, he done treated me like this." Then, he didn't work for two years. He wanted every weekend. That was to keep me from havin them to help me through on the weekend. So, I told her that I was gonna kill him. I went over there one day. I sent the kids to school, and I goes over to Mother Ewing, and I had to go. I was hurtin so and I was cryin so—I don't know how I got there. And when I told Mother Ewing what I was goin through, she said, "Baby, lets pray." [Laughs] That woman had me on my knees so much that day, I should never want to get on my knees again. [Laughs] I prayed with Mother Ewing, and when I'd get up I'd say, "But Mother Ewing, he doesn't deserve to live" [laughter] and we'd go at it again. She'd say, "Come on, Baby, let's pray again." She had me prayin that day. She'd be doin the prayin and I was down there cryin. And when she get through, she said, "Now don't you feel better?" I say, "Yes Ma'am. But Mother Ewing! He don't deserve to live!" [Laughter]

I knew how I was goin to his house. Door had a hook on this side, and there was a bush. And I was gonna get behind that bush, at the house. When he come up to open his door, I was gonna [gestures as if shooting]. And Mother Ewing said, "No you're not." I said "Yes Ma'am, Mother Ewing." I said, "He doesn't deserve to live." And she said, "Baby," she said, "how you gonna get out of that?" I said, "Mother Ewing, I'm gonna do that, and then I'm gonna get my sons, and I'm gonna—" She said, "Baby, don't you know they come to you first?" "I'll say I don't know anythin about it." She said, "They'll see it all over you."

She kept me there *all day* till my kids got home from school. I was so upset. So she called my oldest son, and he was drivin. I had learned him how to drive. She called him, she said, "Everett," she said, "this is Mother Ewing." He said, "Mother Ewing, can you tell me?" She said, "Yeah, your mother's here, and she been here all day." He said, "Mother Ewing, is Mama alright?" 'Cause I left the house, excited, I just got all upset and left that house! The kids had never come to the house and found it like that. I didn't make a bed, or wash the dishes, or do nothing. I got out to Mother Ewing's. That woman kept me from goin crazy.

'Cause if I'd a did that, I wouldn't a finished raisin my kids. So, when she told my son that, he caught the bus and came over there, and he drove me home. It was lucky, I had done learned him how to drive. And she told him, she said, "Everett, don't leave your mother this week, stay 'round close." She said, "Because she's been here all day, and she's very upset."

So, he came and got me, and he drove me home. When we got home, he said, "Mama, what is it?" He said, "Mama, you can tell me." I said, "No, Baby." He said, "Mama, if you please tell me, I can take it. But

Chapter 23

if you don't tell me, I don't know what I'm gonna do." See and I seen that was upsettin him. I said "Well, I might as well tell you," I said, "but I don't want you to get no more upset, at what I tell you." So, he said, "What's that, Mama?" I said, "I went over to Mother Ewing's, and I was gonna—" He said "Mother!" He said, "Why?" And I told him. He said, "Mother, leave it alone." He said, "Mama, I love you and I can't get along without you." And that stopped it. When he told me that.

She [Mother Ewing] didn't have any children. That woman taught me *a lots*. And I used to take her shoppin. She was crippled, and she was heavy on her feet. That woman could cook. And I learned a lots from her, too. I used to take her shoppin. I'd take her shoppin—and what that woman would get in the month, with no money. I couldn't see how she was livin on it. And she'd make out her list, and I used to take her shoppin. And she'd have to lean on her pushin basket, and she'd say, "Baby, get me this." She did so many pounds of meat. Her biggest meat was wieners. She bought chicken, and sometimes different people was raisin chicken and these ones would bring her chicken. But Mother Ewing, she'd buy her bacon. The food that that woman was buyin, I used to look at it, and I don't know. And she would say, "Now this'll do me for so many days, and this'll do me for so . . ." till her month would be up for her check to come again. I don't see how she made it. She was eatin the same thing every mornin for breakfast, most all the time. And the way she would plan it, she'd plan it out before she go buy it.

༄

And, that's one thing that hit me hard. I was visitin my children— I was at Andrew's and I was helpin him in Virginia—and Mother Ewing passed away while I was gone. I got back home. I was wonderin about Mother Ewing. I had been callin the house, and I don't understand why they didn't cut that phone off. Where she was livin, I called and that phone was ring, ring, ring, ring. I said, "I wonder what's wrong with Mother Ewing? She must be in the hospital. She must be gone somewhere." 'Cause, she would take little trips and go visit friends. And so, finally I went to the post office one day and one of the members of the church was there. I said, "How you doin?" He said, "Fine, how you?" I said, "Fine." I said, "Can you tell me where Mother Ewing is? I been callin and the phone rings and rings." He said, "The phone ringin?" I said, "Yeah, and nobody answers." He said, "Sister Hudley." I said, "Yeah?" He said, "Honey, Mother Ewing is dead and buried." I said, "When?" And when he told me, I could have went through the floor.

༄

But, Honey, I'm tellin you, my life, it has been somethin. I looks back over there and I say, "Lord, you done brought me a long way." But, one thing I thank God for is that He give me the knowledge enough to reach out and get me some mothers after mother died—in the church. And the mothers that I chose helped me a lot, and I helped them a lot. Because after I married and went to beauty school and everything and I came out and used to go to their homes and do their hair. And I used to take them to the doctor and the clinics and things like that. I did a lot of service to those that was in need and they gave me knowledge of what they had been through, and guided me along to what I had to go through, and it made it better for me. Because a lot of times, I was lonely, because it was nothin but boys and me at home, and when I chose these people, even after I married, I chose women to be mothers to me. I would have those problems and I'd go talk it over with them, and I'm thankful to have those women.

Interlude 3

MENTORING

Like many individuals who have created meaningful and productive lives despite their struggles with oppression, Edith Hudley gives credit to supportive adults, such as special aunts, neighbors, and teachers (Anderson, 1991; Freedman, 1995; Levine & Nidiffer, 1996; Williams & Kornblum, 1985). In sharing her life story with us, she emphasized repeatedly, "I had many mothers and I have been a mother to many young women." Throughout African-American history, such intergenerational relationships have been recognized as an important resource (Martin & Martin, 1978). Collins (1987), for example, described African-American "othermothers" who guide younger members of the community, often acting as surrogate parents and mentors. One of the most striking features of Mrs. Hudley's life is that such relationships did not end with childhood but continued to play a critically important role in her adult life. These relationships also came to define her identity. She introduced herself to her future in-laws with the announcement, "I had a wonderful mother and a father ... I had a lot of other mothers after my mother passed away."

Over the past twenty years there has been a growing interest in mentoring in the psychological and social work literatures. The early literature on mentoring focused on men's relationships and emphasized its more cognitive and instrumental components (Levinson, 1978). Like these male mentors, the female mentors in Edith's life taught, advised, guided, and supported younger people. More recently, mentoring research, particularly studies focusing on women, has emphasized the relational and affective qualities of mentoring. As Mother Ewing did for Edith, and Edith, in turn, did for Edna, successful mentors also provide emotional support and lasting relationships. Edna came to call Edith "Mama" and later taught her daughter and grandchildren to do the same. Emotional support and connection are characteristics that Mother Ewing and Mrs. Hudley share with the successful mentors identified by the pregnant and parenting adolescent girls in Rhodes and Davis's study (1996). These girls described their mentors—older adult women in the communities with whom they had spontaneously developed relationships—as caring deeply about them and inspiring them to do their best. Similarly, Sullivan's (1996) research suggests that mentors possess an ability to listen, understand, and accept the younger person.

Another important characteristic of many successful mentors is that they are part of the broader community to which the younger person belongs. They understand the values and beliefs of their protégés, and the guidance they provide is congruent with the meaning systems of the community. Miz Cavanaugh, Edith's beloved eighth grade teacher, provided her with needed perspective and encouragement during a difficult period of transition. Miz Cavanaugh not only appreciated the needs and values that compelled Edith to leave school and return home to help her father but also offered advice that was consonant with Aaron's: "If you try and don't succeed, try, try, try, and try again." Similarly, the lifeline that Mother Ewing extended to Edith at a moment of moral crisis is unlikely to be deployed by professional helpers from outside the community: Mother Ewing prayed with Edith.

Research suggests that relationships with caring adults can make an important difference in the lives of vulnerable children and youth (for example, Cowan & Work, 1988; Garmezy, 1985; Rutter, 1990). In their book, *Vulnerable But Invincible*, Werner and Smith (1982), report the results of a thiry-two-year longitudinal study of children exposed to poverty and family instability. They found that the children who thrived had at least one adult who provided consistent emotional support. Support from natural mentors—more experienced people from family or community with whom the youth has an informal, supportive relationship—is associated with improvements in the psychological, social, academic, and career functioning of at-risk adolescents (McLearn, Colasanto, & Schoen, 1998; Munch & Blyth, 1993; Rhodes & Davis, 1996). For example, natural mentors have served as important protective influences on the lives of young, low-income, African-American and Latina adolescent mothers (Rhodes, Ebert, & Fischer,

1992; Rhodes, Contreras, & Mangelsdorf, 1994). Latina adolescent mothers with natural mentors reported lower levels of depression and anxiety than those without mentors despite similar levels of stress and overall social support.

Despite these benefits, relatively few adolescents actually develop relationships with mentors (Rhodes & Davis, 1996). Like Edith Hudley, those who seek out mentors tend to recall their childhood relationships with their mothers as positive and accepting. Perhaps these early relationships instill the motivation and skills that allow individuals to reproduce them with other adults. Mrs. Hudley's account suggests another potentially important factor: parental support. Aaron not only encouraged Edith to develop such relationships but steered her toward older women of the church, "Those is the ones that's got experience, and can give you the right kind of advice...." Heeding his guidance, Edith sought out and benefited from relationships with the mothers of the church throughout her life. For adolescents who are struggling, teaching and encouraging them to recruit support from helpful adults in their own social networks may be an effective intervention strategy.

An alternative approach to intervention has been to develop formal programs to pair supportive adults with vulnerable youth. In the past few years, thousands of mentoring programs have emerged. Beyond their intuitive appeal, there is growing evidence that such programs promote social and emotional growth and school achievement, provide critical support to pregnant and parenting teenagers, and reduce delinquent behavior and substance abuse. (For example, Davidson & Redner, 1998; DuBois & Neville, 1997; Grossman & Tierney, 1998; LoSciutp, Rajala, Townsend, & Taylor, 1996; McPartland & Nettles, 1991; Morrow & Styles, 1995; Quint, 1991; Reisner, Petry, & Armitage, 1998; Rhodes & Davis, 1996; Rhodes, Ebert, & Fischer, 1992; Rhodes, Contreras, & Mangelsdorf, 1994; Rhodes, Haight, & Briggs, 1999; Sullivan, 1996). Of course, mentoring is a complex process, and not all outcomes are so positive. Mentoring can be harmful when a mentor does not keep her promises to a young person with a history of problematic relationships. And there are many situations in which professional help is more appropriate.

Communities for Positive Development

Edith Hudley's life story dramatizes an important issue for parents, social workers, and educators: where are the mentors and protected spaces to which children of color can turn for help in developing their strengths and facing challenges? As discussed in Interlude 1, African-American churches traditionally have served as havens for children, youth, and their families. Edith benefited, as do many children and youth today, from the educational and cultural programs, relationships, and socialization practices within black churches (Haight, 2002).

African Americans have also formed a variety of other kinds of supportive communities. In *Call to Home*, Carol Stack (1996) describes rural, southern communities to which African Americans have returned, bringing with them the skills they learned while living in northern, urban areas and fashioning new, vibrant programs for children. Gregory Dimitriadis (2001) describes an urban community center in which African-American children and youth drew upon relationships with adults and peers, as well as resources from popular culture, to create their self-identities. Staff at the community center helped these young people to develop strategies to deal with racism, including responses to a planned local rally of the Ku Klux Klan (KKK).

Shirley Brice Heath (1995) describes a number of nontraditional and ethnically mixed communities. For example, "BEST" is an outreach program of a white church situated in a low-income, urban neighborhood. In the BEST program, children and youth from a variety of backgrounds, including African Americans, Caribbean Americans, Puerto Rican Americans, and Mexican Americans, had a safe place to come to after school. Here, young people benefited from caring, adult mentors who supported them throughout their school years and provided tutoring, career counseling, and a wide variety of enrichment activities. Heath also describes an informal social network of ethnically diverse street children living in a university town. These young people formed supportive relationships with one another and with adults at a local Teen Feed program that provided a free evening meal.

INTERLUDE 3

Mentoring and Adult Development

Thus far, formal mentoring research and interventions have focused on adolescence and young adulthood. In their classic work, *The Seasons of a Man's Life*, Levinson (1978) and colleagues describe the mentoring relationship as one of the "most complex and developmentally important, a man can have in early adulthood." From this perspective, mentors are seen as "transitional figures" between adults as parental figures and adults as peers. When a young man reaches a level of competence, the mentoring relationship is, essentially, outgrown.

In contrast, Edith Hudley describes important mentoring relationships that extended well into her forties. Her life story challenges researchers to examine their assumptions about the developmental trajectory of mentoring and to consider the possibility that mentoring is a lifelong phenomenon. Individuals further along in life can provide perspective, guidance, and emotional support for younger adults who are dealing with the inevitable stresses and complexities of the adult world. They can support single parents, parents raising their children away from their own extended families, parents involved in the child welfare system, and adults caring for their own ailing parents and spouses. Adults with ample financial resources have long sought out the paid advice of therapists and other counselors. Others have joined support groups. For example, individuals with substance abuse problems have benefited greatly from "sponsors," former substance abusers well into their own recovery who can provide guidance and perspective to others. Mentoring within the context of adult life may turn out to have some features in common with these other forms of help seeking.

To harness the potential of mentoring relationships into adulthood, however, future research will need to determine how the mentoring of adults compares with the mentoring of young people. Edith Hudley's relationship with Mother Ewing in middle adulthood shared some characteristics with the mentoring relationships of her youth. She benefited from Mother Ewing's greater wisdom and experience, and the two formed a deep and lasting emotional tie. Mentoring relationships involving youth and young adults, however, tend to be unidirectional, focusing primarily on the young person (Sullivan, 1996).

On the other hand, Mrs. Hudley described a greater degree of reciprocity in the mentoring relationships she enjoyed in adulthood. Mother Ewing and the other mothers of the church gave a great deal to her, but she took them shopping and to the doctor, helped them with other errands, and shared her many skills, such as hair dressing.

Edith Hudley's life also raises questions about the characteristics of individuals most likely to benefit from mentoring in their adult years. Scholars have suggested that adolescent girls who, like Edith, participated from childhood in an intergenerational world involving their mothers, aunts, grandmothers, and other female kin may be especially eager to seek out and listen to advice from older women (for example, Konopka, 1986; Strommen, 1977). Similarly, during adulthood certain individuals may be less inclined to outgrow their mentors but to continue to seek out the counsel of those who are more experienced.

References

Anderson, E. (1991). Neighborhood effects on teenage pregnancy. In C. Jencks & P.E. Peterson (Eds.), *The urban underclass*. Washington, DC: Brookings Institution.

Collins, P. (1987). The meaning of motherhood in black culture and black mother/daughter relationships. *Sage, 4,* 3-10.

Cowan, E., & Work, W. (1988). Resilient children, psychological wellness, and primary prevention. *American Journal of Community Psychology, 16,* 591-607.

Davidson, W,. & Redner, R. (1998). The prevention of juvenile delinquency: Diversion from the juvenile justice system. In R. Price, E. Cowen, R. Lorion, & J. Ramos-McKay (Eds.), *Fourteen ounces of prevention: Theory, research, and prevention.* Elmsford, NY: Pergamon.

Dimitriadis, G. (2001). *Performing identity/performing culture: hiphop as text, pedagogy, and lived performance.* New York: Peter Lang.

DuBois, D., & Neville, H. (1997). Youth mentoring: Investigation of relationship characteristics and perceived benefits. *Journal of Community Psychology, 25,* 227-234.

Freedman, M. (1995). *The kindness of strangers: Adult mentors, urban youth, and the new volunteerism.* San Francisco: Jossey-Bass.

Garmezy, N. (1985). Stress resistant children: The search for protective factors. In J. Stevenson (Ed.), *Recent research in developmental psychopathology.* Elmsford, NY: Pergamon.

Grossman, J., & Tierney, J. (1998). Does mentoring work? An impact study of Big Brothers/Big Sisters program. *Evaluation Review, 22,* 403-426.

Haight, W. (2002). *African American children at church: A sociocultural perspective.* Cambridge: Cambridge University Press.

Heath, S.B. (1995). Ethnography in communities: Learning the everyday life of America's subordinated youth. In J.A. Banks & C.M. Banks (Eds.), *Handbook of research on multicultural education*. New York: Macmillan.

Konopka, G. (1986). *Young girls: A portrait of adolescence*. Englewood Cliffs, NJ: Prentice-Hall.

Levine, A., & Nidiffer, J. (1996). *Beating the odds: How the poor get to college*. San Francisco: Jossey-Bass.

Levinson, D., with Darrow, C., Klein, E., Levinson, M., & McKee, B. (1978). *The seasons of a man's life*. New York: Knopf.

LoSciutp, L., Rajala, A., Townsend, T., & Taylor, A. (1996). An outcome evaluation of Across Ages: An intergenerational mentoring approach to drug prevention. *Journal of Adolescent Research, 11*, 116-129.

Martin, E., & Martin, J. (1978). *The black extended family*. Chicago: University of Chicago Press.

McLearn, K., Colasanto, D., & Schoen, C. (1998, June). Mentoring makes a difference: Findings from the Commonwealth Fund 1998 survey of adults mentoring young people. Paper presented at the State and Future of Mentoring Symposium, Washington, D.C.

McPartland, J., & Nettles, S. (1991). Using community adults as advocates or mentors for at-risk middle school students: A two-year evaluation of project RAISE. *American Journal of Education, 99*, 568-586.

Morrow, K., & Styles, M. (1995). *Building relationships with youth in program settings: A study of Big Brothers/Big Sisters*. Philadelphia, PA: Public/Private Ventures.

Munch, J., & Blyth, D. (1993). An analysis of the functional nature of adolescents' supportive relationships. *Journal of Early Adolescence, 13*, 132-153.

Quint, J. (1991). Project Redirection: Making and measuring a difference. *Evaluation and Program Planning, 14*, 75-86.

Reisner, E., Petry, C., & Armitage, M. (1998). *A review of programs involving college students as tutors or mentors in grades K-12*. Washington, DC: Policy Studies Associates, Inc.

Rhodes, J., Contreras, J., & Mangelsdorf, S. (1994). Natural mentor relationships among Latina adolescent mothers: Psychological adjustment, moderating processes, and the role of early parental acceptance. *American Journal of Community Psychology, 22*, 211-28.

Rhodes, J., & Davis, A. (1996). Supportive ties between nonparent adults and urban adolescent girls. In J. Leadbeater & N. Way (Eds.), *Urban girls: Resisting stereotypes, creating identities*. New York: New York University Press.

Rhodes, J., Ebert, L., & Fischer, K. (1992). Natural mentors: An overlooked resource in the social networks of adolescent mothers. *American Journal of Community Psychology, 20*, 445-61.

Rhodes, J., Haight, W., & Briggs, E. (1999). The influence of mentoring on the peer relationships of foster youth in relative and nonrelative care. *Journal of Research on Adolescence, 9*, 185-201.

Rutter, M. (1990). Psychosocial resilience and protective mechanisms. In J. Rolf, A. Masten, D. Cicchetti, K. Neuchterlein, & S. Weintraub (Eds.), *Risk and protective factors in the development of psychopathology.* New York: Cambridge University Press.

Stack, C. (1996). *Call to home: African Americans reclaim the rural South.* New York: Basic Books.

Strommen, E. (1977). Friendship. In E. Donelson and J. Gullahorn (Eds.), *Women: A psychological perspective.* New York: Wiley.

Sullivan, A. (1996). From mentor to muse: Recasting the role of women in relationship with urban adolescent girls. In J. Leadbeater & N. Way (Eds.), *Urban girls: Resisting stereotypes, creating identities.* New York: New York University Press.

Werner, E., & Smith, R. (1982). *Vulnerable but invincible: A study of resilient children.* New York: McGraw-Hill.

Williams, T.M., & Kornblum, W. (1985). *Growing up poor.* Lexington, MA: Lexington Books.

Wilson, M.N. (1986). The black extended family: An analytical consideration. *Developmental Psychology, 22,* 246-58.

Part 4

Raising Children

In this part of Mrs. Hudley's oral history her oldest son is born in 1948 and her youngest son graduates from high school in 1969. It takes place primarily in Oakland, California.

This portion of Mrs. Hudley's oral history occurs during the Civil Rights movement of the 1950s and 1960s. In the 1960s the Bay Area African-American community organized politically, and several African Americans were elected to public office. In addition, the Congress for Racial Equality (CORE) was organized in the early 1960s. CORE led opposition to police brutality and advocated for better jobs for blacks and more effective integration of public schools. In 1966, Oakland residents Bobby Seale and Huey Newton formed the radical Black Panther Party. Their intent was to defend local black communities against racism and capitalist exploitation. In addition to providing the black community with protection from the police, the Black Panther Party provided information regarding civil rights, developed health care programs, provided free breakfast programs for black school children, and started a housing center for the homeless (Mendelsohn, 2002; Carson, 1991). Edith went to several lessons taught by the Black Panthers but found the anger and militancy inconsistent with her Christian beliefs.

Given her Baptist faith and her experiences growing up in the South, it is not surprising that Mrs. Hudley was most profoundly moved by the philosophy and tactics of Dr. Martin Luther King, Jr. A child of the segregated South, Dr. King, like Mrs. Hudley, insisted that whites were capable of loving their black neighbors. Dr. King was profoundly influenced by Mahatma Gandhi's philosophy of love and nonviolent strategies for social change. He applied this philosophy and strategy to the plight of American blacks. Dr. King came to view noncooperation with injustice as a moral duty. Like Gandhi, King believed that the most effective way for the oppressed to gain liberty is through nonviolent resistance (Gates & West, 2000). King said, "I had come to see that the Christian doctrine of love operating through the Gandhian method of nonviolence was the most potent weapon available to the Negro in his struggle for freedom" (quoted in Carson, 1991). King's leadership contributed to the passage of the Civil Rights Act in 1964, which outlawed segregation in public facilities and racial discrimination in employment and education, and the Voting Rights Act of 1965, which greatly increased the number of southern blacks able to register to vote. In 1964, Dr. King won the Nobel Peace Prize.

Once again, readers are directed to Appendix A for a summary of key events. This portion of the oral history focuses on Edith's sons, who were born in Texas in 1948 and 1951. In the early 1950s Edith worked energetically for better schools for African-American children. In 1956, Edith and Eugene moved their family to Oakland, California, in search of better schools for their children. They divorced shortly thereafter in 1961. In 1963, Edith married a sailor who was a wonderful stepfather to her sons. In 1968, she divorced him because he began drinking heavily after his retirement and became abusive toward

Edith. By 1969, both of Edith's sons had graduated from high school and were attending Howard University in Washington, D.C. Edith remained in Oakland until 1988.

Appendix B lists a number of important people. In addition to Mrs. Hudley's many friends and Eugene, the main characters in this portion of her oral history are her sons, Everett and Andrew, and her second husband, Ellis.

Students and teachers may again wish to consult Appendix C for suggested issues for study, discussion, and further research.

References

Carson, C. (1991). Civil Rights movement. In E. Foner & J. Garraty (Eds.), *The readers companion to American history.* Boston: Houghton-Mifflin.

Gates, H., & West, C. (2000). *The African-American century: How black Americans have shaped our country.* New York: Simon & Schuster.

Mendelsohn, J. (2002). African American history of San Francisco and Oakland, California. http://www.Africana.com.

Chapter 24

RAISING SAND ABOUT SCHOOL

My oldest boy [Everett] after he got through kindergarten and everything, I had to put him in another school. When it rained, it was mud and slop and everything. And they had to go out of the building into a house. And they let the big kids eat first, and the little kids who wanted to have hot lunches, they'd go last. And then they'd cut half. They would get half of what the larger kids was gettin, and we'd be payin the same thing. So, I worked with them on that, and I said, "Hmm mmm, I can't be havin my kids doin this."

So, I put him in another school where he wasn't in the district where I was livin, but my sister was. And they knew how smart he was—Everett was real smart—and the word got out. They was runnin me down, tryin to find how to take Everett out of this school. And I told 'em, I say, "You know what," I say, "I'll leave this place before I take my child and put him out there in that world."

'Cause I had worked with the teachers, I was the secretary of the PTA. They wanted me to be the president. I wouldn't do that at that school 'cause I had already did it once. So I said, "Uh uh."

So when I went with my oldest son to the school that he was goin to, then I was workin with the teachers, with the other kids. And so I put on "plattin the Maypole." Have you ever heard of that? That was a beautiful thing. So we used to plat that when I was in school, so I taught it to them. And this other school heard about it where he was supposed to been goin. They got angry because he was in this school, and this school's grades was goin up with the little childrens 'cause I was workin with them some. And they wanted Everett in that school.

I went over there and worked with those people, and I told 'em, "Look, let me tell ya'll one thing." I said, "I'm not bringin my kid in this school to walk in mud and water and goin to this house out here, and you gonna let the older kids eat first." I said, "You should be lettin the new kids eat first." I said, "And then you cut in half." What one big kid eat, they was givin it to two little ones. And was havin to pay the same thing. And I told 'em, I said, "I'm not gonna do that."

So they got behind me. And then I got with one of the ladies, and she said, "I want you to work in with the school district," and so we did. Oh, Honey! We started diggin out all the things of that school district. They threatened our lives! Oh yes. Yeah, that was just before the Civil Rights. They threatened our lives. We went at nighttime to meetings. And the school that they had for their white children—they had a umbrella arch from their cafeteria, they had cement walks all around. And another thing, we was payin more money in the school district.

*

I worked with them till we got another school. And when that school was built—when Carver Junior High School was built—they said, be sure to have Miz H. to walk through that school first [laughs]. I had raised so much sand with those people, and fussed. You know what they did, they sent a car to pick me up at my house to drive me to that school! When this car come, I said, "Who's this comin here?" We was in the store business then. I thought it was somebody comin to the store, and they said, "We've come to pick up Miz H." I said, "For what?" "Well, they sent us to come pick you up."

And they was gonna march from the old school to the new school. Well, I had been workin with them, but they didn't give me the day that they was gonna march from the old school to the new school. And they picked me up and carried me, drove me, and then had me to march in before some of those pupils did. They said, "She done raised so much *hell* about this school that we wanted her to see the school first."

So, I had to go through this school. I was embarrassed in a way, but I was glad I did what I did 'cause it helped the school and helped the

Chapter 24

kids. So I went through that school, and they told me, "Anything you find wrong, you write it down. We'll straighten it." So I had raised a lot of things 'cause I had been goin to meetings in the school district, and I was tellin them everything that we needed in the school. I said, "In fact, we need a new school." I say, "Now we payin more tax where we are than where you all live, and ya'll have the best school." I said, "You know that's not right."

~

One man, he threatened me and another lady one night. And we was almost scared to leave that building to go home. But I was drivin and I told her, I said, "If you watch out, I'll do the drivin." I said, "Anybody get in my way, now." She said, "Don't try anything." I said, "I'm gonna run over 'em." I say, "Ms. Nelson, you all right?" She say, "Yeah." But she's the one got me into the thing.

~

So, after I fought so much and helped them get a new school, when it was time for my son, I told him, I said, "We's leavin here." And takin my kids and went back to California, and that's where I schooled them, in California. I told my husband, I said, "I done fought too much." And when I got to California, it was better in Oakland, but I had to work too.

Now their dad wasn't the type like my dad was. My dad would go and visit the school and see how the childrens comin on. My mother, when she was livin, she was active. But, my kids' daddy, he didn't have no time. He'd say, "They doin all right. Check up the work at night." Well, that wasn't it.

And so, when I takin my oldest son—my youngest son wasn't old enough to go to school when I left and went back to California—my son went to school one year. And then when they would come I'd go in there and I helped them get that school, and I said, "Huh uh," I said, "I'm leavin here. I'm gonna take my child where I can get him a better education." So I did.

~

I was scared [in Houston]. Really, I really got scared because I had gotten some threatenin remarks in the meetings. And where we had to go in these meetings, I didn't know my way around. I would get with somebody else that would guide me into where we was goin. If they'd a went off and left me, or got 'em a way some other way, I wouldn't a knowed my way out. So, I told 'em, I said, "I don't mind workin." And I said, "I'll do everything I can," I said, "because I walked four miles to school," I said, "when I was goin to school." And I said, "I want all children to have somethin better if they can." But, it was hard. It was hard.

We'd take *lies*. And I couldn't understand it. And then when I started to questionin about why, I said, "Well, I'd like to know this." I say, "Ya'll have a good school here. How much tax do ya'll pay, school tax?" And that shut 'em up. Nobody didn't want to say anything. And I said, "I know tax you pay goes towards helpin the school, buyin stuff for school, that the school need and all." I said, "We got some bad buses," I said, "and I see ya'll have a line of nice buses."

So, I was just linin out everything, you know. And so [laughs] one lady told me, she said, "Girl, you better hope, for we may not get outa here." And I didn't know that they had got some threats at the meetin before. And that's the reason they was tryin to get as many parents to go, see. Because some of those that had went, they had got threats, so they tried to get as many parents to go.

So, me and Miss Bertha, she was one of the ones that got the threats, so she wanted me to go, but she didn't tell me that they had got the threats. They wanted all those in that district to support them, and that's what I did.

And when I got to askin questions, one man got up and looked at me, and he says, "Why you askin so many questions. Do you have one goin?" I said, "No, but he'll be goin pretty soon." And he says, "Just where are you from?" And I said, "I'm the lady that have the H.'s Grocery Store and Market on 1719 Desota Street." He looked at me and he said, "Oh, you're in business." And I said, "Yes." And so, he looked at me real funny, and one lady said, "Don't tell him too much." And I said, "No," I said, " 'cause if they come around me," I said, "I'm gonna be

Chapter 24

ready for 'em too." They said, "No, Baby, don't talk like that," she said, "because you don't know. They can blow you up." I didn't think about that. I'm just thinkin about workin with these kids [laughs].

So finally I said, "Mister, I'd like to stand up and say this much." I said, "Would ya'll give me a, a few minutes?" I say, "I won't take long." So they said, "Yes." There was an elder man there, and he was guidin me along, you know. He was the one that was pullin, that had coaxed the whole thing. He said, "Why not give her as long as she needs?" He said, "This is a lady that's in our community. She helps people. She help the sick, she carry 'em to the hospital. She go and get them." He said, "She help people's children." And he said, "Where the children's catchin the bus for school, if it's raining, they's in the store until they get the bus."

So, they felt like, well, if she can help, well, we'll give her that time. And when I got through tellin them how I felt about it and how far I had come, and my parents, and my brothers in service, and I said, "And I lost a brother in service." When I got through tellin them the way I felt, I said, "Our children do need a better education. But how can they get it when they don't have the proper things?" And so when I got through, it was an elder man there, he was the one that's helpin get the people in that district to go to the meetin, he came to me and put his arm around me and he said, "Baby," he said, "you did it tonight." He said, "I think they see it." I told him, I said, "I don't have a child that's goin here now, at this school that we're workin for." I said, "But I wouldn't want my child to go there," I said, "what I have gone and seen." And I had worked with them and didn't have no child goin to that school, but I was in that district. And after I had went and visit and seen the condition, I didn't want my child goin there.

Chapter 25

WORKING WITH THE TEACHERS

When my kids was in school, I used to tiptoe in their class, and they didn't even know I was in school. I be sittin back in the back. I didn't want them to know I was there, so I could see how they was doin. And my youngest son, he's always busy. And when we was in California at the school he started in—Andrew was smart, but he was the busy bodiest little child you ever seen! He couldn't set in that seat. And I would tell him at home, "Andrew, you have to stay in your seat." "Mama, I gets my lesson. I do all my work and everything!" He was good at that. But sittin in a seat and obeyin and stayin still, he couldn't do it.

And so I carried him to the doctor. I told the doctor, why was it that Andrew couldn't sit still in his seat at school? I said, "Doctor, I have gone to his school, and Andrew would be tickin across the room."

The teacher, she would have 'em in sections. So she'd have this group, and this group is with her, this group is sittin here and there's another group over here. One teacher would sometimes have four and five groups of kids that she had to get 'round to. And I walked in his room one day, and I eased in, set at the back. Here Andrew was, goin away, I said, "Now, where is he goin?" That hurt me! I said, "Now I have told him, 'You have to stay in your seat.' " I felt so bad. I said, "Now he knows I been tellin him to stay in his seat, 'You have to listen to the teacher, you have to pay attention to what the teacher said, so you can learn, Andrew. Be quiet. Study your lesson. Do what the teacher tell you.' " I walked in there, and here he's clear across the room. I said, "Oh Lord," I was so hurt.

But after that, he knew that I was gonna be comin, off and on. Andrew got to where he was comin home, "Mama, this is what the teacher gave me today. She said I was a good boy!" I said, "Good, Andrew." I said, "Now when you be naughty, you tell the teacher I said send me a naughty note too, OK?" "Mama, but I'm gonna be good." I said, "I want you to be good." I said, "I want you to listen to the teacher."

❧

So I tried to instill that [if you start hating, hate will destroy you] with my two kids and workin with the two PTA presidents in the school, and then I ended up PTA president [laughs]. And I seen what the poor teachers—Lord have mercy—went through in those schools with those children. And I said, "Lord Jesus," I said, "these poor teachers."

Now, I worked with the teachers a lots when my kids was comin up. I was there! When they'd say, "We need some parents," I was there. I always made time. If I had to take off from my job, I'd tell 'em, "Now, my childrens is in school, and I work with the teachers, and whenever they call me or need me, I may have to ask you for a day off." I taken the time. I said, "I was gonna give my kids the best that I could," but, when I seen what those teachers was goin through, I say I was gonna give those teachers all of the service that I could.

❧

So, then I ended up bein [laughs] a PTA president! But, when my oldest son came out of elementary goin to junior high, when I came home from work ... I had never been to that school or nothin, but I knew the school he was gonna be goin to from this elementary [school]. Here they had done got all of the PTA president papers and everything, and there was a box sittin at my door, where I live, because the school had sent my son's name over. They knowed he was goin to that school.

They had got together at that school and elected the officers for the next year that my son was comin in, and they knew Everett was comin there, and they put me for president of the PTA. I didn't know, because I had never been to that school, and that was gonna be his

[Everett's] first year. And I had been there and seen and visited, you know, and seen the school. But, I came home from work and there was all these papers from the years past of the PTA, and sayin, "You are the elect PTA president to lead these people."

But I had never been a president. I had worked with the president. But I went to them and told them, I said, "Now, my dad taught me, and my mom, 'never say what you can do till you try.'" So that was in there. And he say, "You never know what you can do until you try, try, and try again."

So I told 'em, I said, "Now, I've never been a president of the PTA." I said, "Now ya'll have got all this at my house, but when I come in," I said, "all this was at my door and sayin I was president of the PTA," I says, "when I work, I work." I said, "Now if ya'll are gonna work with me." I said, "I've never been, but I'll try." I said, "But I want all the help I can get." So they laughed at me. I said, "Now, if you start to flunkin on me," I said, "ya'll are gonna hear from me."

I had to go to doors in the evenin time, to knock on the parents' doors. But the parents mostly had stopped goin to the PTA meetings, and we *needed* those parents there, Honey. I went knockin on doors and lettin the parents know: "We have a PTA meetin at such and such time and such and such school, in such and such a room or wherever it was gonna be, and *I want you there!*" I says, "Now they elected me," I said, "I want you mothers to show me you care about your children." And got more mothers out that year than they had *ever* had! That made me feel good! But I got out of that [after] one year, and I said goodbye!

Chapter 26

CHASTISING CHILDREN

That's what I had to fight [for] with my kids. When they [educators] started sayin that you couldn't spank your children. They didn't birth the child. They didn't have anything to do with the child comin here, and for the parents to chastise their own child—who knows what they need—I feel like they have destroyed the youth. Because my youngest son, bless his heart, he was a hard-headed child. He was gonna do it his way or no way. My oldest one was just the opposite. I didn't have much trouble with him at all. But the youngest son, he was determined to do anything like he wanted and had nerves enough to front me and was gonna tell me what he was gonna to do and what he wasn't gonna do.

We was livin in California where you couldn't spank your kids, and I went to the [school] board with a group of school members and mothers and I protested that a parent couldn't spank their child. But they did it anyway. And they asked me, "Why?" and I explained it to them. I had a lots out of the Bible where it says, "Raise up a child in the way he should go and when he gets older, he won't be far from it." And if a child do wrong, you chastise that child with the love that you have for that child, and I knew I had given love to my kids.

~

Everett and Andrew was in elementary [school]. That was in the late fifties or the early sixties this happened. See, we was comin from church and they said these two little boys broke in a place and the police was comin and the kids was runnin and they [police] hollered, "Halt, halt!" And you know kids who did something when runnin, they don't pay attention to "Halt." They was tryin to get home. And he shot at those kids and shot one of them and killed him.

And we was comin from church that time, and we saw this incident that happened, and I tried to get my husband to stop so we could be eyewitnesses in the case if it was needed. [Eugene said] "I'm not gonna bother those folks." That hurt me because we had two sons then, and that was a little boy that got killed, and it was two little boys that was runnin. Although they may have been doin things that they shouldn't have done, it wasn't that bad that the police had to shoot and kill one of them. That was the first incident that I saw.

Then, another one, we was comin from church, and it was on another street, this was on Market runnin into Washington. So, we was gonna stop, and they made good hamburgers, oh, they had the best hamburgers you'd want, but anyway, we was gonna stop there and get a hamburger. Just as we pulled up, we saw the police there and young people were screamin and hollerin, "He didn't have to do it, didn't have to do it!" This little boy, his mother had sent him down there to get some hamburger. The little boy had give the order and gave the money, but when they got the hamburger ready, another little boy got in and said, "Are these my hamburgers?" And he said, "No." So, he's takin the hamburger and this other little boy said those was his hamburgers. He started off and that man shot and killed that child.

And it hurt me to the point to where I was almost afraid for my kids because so much was happenin to little boys. And I had to sit down and talk to my kids, and they would say, "Mama, it won't happen to me, it won't happen." I said, "Well, you know you never can tell," and I started to tellin them the best places that I wanted them to go and not.

So, my youngest little boy, he'd take me serious and he started readin his Bible. I was a Sunday school teacher for the kids, and one Sunday, he got up in the class—he wasn't in my class—and told about what happened. Then he said, "If this is what God is gonna do for us, I don't want to be God's child."

˜

I was the one that had to chastise the kids. He [Eugene] would say, "Go to your Mama." If they got into something, I would try to reach them first—before he would know anything about it—chastisin and

Chapter 26

such. But, my youngest son used to run everytime I started to whup him, but the oldest one, he would stand there and just flinch. With a switch you don't have to hit hard. That's what I was raised up on.

It hurted me, and when I would chastise them, I would say, "Do you know this is hurtin me more than it is hurtin you?" I would talk to them the whole time. I said, "I feel it all over." I says, "This is hurtin me and hurtin my heart to have to do this to you." I said, "I talk to you and I know you know better." I said, "Why can't you just follow what Mama tell you and keep from gettin these spankings?" I said, "But when you disobey and go against my rules, you're gonna end up gettin a spankin."

∾

So, it ended up that Andrew got so naughty in school that I had to visit his school, because he had it in his head that you couldn't whup no child, see? They had done passed the law.

So, I went to a meetin and they had this man speakin there about raisin up children and all, and that parents don't know when to whup and chastise and whatnot. Boy, you talkin about some blood boilin up. I could taste blood in my mouth. And I held my hand up and he said, "We have a young lady there." And I said, "No, you have a mother here." And so, when I got through tellin him, I said, "You talkin about what parents can't do, you're not with our children. We're the ones raisin our children. We know what our children is doin and what they're capable of doin and what they don't have to do." I said, "And you gonna tell me that I can't whup my own child?" I said, "And you gonna chastise them and you don't know what it's all about?" I said, "This is a law that y'all need to cut out and throw it in the garbage can."

That man looked at me so funny, and he said, "Well, why would you say that? Did you get whupins?" I said, "I did when I needed it." I said, "And I thank my mother and father for everything—every lick that they gave me—because it taught me a lesson." I said, "And it didn't kill me and it didn't blister me up."

"Well," I said, "the reason why some of these parents go overboard when they chastise the kids is because too much has done piled up in them and it all come out at one time." I said, "But if you all would just help the parents to raise the kids, the children would be better."

I said, "But, I'm gonna tell ya'll one thing," I said, "I don't care what ya'll say to me, and how many times you come to my house, I'm gonna raise mine." I said, "Because, if I don't, the next thing ya'll will be puttin a bullet in them or a billyclub up against they head." I said, "I've seen you do it." He says, "Are you sure?" I said, "Yes." I said, "Officer, would you like for me to take down what I see from now on and turn it over to you?" I said, "But, I'm quite sure ya'll wouldn't do anything about it but sweep it under the rug, would you?" Everybody went to laughin. It wasn't no laughin thing to me. I wanted some sincere answers.

And I asked him, I said, "How is it that a mother carry a child nine months and they always told me to be careful what you do and your actions and all carryin the baby, because it will fall on the child." I said, "Now, Officer," I said, "It's for the parents to straighten the child out, not me come tellin you about what my child is doin." I said, "My child is with me and he's not with you. So, if I can't chastise him, how is you gonna chastise him and don't know what it's all about?"

The place got silent. The man didn't know what to say. He stood up there and looked at me and he [mocking the man huffing and puffing]. When I asked him the question, "You gonnna chastise him, but you didn't birth him? You are not livin with him, you don't know. But, you're gonna chastise my child for what he did or what he say and I can't do it?" I said, "Officer, ya'll got something goin wrong."

ဢ

And that still hurts me today. That's why we have lost a lot of our young people. I've known some that cuss out the parents, talkin about what they'll do. One lady come to me cryin—come from work, done worked all day—and the little boys done taken something. Those was long hours parents had to make then to make ends meet. They couldn't go to a job at eight and get off at four and come home. If they did, they was a distance, and by the time they get home it may be an hour or more.

Chapter 26

And there was a lady, out in public, and the child got a little restless and everything, and the mother snatched the child from back here—caught the clothes she had on and snatched. And before I could compose myself, I had done ran and taken that child from the mother. I said, "Give me this child here." She looked at me. I said, "I can't help it, lady, but you're doin the wrong thing right now." I said, "Calm yourself down." I said, "I'll help you with her." She [mother] was takin her back here like this and had pulled her hair and sat her down on her seat real hard, and that baby screamed out. And I told her, "Honey, let me tell you something," I said, "don't ever sit your child down like that," I said, "Do you know that your backbone runs all the way out and it comes out to a little tail?" I said, "At the end of your backbone is a straight little tail and you sat that child down," I said, "and that could fracture her tailbone." And the little child grabbed herself when she sat her down, you know. It hit hard and when I got through with her, that lady was sittin there just tremblin. She said, "Well, she gets on my nerve." I said, "Honey, when she gets on your nerve, go and put her in her room and tell her to take a nap or give her something to do."

~

I talked a lot to my kids and then when they didn't heed to my talkin and it went so far to where that I had to spank them, I got the switch. I didn't get no strap. I didn't pick up no chair. I didn't take no pot—a lot of people just go after anything that they can. I had my switch. I didn't have no big switch, I had this little switch. They had an undershirt on, and I would get they back part. And I gave them they lashings.

I would talk to them every time I was hittin them a lick, and I would let them know how I felt. I would tell them, "I'm doin this because I love you and if I don't chastise you and you keep doin what I say don't do, you disobeyin me." I just sit down and read the Bible to them—that scripture "Honor your father and mother"—that was my main one, "Honor your father and mother that your days may be longer." I say, "God gave ya'll to me to raise, and if I fail to raise you, I have failed God." And I said, "I have to suffer the consequences."

That's what I think the parents don't do all that they are supposed to do. They got to sit down and talk to they children first and let them know how much I love you and what I expect of you and if you have any problems, come to Mama, come to Daddy, talk it over. Don't be afraid and not talk about it. But if you disobey me, then, we are gonna to have to have some problem solvin and my switch was my problem solvin."

༄

Now, when my kids was comin up, they would rather for me to talk, talk, talk. "Mama, don't get the switch. Mama, please, please." But, I said, "Well, I done talked and talked till I'm tired now." But, when I get the switch, then they say, "Mama, but it hurts so bad." And I say, "Do you know it's hurtin Mama's heart worse than it's hurtin you?" I said, "I'm hurtin, I'm hurtin, too. I'm hurtin because I have to do this to you."

I didn't have to whup my kids that much. It was long in between that I whup them. I can almost count on one hand, for each one of them, that I had to whup them. But, I talked to them and I would tell them, "Ya'll done hurt Mama's heart. My heart is hurtin and my heart is heavy and sometimes I have to go in the back room and cry."

The kids got to worryin. They got concerned. You have to get them concerned about you and them, let them know how it's hurtin you and how it hurts you to have to chastise them and that's the way my boys were.

Chapter 27

TWO DIFFERENT CHILDREN

Everett, from a baby, was a good baby. And I started him to preschool, kindergarten, and whatnot. But I started him at home. He was eager to want to learn, and I started him at home, a learnin. When it ended up with Everett and Andrew, it was just as different as night and day with those two kids. Andrew has been so much like his dad's people, on that side. Everett is more comin up my grandmother's side of the family. It's just different. It's as much difference in the boys as night and day.

Because my youngest son—bless his heart—he was a hardheaded child. He was gonna do it his way or no way, and my oldest one was just the opposite. Now, my oldest son, I didn't have much trouble with him at all, but the youngest son, he was determined to do anything like he wanted.

And Andrew used to tell me I cared more for Everett than I did for him, but it wasn't that. Everett paid attention. If I would tell Everett something—"I wouldn't do this," or "I'd do thus and so"—he'd listen. If I started tellin Andrew that, he'd say, "Mama, I know, I know, I know, you don't have to tell me." You see? That was the difference in the two sons, so I had to handle them both in different ways.

So, I got to where I said, "OK, Andrew, whenever you need me, you let me know." And when he finally realized that, he was in school at Howard [University]. He messed up. He called me cryin. I said, "Andrew, you didn't listen to me. So Mama can't be still tryin to pay and you flunkin." "Mama, they did this to me!" I said, "Andrew, don't tell me what they did to you. Tell me what you didn't do for yourself."

See, he didn't know they were sendin me his grades. When he started to flunkin, they were sendin me his grades. And, "Mama, they did this—they marked me this way and I had this, and I know I did." I say, "Andrew, I got the same thing you got." Then he hushed. I said, "Andrew, you know when you had to give them your mother's and father's [address] and whatnot." I said, "I got just what you got," I said, "I know what you doin," I said, "Now it's up to you," I said, "I'm tryin to help. But if you don't keep your grades up, and they flunk you out of school," I said, "you gonna be on your own 'cause Mama's *not* gonna do it." I said, "I'm workin hard, tryin to help you get what *I* didn't get."

And he was smarter than my older son. My older son had to dig, dig, dig. Andrew could look at it—he was quick on the money—but he didn't put it to good use. So I told him, I said, "When you flunk out, don't come back home." And I meant that, 'cause I was workin two jobs. I'd go to work in the mornin, I'd get home at twelve, one o'clock at night.

∾

He was smart, he was. The doctor told me that Andrew was almost too smart for his own age, you know? What they was doin was borin to him, and he just couldn't sit still. And he used to help Everett, the oldest boy, with some of his lessons. And Everett had been goin to school before he was. And he would come home, "Mama!" Everett was askin me something. "Everett, I can do that!" I say, "You can't." "Mama, I'll show ya!" And he would take Everett's work and do some of it. And Everett would look at him and look at me and he'd say, "Mama, how come?" I'd say, "I don't know. Andrew, where'd you learn?" "I learned at school." Now we couldn't ask him who taught him at school. We knew what grade he was in. He was just more apt in everything to pick up and learn. But those two kids was somethin else. And now, he's [Andrew] like that now. That boy can pick up from one thing to another and just go with it.

But, I don't know, if I had to go all over it again, I don't think I can make it. If I had to go through this again with the children, with my boys, I don't think I could make it. I think my patience would run out. 'Cause Andrew gave me a runaround. That boy was somethin else. And he always had the answer, regardless of what it was, he always had the answer. "But Mama, so and so and so!" It was always "but." He had to put that "but" in there and he had the answer right, but it wasn't right. But, I loved 'em for bein as active as they were. And I told Andrew that he was a little too mouthy. [Laughs] And my brother told me, he said, "Where do you think he got it from?" [Laughs] I said, "Brother, I wasn't." He said, "Yes you were. When you was comin up, you was the mouthiest little thing and you was always sayin, 'Mama, I can do it!' "

Chapter 28

FATHERS

When I was tryin to get his [Everett's] daddy [Eugene] interested, I had put him in Cub Scouts. I had to go with him. I had to be the Den Mother, and I had to work with them. When they got scouts, they were goin on field trips, and they went up in the hills in Oakland. Everett come back so scared and told me he didn't want to be in the Boy Scouts no more. I say, "Why Everett?" I said, "You've been enjoyin it." "I can't sleep out there no mores by myself, and Daddy said he wasn't gonna go with me no more." See, they had to have fathers to go along with the boys. He [Eugene] started to say he wouldn't go out there or nothin. He went with them *one* time, and it was in the daytime, and they come in that night. They didn't spend the night. And his daddy told him he wasn't goin back out there and never was gonna go with him. And that's when Everett told me, he said, "Mama, I don't wanna be in the Boy Scouts no more."

So, I pushed him a little while longer, and then he gave it up. But when Andrew came along, he was eager for all of this—outgoin. But that's when I found out that Gene didn't want them to excel under me. Because when he carried Everett up there, I don't know if that was just before we separated or right after we separated. It was *before* we separated. He carried Everett up there, then he started up. He wasn't gonna do this and he wasn't gonna do that.

So, I told him, I said, "Well, how do you expect for these boys to grow up, to be able to stand on their own, when you're not teachin them to stand on their own?" I said that everything is not gonna be peaches and cream for 'em. Everything's not gonna be like they want it. I said, "They're gonna have to learn that they're gonna have to take as well as give." I said, "And Gene, you're not layin that pattern for them." I said, "You're tellin them what they *can't* do, and I'm tryin to push them and tell 'em what they *can* do."

That man wouldn't even take 'em to a ball game or nowhere by themselves. If he take 'em to the ball game, I had to go. Anything that was participatin or pertainin to fathers and sons, I was gonna be taken to go. And I remember we went to something, and Everett had got some tickets for fathers and sons. I had to tag along. And when I got there, I was embarrassed because they said, "This is father and son." You know what I had to do? Stay in the car until it was over."

My young son was a ball player from his heart, playin ball and all that. When I get ready to take him to play ball I had a car full of boys. I didn't have but one in the game, but I had a car full of boys. They knew if Andrew was gonna play, they had a way to go, and some of those kids' parents never did go play ball, and that's what hurts a lot of kids, too. When you got kids and they're in something, you participate with them and let them know that you are concerned, too, and that you want to see them excel. Then the kid has more zip to want to do and if they make a mistake, [say,] "Well, son, daughter, it's no perfect one on earth. Everybody makes a mistake sometimes. Pick up the pieces and go on."

༄

You know what he [Eugene] told me? "I'll tell 'em some things [about the facts of life] when they get nineteen, or twenty, twenty-one, but the rest of it they have to find out for theirselves." That was their daddy! Now, they were fifteen, it was time to talk to those boys! I had to be the one. So I got them what they called *The Growing Up Book for Boys*. Their daddy caught 'em, saw 'em readin it one time, and tried to take it away from 'em. And I had to intervene. And he got angry at me. Told me I was just raisin them up to be a nobody.

And I told him, I said, "Look Gene," I said, "Now you're not tellin these boys about the facts of life." I say, "It's too much out there now." I say, "I had a mother to tell me some things before she died, and my dad." I said, "I asked my daddy questions and things, and my daddy said, 'I'll get back to you.'" I said, "When it come back to me it was a woman bringin it back to me, 'cause he'd go and tell them what I had done said. I didn't know!" And I said, "They brought it back to me." And then I had a godmother. She said, "Now, Baby, when you want to know things, you come and ask me." 'Cause I didn't know. I didn't know what's goin on.

༺

Everett was talkin and he said, "If it hadn't been for you, Mom." And I didn't know he was payin that much attention. "I can remember some things Dad said to you, I remembered." I said, "You heard?" He said, "Yeah, Mama." He said, "I remember when we'd want Daddy to take us, and he'd say, 'Go ask your mama, go ask your mama. Tell your mama to do it.'" He said, "Mama, I'll never forget that." He said, "And you know what, it hurts me now?" I said, "What?" He said, "Dad has made everything like he wants to be put away." He has sent everything to him and if anything happens to his dad, he has to go to Texas and bury him. He said, "Mama, I looks back over when I was there and we all could have been together, couldn't we?" I say, "Yeah." He said, "If Daddy would've did right." I said, "Yes."

And so, that way we had a long talk. He said, "Mama, you don't know how much you did for me and how I dealt within me. When you left Daddy, that was one of the best things you ever did for me." His daddy had him so nervous, till Everett was wettin the bed and that's something he never did. He said, "Every time we'd ask Dad, he'd say 'Go to your mama.'" He said, "Mama, I can't forget that, and then Daddy promised me a car if I kept my grades up when I graduated, and it ended up Ellis givin me my car. But, Mama, I thank you. I can't thank you enough, because you did one of the best things for me you could have when you left Daddy."

༺

Now, that was the first thing he [Ellis, Edith's second husband] told them, and that is what made me know that that was a good man. He said, "You got to obey your mother and I'll help you anyway I can." He said, "We just get along together, OK?" Those kids got to where they leached to him and didn't want to even go see they father when it was time for them to go visit they father. And if Ellis come in on that Saturday morning, if Saturday they was supposed to be goin to they dad's,

Chapter 28

they would not go. They would say, "Mama, we ain't goin over to Dad's today. We gonna be here with Ellis." And I didn't bother them because he was doin more for them than they daddy was.

And when we separated, I said, "You and I weren't separated when we got the kids. We was together. Now, I'm not gonna run you down and I'm not gonna be runnin backwards and forwards sayin that you haven't supported the kids, because you know what you supposed to do, and if you don't, I'm gonna make a list of it and turn it in and that's gonna be it. I'm not gonna be runnin and spendin out money carryin you to court to try to make you pay for these kids." He did a little bit. He didn't do what a daddy should've did. And he had promised my oldest son that if he kept up his grades, he could have a car when he graduated. He went back on that. So much he went back on, they lost all confidence. Then they went to clingin to Ellis.

If they wanted something, they went behind my back. "Ellis, we want so-and-so and so-and-so. Ask Mama! Tell Mama! What you think she would do?" They'd talk it over with him and then he'd come and say, "Honey bunch, I got something to talk to you about." I say, "What's that?" And then he'd tell me what the kids done said to him. He say, "What you think about it? I'm not gonna go over what you don't want me to do now. You tell me if I can or if I can't." Those kids clinged to him like white on rice.

༄

When my oldest son graduated from school, his daddy had promised him if he made the grades, with the honor roll in school, he'd buy him a car. When the time come, Everett was on a scholarship roll. And he talked about it. He said, "Daddy, I'm gonna get a scholarship, and you promised me a car if I keep up my grades." He said, "Hmmph. I can't buy you no car." He said, "Well, Daddy, you promised it." He come back tellin me, "Mama, Daddy said he couldn't buy it."

And Ellis was there, and he heard, and he said, "What did you say?" He said, "Well, Son, don't worry. I'm gonna help you get your car." He said, "He promised it," he said, "he don't have to give it to you." He said, "I'm gonna give you your car." And so he told him, he said, "I can't give you a new one," he said, "because, see, I'm payin for this house." He says, "And ya'll be good to Mama," he said, "you gonna be alright."

∾

Then he got the newspaper. He showed my son how to look for a used car. So Ellis came in [from a trip to sea] early Monday mornin, and he called me. And I went and picked him up. I had to go there [to the owner's house] before I took him home so he could see that car. So when I went by, I taken him by and he looked, he said, "Oh, yeah, he gonna get that," he said. Then he said, "Wait a minute. I'm goin back to my credit union." All this he did before he went home. "He's gonna have this car for his graduation, and I don't want nothin to pass before he get it."

What he was really tryin to do, he was tryin to get that car to be at the house when he [Everett] came home from school. But he couldn't do that. But he got it so that he could take him down there and he'd drive the car. And I thought, "Now do you know anybody'd do somethin like that? How sweet it was. Weren't his child, but he loved me that much, to do this."

And his [Everett's] own daddy been treatin him that way, you know. And Everett had been a A student in school. That was the thing that hurts. So when Ellis gave him the car, he [Eugene] got mad because *Ellis* gave him the car. "Now I know he's gonna flunk now." And Everett came out with a scholarship to Howard University.

∾

My two sons cried. When Ellis was a certain age, they retired him from the sea. He had been a seaman for years—a cook on the ship—and he had been carryin the boys. When he come in he'd pick the boys up on Saturday, sometimes, and he'd take them down, and they learned about the ship from him—he carried them all over the ship and tell them everything about it. He'd tell them people, "These are my sons."

And when they retired him—bless his heart—he couldn't take it. He had been a seaman for so long, he just started drinkin, drinkin,

CHAPTER 28

drinkin, drinkin. It got so bad we had tried to dry him out. They told him what he couldn't bring [to the rehabilitation center] no knives, no watches, and, different things. Do you know I carried the man in and I said, "Baby, I'll be comin back and I'll be callin. I can call and talk to you." The man had a knife in there, and the nurse came in his room for something one day and he asked her for something. I don't know just what it was, now. When she come back, he told her, "I said so-and-so-and-so and you put me off and I don't have to take this." He pulled his knife out. Well, I got a call. I had to go pick him up because he wasn't supposed to carry no knife. They told him in the beginning, "No knives and no straight razor." Now, if you shave, you could have your safety razor, but no straight razor and no knife and no scissors. Those are things that you cannot take in there. And he slipped that knife in there and pulled it on this worker, and they called me and I had to go get him. He stayed pretty good for about a week and a half.

I was workin, and he got to where he would come on my job and set and watch and set and watch. The people I was workin for then—Pitts and son—had a business where he cleaned the airplanes when they come in, and that was the job I was doin then. He had some buildings where his two sons and his stepdaughter were takin care of those buildings. So, the man was doin good, and he was givin other people jobs. Ellis could not stand comin in that little old office when he first got there and he introduced hisself. Mr. Pitts, he was just a noisy talkin person, he said, "Man, how did you get that little fiery woman? I mean to tell you that she is the best worker I got on this job. How did you get her? I hope if I get single, I can find somebody like her."

And it got next to him. He couldn't take that, the compliment that the man was [giving to me]. He couldn't take that, and he got to the place where he didn't want me to work out there. I said, "Ellis," I said, "You know the children's daddy is not doin what he's supposed to do, and I got to keep those kids in college." I says, "And I don't want them to feel that Mama don't care." And the thing what made it so sweet and all, [from the] time we got married he put those boys on his payroll, and they was gettin a check when they retired him. Those kids was gettin a check from Social Security. When Everett left and went to

Howard, he was gettin a check off of what Ellis had made. Andrew was, too. They daddy wasn't doin anything. Looked like they daddy just tryin his best to make them be a failure. But they pulled through and did better than they daddy expected them to, and Ellis was the backbone.

And that's what hurt me so bad, when he [Ellis] tried to hurt me and he come behind me. He was arguin in the kitchen. I said, "Ellis, Honey, I'm not gonna argue. I'm so tired." I started walkin out of the room and I happened to turn around. He was comin down with—it looked like a bamboo cane, but in it was an iron rod, and he fractured my nose. He hit me across it. I throwed up [my arms] and if I hadn't broke the lick, the police said he'd of beat me to death. He said, "When he had got so angry that he come behind you with that, he wouldn't have stopped." If I would've fell, he wouldn't have stopped. He had roused up all that envy, and for what? It was untold.

∾

So that ended our marriage from that. I said, "I can't." I said, "My daddy told me if he hits you once, he'll hit you again." So, if they start to bein abusive to you, he said, "When they say, 'Until death do us part,' " he said, "you'll be the one partin." He said, "So get out." That what my daddy told me. Whenever I married my first husband, he said, "Baby Rae, I want to tell you this. I'm your father, and I never hit your mother." He says, "And in the Bible, it says, when you get married, 'Till death do us part.' " He says, "If they start to gettin too rough and fightin," he says, "I've had relatives that was gonna stay in it and stay in it." Said, "They's gone." But he said, "They life was cut off. Because they was tryin to stay in it. Where if they'd a left," he said, "they'd a been livin." He said, "So, if it gets too rough," he says, "no man is supposed to be hittin on no woman." He said, "If they love you, they're not gonna abuse you."

Chapter 29

OTHER PEOPLE'S CHILDREN

The Board of Education and the school district, they set up a class where they were tryin to educate them little parents that didn't get much [education]. I had a job goin from house to house tryin to sign up these mothers to go to this school. I had to go to knock doors, doors, doors. And then I had to go and check out and see how many of those people I had contacted to see how many of them was there [at the meetings]. I had to report this back to the school board.

But, I did some dangerous things, too. I went to a house and they had told me in that project that they had dope and stuff in there, but I had never seen it and I didn't know what it was all about. And I went to one door and knocked and one young man opened the door. They had a special knock—the way I knocked wasn't that special knock and this young man opened the door and said, "What do you want?" I said, "Is your mother home? I would like to talk to your mother." And I went to tellin him I was from the Board of Education. "No, we don't need you." And the mother said, "What is it?" "It's nothing, Mother." I said, "I'm from the Board of Education and I'm tryin to enroll parents if they would like to go to school—those who didn't get their high school diploma." They said, in school, they was havin more trouble with children that parents didn't get enough education. That young man told me, "Get away from the door," and told his mother, "Go back and sit down." So he was runnin that house, but he had been runnin dope, see? And he didn't want me in that house. And she shook her head and turned around and went on back and he told me, "You don't need to come back here anymore, and I don't want to see you at this door anymore." I wrote everything down, the number and everything. They was givin me a list of the homes that I had to visit, and I marked an "X" on this one.

So, when I turned it in, I said, "I don't know what you're goin to do about this, but something needs to be done." I said, "A young man answered the door and when I went to explain, his mother come to the door and he made her go sit down and he told me that he didn't need me to come back no more." I says, "Now, it's a project and I wasn't nowhere from the projects." I says, "This is jeopardizin my life, because these children will see me and know me and recognize me when I won't recognize them and they could get it in for me," and I said, "I could be killed and leave my two sons." And I said, "If y'all can't give me anything different," I said, "I won't work it."

But, it was hurtin me to know that there were so many little children runnin around in the streets when they should've been in school and my kids was in school. So they said, "If any young man comes to the door and you can't talk to the mother, just say, 'Goodbye' and mark it, and they will have a policeman to go there and give them this notice of what they can do."

I went to one lady's house one morning. She called me and asked me could I come down there right away. Well, it wasn't [far] from where I lived, and I rushed down there and I was gettin ready to go on my tour of the homes. Her son was in the bed and it was time for him to get at the school and he was still in bed and wouldn't take no heed to her. She said, "I don't wanna get thrown out of here just on account of him."

Because they had run it up to where, if the parents couldn't keep these kids in school, they couldn't live in that low rental, see? In the projects, they couldn't live there. If those kids couldn't go to school, they had to find somewhere else to live and that woman was a single mother and this young man was smart. My son would come home and say, "Mama, that boy is smart." He would tell me about it. He would say, "Mama, if I could just do like him." He said, "It looks like he don't have to study and he knows it."

That child was layin up in the bed when she called me, and I went down to her apartment and she was tellin me, "I want you to come in here and talk to him. Maybe you can get him." I went and knocked on the door, and he said, "Yes, who is it?" And I told him and I said, "May I come in and talk to you?" "Yes!" So, I went in there and talked to him. I said, "You know, my son goes to the same school you go to and he's always tellin me how smart you are and how you come up with your lessons, and he says it looks like you don't even study, and my son is diggin like everything tryin to be good in his school like you." I said, "Son, why would you want to hurt your mother's heart? Don't you know she wants you to go as far as you can?" I said, "It's your mother." I said, "Where is your father?" "I don't know where my daddy is and I don't ask Mama." I said, "Well, don't you see how you're hurtin your mother now?"

I said, "Son, get up and put your clothes on and let me take you to school." I said, "Don't mess up." I said, "If you do, you're goin to mess up my oldest son's life." He said, "Why?" I said, "Because, he's tryin to be like you in that class. He's tellin me how smart you are and you know all of the answers, and my son is diggin like everything tryin to be like you, but you want me to tell him to stop now and not go to school anymore?" Then, he said, "No, Ma'am." I said, "I'll take you to school. I'll tell them you was late. I'll make an excuse for you."

So, the young man, he got up and he said, "Yes, Ma'am." I said, "Son, when your mother is concerned about you, obey your mother." I said, "I have something to tell you when I take you to school." So, I went back home and got my car ready and everything and I said, "When you get dressed"—he know where I live, it wasn't far from him—I said, "You come on up to my house." I had no more than got back home good and got the car started up and here the child comes walkin up, just as fast as he could. And on the way to school, I told him how I wanted to go to school and how I didn't have the opportunity to go to school and how my mama died when I was ten and he still had his mother. That worked him all over.

That boy came out victorious when he graduated. I lost track of him because my kids went off. I lost track because I wasn't workin for the Board of Education then and I wasn't surveyin to see how many kids went on to finish, but he was in the march and graduated with the other kids, high. And Everett told me, he said, "Mama, I don't know what you said to that young man," but, he said, "he ain't gonna ever stay out of school no more."

Interlude 4

PHYSICAL DISCIPLINE

There is perhaps no single child-rearing issue about which Edith Hudley feels more strongly than the importance of "chastising" children. For her, physical discipline, in conjunction with explanation and love, is an important tool for curbing deliberate disobedience and defiance of parental authority. Her advice to parents is ". . . sit down and talk to . . . children first and let them know how much I love you and what I expect of you and if you have any problems, come to Mama, come to Daddy, talk it over. Don't be afraid and not talk about it. . . . But if you disobey me, then we are going to have some problem solving and my switch was my problem solving." This "problem solving" was sharply distinguished from abuse. "I love children, period. And I can't stand to see anyone mistreat children." She recalls the spankings she received while growing up as a painful deterrent to future misbehavior, but they certainly didn't "blister me up."

According to Mrs. Hudley, appropriate chastisement is not done in anger and is accompanied by a discussion of the transgression and the parent's love for the child. Of course, physical discipline is but one tool for guiding children's behavior. It is reserved for the most serious offenses such as defiant misbehavior, endangering self or other, or being willfully destructive. Edith estimates that each of her sons was spanked no more than five times while growing up.

Although Mrs. Hudley rarely used physical discipline, she views it as indispensable. This was especially true in raising her beloved second son, a "hardheaded child" who was "determined to do anything like he wanted and had nerves enough to front me and was gonna tell me what he was gonna do and what he wasn't gonna do." From her own experience, Edith knew how dangerous such a stance can be for a young, black male. She had witnessed, firsthand, and heard many stories about violence, including police violence, against black youths in the rural South as well as in Oakland, California. "And it hurt me to the point to where I was almost afraid for my kids—my boys—because so much was happening to little boys." In Edith's view, such dangers necessitated strong and effective deterrents in a social and cultural context unforgiving to errant black boys. Although she found spanking her sons difficult, "This is hurting me and hurting my heart to have to do this to you," she also believed that it was a parental responsibility she would have been remiss to shirk.

The position of Mrs. Hudley and other parents in her community, however, conflicted markedly with white, middle-class educators who advocated abolishing all physical discipline at home as well as at school. She found their position to be uninformed by the realities of her children's lives. "That's what I had to fight for with my kids. . . . When they started saying that you couldn't spank your children . . . they didn't birth the child, they didn't have anything to do with the child." From Mrs. Hudley's perspective, the white authority figures were attempting to strip parents of the authority they needed to keep their children out of harm's way. She expressed grave skepticism concerning the motives of those who would do away with physical discipline. She quoted the argument that she presented at a school board meeting, " 'I don't care what ya'll say to me, and how many times you come to my house—I'm gonna raise mine.' I said, 'Because if I don't, the next thing ya'll will be putting a bullet in them or a billyclub up against they head.' I said, 'I've seen you do it.' "

Today, approximately fifty years after the conflict between Edith Hudley and school officials, the debate surrounding physical punishment rages on. Some scholars, and many parents describe physical discipline much as Edith does: used judiciously, it is an important tool that can help to curb children's unsafe, defiant, and disobedient behavior (Baumrind, 1996a; 1996b). According to some surveys, over 90 percent of U.S. parents report that they have spanked their children (Holden & Zambarano, 1992). In contrast, some U.S. pediatricians, child advocates, and developmental researchers argue for the abolishment of physical punishment not only by educators in schools (twenty-seven states have banned physical discipline in schools), but in the home as well.[1] The ban on physical discipline in Sweden (the "aga" law) and Norway has been lauded by some as a model for U.S. families.

Much of the professional discussion around physical discipline is highly emotional and polarized. For example, even when the American Academy of Pediatrics provided explicit instructions to a group of nationally known researchers and scholars for objective rather than emotional or moral debate, some resulting conference papers characterized physical discipline as subabusive violence, immoral, an evil, and a serious risk factor (Graziano, 1996; Straus, 1996; Cohen, 1996). On the other hand, some conference participants supported physical discipline with statements such as, "I was spanked and I turned out all right!" (Friedman & Schonberg, 1996). Even during a professional discussion of empirical research, our culture and personal experience clearly shape the questions we are able to ask and the answers we are able to hear (Polite, 1996).

Unfortunately, polarized, decontextualized debates do little to advance our understanding of why parents choose to use physical discipline, what it means to parents, how it affects children, and how these practices evolved in context. These contextual issues are precisely what Mrs. Hudley's life story helps us to address.

Different Values about Physical Discipline

As Mrs. Hudley's conflict with European American school officials illustrates, there is variation across communities in the United States as to whether physical discipline is an appropriate child-rearing practice. Although there is considerable variation *within* communities as well, spanking is more likely to be endorsed by African Americans than by European Americans.[2] For example, in a recent pilot study,

---

1. For example, see pediatrician B.D. Schmitt (1987), child advocate I. Hyman (1996), and a review by developmental researchers E.E. Pinderhughes, K. Dodge, J.E. Bates, G.S. Petit (2000). Hyman (1996) advocates the abolishment of physical discipline in the home as well as school.

2. For discussion of variation within communities, see, for example, Abell, Clawson, Washington, Bost, & Vaughn (1996); Kelley, Sanchez-Hucles, & Walker (1993); Kelley, Power, & Wimbush (1992). For evidence that African Americans are

African-American women generally viewed physical discipline and reasoning as equally appropriate and nonabusive strategies, while European-American women viewed physical discipline as indicative of less concern for the child and more abusive parenting. There is, however, no evidence that normative, culturally based views on physical discipline are associated with child abuse (Baumrind, 1996a). If this were the case, rates of child maltreatment would be higher among African Americans. Data from the National Center on Child Abuse and Neglect, however, indicate no association between race or ethnicity and child maltreatment (Fisher, Jackson, & Villarruel, 1998). Furthermore, there is no evidence of an association between culturally based views on physical discipline and the tolerance of harsh treatment toward children. Giovannoni and Becerra (1979) presented ethnically diverse adults with vignettes representing a wide range of situations with potential for child maltreatment. Although less likely than European Americans to rate spanking as having a high potential for maltreatment, African Americans and Hispanics judged more situations to have such potential.

Mrs. Hudley's views about the value of physical discipline are echoed in a study of elderly African-American women serving as volunteer mentors to parents involved with the public child welfare system because of child maltreatment (Mosby et al., 1999). Like Edith, these mentors viewed physical punishment as a better and more effective method of discipline with young children than the methods, such as time-out, advocated by many social workers. Again, like Edith, they were very clear that they were endorsing a "little chastising," not physical abuse. They also were well aware that spanking is at odds with what social workers typically advocate. They emphasized the importance of controlling a child's behavior in public, as well as adapting child-rearing methods to the individual child. For these elders, raising children involves nurturing, talking and listening, teaching, and dispensing small doses of physical discipline, as needed.

---

more likely than European Americans to endorse physical discipline, see, for example, Bradley (1998); Deater-Deckard & Dodge (1997); Jackson (1997); Pinderhughes et al. (2000).

The Variable Effects of Physical Discipline

Among scholars, there is a growing recognition that child-rearing practices, including physical discipline, cannot be understood apart from the broader context of the neighborhood and cultural community in which the parent-child relationship is embedded (Abell et al., 1996; Deater-Deckard & Dodge, 1997; Kelley et al., 1993). As expressed by Diana Baumrind (1996a), "The cultural context critically determines the meaning and therefore the consequences of physical discipline" (p. 629). John Ogbu (1981) and others have argued that parents teach their children those instrumental competencies required for functioning within their particular physical, social, and cultural contexts. For example, within certain low-income, urban neighborhoods, even mild levels of disobedience to parents may result in serious consequences to the child and therefore require a more forceful method of discipline than those applied by more affluent parents (Kelley et al., 1992). Further, as Mrs. Hudley's story illustrates, African-American parents have to prepare their children to function in a society that is often hostile, racist, and discriminatory. Demanding obedience from African-American children in some cases is imperative, given the life circumstances imposed on black youth by American society (Bradley, 1998). Finally, communities vary in the value placed on particular psychological and social attributes. Within some African-American communities, respecting others, particularly elders, is considered to be extremely important. Some African Americans have expressed concern at what they perceive to be the disrespectful stance of some middle-class, European-American children towards their elders, and suggest that their parents have been too permissive in their disciplinary practices (Polite, 1996).

Given variation in beliefs about physical discipline, it is not surprising that its use is associated with different parenting styles across cultural communities. For example, African-American parents' use of physical discipline is positively associated with warmth and use of reasoning. This has generally not been the case in European-American communities (Baumrind, 1996a).

Also consistent with this contextual view of discipline is evidence that physical discipline has different effects, depending on the community that the child inhabits. For example, a positive correlation has been found between physical discipline and child aggression for European-American children, but the correlation is not significant (and sometimes negative) for African-American children. Deater-Decker and Dodge (1996) conclude that the relationship between parents' use of physical discipline and children's tendency to be aggressive may be moderated by the different meanings that parental practices have in different cultural groups.

Physical Discipline, Not Physical Abuse

In distinguishing physical discipline from physical abuse, Edith Hudley describes intervening in a grocery store on behalf of a toddler whose frustrated and angry mother mistreated her. The judgments concerning maltreatment that social workers, child welfare workers, educators, pediatricians, and others must make rarely occur with the benefit of such direct observation. In many cases, judgments about child maltreatment are made after the fact and are fraught with complexity and ambiguity.

Yet the task of determining when parental behaviors are excessive, unwarranted, dangerous, and ultimately abusive is vital (Kolko, 1996). Child maltreatment, including physical abuse, is a very serious social problem that has increased over the past forty years. According to The Second National Incidence Study of Child Abuse and Neglect (cited in Wells, 1995), a conservative estimate of maltreatment would put the number of cases at 1.4 million children nationwide in 1986. Of maltreated children, 64 percent were neglected and 41 percent were abused. The most frequent category of abuse was physical abuse (Wells, 1995). A substantial body of research has documented the devastating effects of abuse on children's well-being, development, and survival (for example, Cicchetti & Carlson, 1989).

Susan Wells (1995) has argued that one of the reasons that judgments about physical abuse are complex is that child abuse and neglect are legal, social, cultural, and historical constructs. For example, the acceptance of infanticide in ancient times is remarkable to us today, and many practices and conditions currently tolerated in the United States will no doubt seem barbaric in another time and place.

In addition, definitions of abuse and neglect vary not only internationally but also among the states within the United States (Wells, 1995). Korbin (1987) succinctly presented the dilemma of child welfare professionals and made a case for cultural context in evaluating abuse and neglect:

> Failure to allow for a cultural perspective ... promotes an ethnocentric position in which one's own ... cultural beliefs and practices are presumed to be superior to all others. Nevertheless, a stance of extreme cultural relativism, in which all judgments ... are suspended ... may [be used to] justify a lesser standard of care for some children (p. 25).

How social workers and other professionals actually implement a cultural perspective to differentiate cases of physical discipline from physical abuse, however, is an area requiring more thought and research. A number of practitioners have suggested guidelines for making such distinctions (see, for example, Schmitt, 1987; Downs, Costin, & McFadden, 1996). In deciding if physical discipline is reasonable in a given cultural context, the professional can consider (Downs, Costin, & McFadden, 1996): 1) What are the consequences for the child? Was there a reasonably foreseeable consequence of serious injury to the child, for example, broken bones, lacerations, burns, or other injuries requiring medical attention? 2) What is the purpose of the discipline? Was the discipline intended to train and educate the child or gratify the parent? 3) Was the punishment unnecessarily degrading, brutal, or beastly in character or protracted beyond the child's power to endure? 4) If physical force was used, was it recklessly applied, for example, directed towards the head as opposed to the buttocks? To this list we, and others, would add: What are the local meanings of the practice? Was an understanding of the corrective purpose of the discipline shared by the child, adult, and other community members? Interestingly, these guidelines are compatible with Edith Hudley's understanding of physical punishment.

What's Wrong with Banning Physical Discipline?

The educators in Mrs. Hudley's school district responded to the complexities of distinguishing physical discipline from physical abuse by unsuccessfully attempting to ban physical discipline, at home as well as at school. Similarly, some recent practitioners (Schmitt, 1987) and child advocates (Hyman, 1996) have recommended that physical discipline be abolished in the United States. Child advocate Irwin Hyman posed the question: What would be the harm in simply prohibiting physical punishment? Given the potentially devastating consequences of physical abuse, such a stance surely has merit if it would save just one child's life. Such a policy, however, is unlikely to be effective and quite likely to be damaging for several reasons.

First, the expectation that the incidence of child abuse would be lowered if physical discipline were banned is not supported by existing empirical data. For example, in Sweden, where physical discipline was outlawed in 1979, corporal punishment has declined, but rates of child abuse have actually increased (see Baumrind, 1996a). In addition, there is little empirical evidence that physical discipline per se is harmful to children. Baumrind concludes that the prudent use of physical discipline within the context of an authoritative child-rearing relationship is well accepted by young children, effective in managing short-term misbehavior, and has no documented long-term effects. Physical discipline is prudent if it is consistent, immediate, calm, private, and specific for willful defiance with children older than eighteen months and prior to puberty. Imprudent discipline involves reprimands delivered late, inconsistently, explosively, publicly, and nonspecifically. According to Baumrind (1996a), disciplinary spanking at home is no more harmful than alternative tactics when used prudently, and it can shape socially constructive behavior, thereby protecting children from the more painful consequences of misbehavior occurring outside the nurturing family setting. The larger point implied by Baumrind's analysis is that any form of discipline—be it physical, time out, or scolding—can be misused by adults or carried to unhealthy extremes.

Thus, banning physical discipline will not necessarily lower rates of child abuse and denies parents the right to use a culturally valid, effective approach to discipline. But there are other important matters at stake in the movement to ban physical discipline, matters that can affect children in ways that are less direct but equally profound. Mrs. Hudley's indignation about her school district's planned shift in policy draws attention to the problems that arise for families when powerful institutions enshrine white, middle-class preferences as the only acceptable standard. Currently, physical discipline is regarded as dubious if not dangerous in most educational systems.

The same is true of most child welfare systems. In the state of Illinois, if a child is a ward of the public child welfare system, physical discipline by biological or foster parents is considered inappropriate. These systems have enormous power over people's lives. Yet, they often operate with little awareness of the extent to which cultural misunderstandings may influence decision making. For example, in one study of staff members working in child welfare, researchers interviewed non professionals and paraprofessionals from various minority groups. They were asked about cultural practices within their own communities that might be misinterpreted by child welfare professionals (Gray & Cosgrove, 1985). Misunderstandings pertaining to physical discipline were emphasized by informants from three different cultural groups, Mexican-American, Samoan-American, and Vietnamese-American.

In a study of the beliefs of parents with young children in foster care, child welfare workers, and foster parents, the issue of discipline also emerged as problematic (Haight et al., 2002). The parents in this study participated in regularly scheduled, supervised visits with their children. These visits were intended to preserve the parent-child relationship while children were in foster care. Both parents and child welfare workers expressed concern about children "running wild" during visits. Parents, however, expressed serious reservations about disciplining their children in front of child welfare workers and were particularly reluctant to use physical discipline to curb children's out-of-control behavior. Some child welfare workers attributed parents' lack of effective response to their indifference or inability to set boundaries. Many child welfare workers also viewed visits as an opportunity to assess parents' mastery of "appropriate disciplinary practices," such as time out, taught in parenting classes. The majority of parents were involved in the child welfare system not because of problems with inappropriate discipline or physical abuse but because of neglect, stemming from poverty, substance abuse, and/or unmet mental health needs. However, in order to be reunited with their children, these parents had to receive positive evaluations of their parenting skills, evaluations that depended, at least in part, on child welfare workers' assessment of their disciplinary practices.

As suggested by this example of parental visits, social workers and child welfare workers may treat a parent's commitment to physical discipline as evidence that she is an incompetent or uncaring parent. Some scholars have even argued that the confusion of physical discipline with physical abuse is one factor contributing to the overrepresentation of African-American children in the U.S. foster care system. African-American parents who express a preference for physical discipline are sometimes seen as resistant and noncompliant. Thus, physical discipline, a culturally valid parenting practice, may be one factor that places certain families at risk for extended involvement with child welfare systems (for example, see Mosby et al., 1999).

Furthermore, when child welfare workers are unaware of the meaning and value of physical discipline within minority communities, they may jeopardize their professional credibility. In studies of families involved with the public child welfare system (Haight, Black, Mangelsdorf et al., 2002; Haight, Black, Workman, Tata, 2001), many parents viewed themselves as in need of help with their families. Many also said that they had not received help but that, instead, professionals had placed onerous demands on their overwhelmed families. For example, parents in families struggling with issues of domestic violence, substance abuse, homelessness, and unmet mental health needs were routinely required to attend parenting classes where issues such as appropriate discipline are a focus. Clients, especially involuntary clients, can rapidly become disillusioned and skeptical that any help is available within the system to meet their real needs.

These families draw our attention to a final issue relevant to the proposal to ban physical punishment: How should monetary and professional resources be invested in order to best support the well-being of children and families? While it is clearly critical that families are helped to provide loving care and sound discipline, there is a danger that a focus on physical discipline will deflect attention from other more daunting tasks. A serious commitment to reducing child maltreatment in this country will require sustained effort to reduce poverty, domestic violence, and substance abuse and to meet the health and mental health needs of families.

As will be apparent in the upcoming chapter, "Little Edith and Lula May," her family's commitment to physical discipline was the very least of the risks facing Little Edith when Grandma Edith stepped up to foster her granddaughter through a troubled period of parental separation, maternal substance abuse, and homelessness. Although Little Edith and Grandma Edith strengthened a loving relationship that sustains both to this day, to the profound sadness of all, Lula May never recovered to parent Little Edith. To Little Edith, her grandmother became "Mama."

References

Abell, E., Clawson, M., Washington W.N., Bost, K., & Vaughn, B.E. (1996). Parenting values, attitudes, behaviors, and goals of African American mothers from a low-income population in relation to social and societal contexts. *Journal of Family Issues, 17*(5), 593-613.

Baumrind, D. (1996a, October). The discipline controversy revisited. *Family Relations,* 405-414.

Baumrind, D. (1996b). Response: A blanket injunction against disciplinary use of spanking is not warranted by the data. *Pediatrics, 98*(4), 828-831.

Bradley, C.R. (1998). Child rearing in African American families: A study of the disciplinary practices of African American parents. *Journal of Multicultural Counseling and Development, 26,* 273-281.

Cicchetti, D., & Carlson, V. (Eds.). (1989). *Child maltreatment: Theory and research on the causes and consequences of child abuse and neglect.* New York: Cambridge University Press.

Cohen, P. (1996). Response: How can generative theories of the effects of punishment be tested? *Pediatrics, 98*(4), 834-836.

Deater-Deckard, K., & Dodge, K.A. (1997). Externalizing behavior problems and discipline revisited: Nonlinear effects and variation by culture, context, and gender. *Psychological Inquiry, 8* (3), 161-175.

Downs, S.W., Costin, L.B., & McFadden, E.J. (1996). *Child welfare and family services: Polices and practice.* (5th Ed.). White Plains, NY: Longman.

Fisher, C.B., Jackson, J.F., & Villarruel, F.A. (1998). The study of African American and Latin American children and youth. In I. Sigel & K. Renninger (Eds.), *Handbook of child psychology (5th ed.).* New York: Wiley.

Friedman, S.B., & Schonberg, S.K. (1996). Personal statements. *Pediatrics, 98*(4), 857-858.

Giovannoni, J.M., & Becerra, R.M. (1979). *Defining child abuse.* New York: Free Press.

Gray, E., & Cosgrove, J. (1985). Ethnocentric perception of childrearing practices in protective services. *Child Abuse and Neglect, 9,* 389-396.

Graziano, A. (1996). Presentation: Middle class families and the use of corporal punishment. *Pediatrics, 98*(4), 845-848.

Holden, G., & Zambarano, R. (1992). Passing the rod: Similarities between parents and their young children in orientations toward physical punishment. In I.E. Sigel, A.V. McGillicuddy-DeLisi, & J.J. Goodnow (Eds.), *Parental belief systems: The psychological consequences for children*. Hillsdale, NJ: Erlbaum.

Haight, W., Black, J.E., Mangelsdorf, S., Giorgio, G., Tata. L., Shoppe, S., & Szewczyk, M. (2002). Making visits better: The perspectives of parents, foster parents and child welfare workers. *Child Welfare LXXI(2)*, 173-202.

Haight, W., Black, J.E., Workman, C.L., & Tata, L. (2001). Parent-child interaction during foster care visits: Implications for practice. *Social Work, 46*, 325-340.

Hyman, I. (1996). Presentation: Using research to change policy: Reflections on 20 years of effort to eliminate corporal punishment in the schools. *Pediatrics, 98*(4), 818-820.

Jackson, J.F. (1997). Issues in need of initial visitation: Race and nation specificity in the study of externalizing behavior problems and discipline. *Psychological Inquiry, 8*(3), 204-211.

Kelley, M.L., Power, T.G., & Wimbush, D.D. (1992). Determinants of disciplinary practices in low-income black mothers. *Child Development, 63*, 573-582.

Kelley, M.L., Sanchez-Hucles, J., & Walker, R.R. (1993). Correlates of disciplinary practices in working- to middle-class African-American mothers. *Merrill-Palmer Quarterly, 39*(2), 252-264.

Kolko, D.J. (1996). Child Physical Abuse. In J. Briere, L. Berliner, J.A. Bulkley, C. Jenny & T. Reid (Eds.), *The APSAC handbook on child maltreatment*. Thousand Oaks, CA: Sage.

Korbin, J. (1987). Child abuse and neglect: The cultural context. In R. E. Helfer & R.S. Kempe (Eds.), *The battered child* (4th ed., pp. 23-41). Chicago: University of Chicago Press.

Mosby, L., Rawls, A.W., Meehan, A.J., Mays, E., & Pettinari, C.J. (1999). Troubles in interracial talk about discipline: An examination of African American child rearing narratives. *Journal of Comparative Family Studies, 30*(3), 489-521.

Ogbu, J.U. (1981). Origins of human competence: A cultural-ecological perspective. *Child Development, 52*, 413-429.

Pinderhughes, E.E., Dodge, K., Bates, J.E., & Petit, G.S. (2000). Discipline responses: Influences of parents' socioeconomic status, ethnicity, beliefs about parenting, stress, and cognitive-emotional processes. *Journal of Family Psychology, 14*(3), 380-400.

Polite, K. (1996). Response: The medium/the message: Corporal punishment, an empirical critique. *Pediatrics, 98*(4), 849-851.

Schmitt, B.D. (1987). Seven deadly sins of childhood: Advising parents about difficult developmental phases. *Child Abuse and Neglect, 11*, 421-432.

Straus, M.A. (1996). Presentation: Spanking and the making of a violent society. *Pediatrics, 98*(4), 837-841.

Wells, S. (1995). Child abuse and neglect overview. In L. Beebe (Executive Editor), *Encyclopedia of social work (19th ed.)*. Washington, DC: NASW Press.

PART 5

Later Years

Part 5 of the oral history encompasses Mrs. Hudley's marriage to Mr. Floyd Hudley and their eleven years in Salt Lake City, Utah. Although African Americans comprise only about 1 percent of the total population of Salt Lake City, they have a strong community and presence. The first permanent African-American community in Salt Lake dates back to the nineteenth century, when black settlements were established with the immigration of the first Mormon pioneers. The building of the transcontinental railroad as well as military activities during World War Two further increased the size of the African-American community (Coleman, 1981). Today, African Americans contribute to all aspects of the development of Utah including the arts, politics, law, business (Wright, 1994), and religion (Haight, 2002). Although racial hatred and violence is minimal compared to other major U.S. cities, African Americans in Salt Lake continue to experience discrimination. During Mr. and Mrs. Hudley's stay, African Americans reported problems renting or purchasing homes (Matthews & Wright, 1994). Employment opportunities, while improved, continued to be limited, and tokenism was common (Coleman, 1981). During the Hudley's stay, the average unemployment for blacks in Utah was 11 percent, twice the state average. The number of blacks living below the poverty line was 31 percent, well above the state average for all Utahns (11 percent). The average income of blacks was $25,000, while the state average was $35,000 (Wright, 1994).

As indicated in Appendix A, this portion of the oral history includes the deaths of Mr. Hudley's sons and the births of Edith's three grandchildren. It also includes the raising of Mrs. Hudley's oldest grandchild, whose mother suffered with drug addiction. In 1988, Mr. and Mrs. Hudley moved to Salt Lake City. Mr. Hudley, born and raised primarily in Wyoming, had lived in Salt Lake City as an adolescent and wanted to be closer to family members. While living in Salt Lake, he worked primarily as a Greyhound bus driver.

Appendix B lists a number of people important to part 5 of the oral history. They include Edith's third husband, Floyd; Floyd's sons, Randy and Ricky; Edith's granddaughter and namesake, Edith; and Little Edith's mother, Lula May (also known as "Sis").

Once again, students are directed to Appendix C for suggested issues for study, discussion and further research.

References

Coleman, R. (1981). Blacks in Utah history: An unknown legacy. In H.Z. Papanikolas (Ed.), *The peoples of Utah*. Salt Lake City: Utah State Historical Society.

Haight, W. (2002). *African American children at church: A sociocultural perspective*. New York: Cambridge University Press.

Mathews, A., & Wright, L. (1994, March 20). Utah's people of color: The east-west wall hasn't fallen in racially divided S.L. Valley. *Salt Lake Tribune*.

Wright, L. (1994, March 27). African Americans: Utah's people of color. *Salt Lake Tribune*.

Chapter 30

MEETING FLOYD

I met Floyd after Ellis and I had separated. I was still in the house that he [Ellis] put me in. Lord I hated that so bad. That man [Ellis] was so good to me. And I hated he changed so. That was my sweetheart. So, I was there at the house. And this lady that had been workin with me, she's the one told me about workin in the bottlin place. Oh boy, I worked there so much! Owens Illinois Glass Company. I worked there, where you make the bottles and jars and all that. Well, she was out of a relationship with a person, but she was with her sister, and her and her sister wasn't gettin along. So Ellis and I had separated, and my kids was off at *school,* so Dorothy came to my house. She said, "Well, could I rent a room with you?" I said, "Yes." So I let Dorothy have a room.

[I] met Floyd while she [Dorothy] was there. She was goin with Floyd's brother and he was married! Morris [Floyd's brother] had a *wife* right there in San Francisco! So, he was after women too. He was a seaman, too, Floyd's brother was. And next thing I knowed, I got to meet his *wife!* And I didn't know that was her husband who had been comin to my house! So, I told her [Dorothy] one day, I said, "You know what Dottie?" She said, "What?" I said, "Dottie, you livin a double life." I said, "You livin a *dangerous* life." I says, "Now, who is this 'Daddy' you're talkin about?"

[Dorothy said] "Oh, Daddy's comin home, and can I fix dinner here for him?" I said, "Yeah." That was before I met him. Floyd's brother was comin in, and she fixed a dinner—man had a wife in San Francisco! We was in Oakland, just across the Bay Bridge. He come in there, and oh my, she was *so* happy. She cooked up this dinner, and there was somethin she had me to make that she couldn't make. And, oh, he come in and I met him and everything. I thought he was a single man until I found out, and then I laid the law to her and told her, "No, no, no, this don't go on in my house."

Well that's where I met Floyd, through his brother, when his brother saw we was these two womens in this house. Floyd was on the ship, and Floyd was comin in, and when Floyd came in, he usually go to [Morris'] house, 'cause that was his brother. So when he come into San Francisco, he'd go to stay with his brother. So Floyd said, "Reckon I can meet her?" He [Morris] said, "I'm sure you can." Said, "She's a single woman." Said, "She got kids, but they're off to college."

༄

So I met Floyd, and when I met Floyd, I says, "Is that your brother?" And Morris had told Floyd not to tell me he was his brother. I said, "Are you all any relations?" He said, "Oh, we're on the same ship together, we work together." So I said, "Oh," I said, "I'm quite sure you have a wife." I went to askin questions, and he [Floyd] said, "My wife and I are separated." I said, "You have any children?" He said, "I have two sons." I said, "Where are they?" I was askin questions. He said, "They're with my wife." I said, "Do you take care of them?" [Laughter] I was readin him down, and gettin it! [Laughter] He said, "Yes," he says, "They gets a check from my job." So I told him, I said, "Well, you know one thing?" I says, "I have had my husband," I says, "Now, I don't want *nobody's* husband." I said, 'Cause I wouldn't want nobody messin with my husband," I says, "so, you're takin bread out of children's mouths." I said, "Now are you sure?" That's what I told Floyd. I said, "You sure?" He said, "My wife and I separated," and he says, "she has the kids, and I supports my kids." Said, "My kids' money goes out of my check to them." He said, "And then when I come in," he said, "I used to try to live close," said, "so they could be with me," he said, "but she got so mean, she didn't want me nowhere around." And I said, "Oh." So when I got it over to him, and I say, "Is this your brother, for real?" And he says, "Yes," he said, "that's my brother," and he says, "I'm gonna take you over to where they live." And I says, "OK."

༄

So we got together. We went out and had dinner, we came back, and we talked and everything, and so his brother came and he says,

"Floyd, what ya think?" Floyd said, "OK." Like that, and I didn't know what they was talkin about, ya know. So I says, "I guess you're gettin the OK on me?" I said, "Is that what you're doin, gettin the OK on me?" And he said, "Oh no," he said, "We were just talkin." So we all got in the conversation, and I said, "OK," I say, "who likes to hear music?" I had records, and I played records. I says, "Now, I could entertain you with my music," so they say, "Oh, OK!" And I said, "I like to go out and eat sometime," I said, "but I have special places where I love." So he said, "OK." I said, "Would ya'll like to go?" They said, "Yes." And, Floyd said, "Well I been eatin out of restaurants and things—do you ever cook?" I said, "Oh yeah, I cook." He said, "Well how 'bout us buyin some food and you cook it—I like a good *cooked* meal." He was testin me out to see if I could cook! So I said, "Oh," I said, "you would like for me to cook you a meal, is that what it is, so you can see what a good cook I am?" I said, "Well I tell you what," I said, "I been cookin ever since I was a little girl." I said, "Before my mother died, now she died when I was ten," I said, "and I been cookin before that, and I been ever since." I just *rattled* it off to him! He said, "Oh, OK, OK, OK." And I said, "Well if you buy it, I'll cook it."

I fixed the dinner, and boy, they was so elated over this dinner I fixed. And his brother said, *"Maaan!"* He's grinnin, he was [lowers voice dramatically], "You know Floyd?" I got to where I couldn't *stand* him afterwards! "Maaan, don't you let this get away from you, Maaan!" [Laughter] And I said, "You all are brothers, huh?" "Yeah, that's my baby brother!" He changed his voice just like that. He said, "That's my baby brother! Of course my baby sister, she passed when she was young." He went on tellin me."

"Oh," I said, "Your family was similar to my family!" I said, "Only though, when my mother died," I said, "my father didn't say he couldn't take care of the family." When *his* father died first, the mother gave up the will to live. And that's when she said she couldn't raise that family by herself. And Floyd said it wasn't no time after his daddy died before his mother died. So I told him, I said, "Well it was a little different with mine." I said, "My dad was a mother *and* a father for us after mother died. I says, "Now, I had a lot a other mothers." He said, "You mean your father—" I said, "My father and my mother is dead," I said, "yes." He said,

CHAPTER 30

"Mine too." And he said, "How old was you?" So I told him how old I was when my father died, and I said "I was grown, but I didn't have any kids. My dad was wantin to see me with children." I said, "But he didn't see me with children." I said, "But my daddy gave me away to my first husband." I said, "And that's my kids' daddy."

And he said, "Oh the ones you got—" I said, "Yes, both my boys are in college." And, so he said, "Mmm hmm! And where are they in college?" I said, "Howard University." His brother said, "M-a-a-an! Two boys in college!" I said, "Yes, two boys in college, and that's all I have is two boys." He [Floyd] said, "I got two boys." I said, "Oh you have?" He said, "Yeah, I have two boys." Said, "What's their names?" "Ricky and Randy." And I say, "Oh." So he was tellin me about his boys, and I says, "I hope some day they get a chance to meet my sons." But they never did.

ɷ

So we ended up goin to the store, havin the dinner, playin the cards, playin records. And so I told 'em, I said, "Well, I'm gonna tell ya, I have to say goodnight." Well, I had three bedrooms. And Dorothy had one room. I had let her have this front room. So she says, "Floyd, where are you stayin?" He says, "Well, I got to go back to San Francisco." And Dorothy said, "Well, I think my sister will let you stay at her house." She said, "I think my sister'll let you stay at her house tonight." I've never told anybody this before. I said, "Well," I said, "I've never had men sleepin in my house, that's my friends." I said, "But I have a extra room." I said, "Now if you want to stay here," I said, "I'm not *sleepin with* you." I said, "I have to have that respect." I say, "You can sleep in this other room." Floyd said, "I don't mind that." He said, "I respect you." When he said that, his brother said, "What did you say Floyd? I thought you was a man!" I say, "Yes he is!" I said, "And I respect him as a man, and he's respectin me as a woman!" I say, "I met him *today*." I says, "I made ya'll welcome in my house—we've entertained here," I said, "but I don't sleep with no man I've just meet him!" I said, "No, no, no, no, no." I said, "That's a no-no with me."

ɷ

I said [to Morris], "Well, I would like to meet your wife." You have a wife?" "Well ye-e-e-s." I said, "Well what are you doin over here with somebody else at my house?" I said, "Now you know what?" I said, "I'm gonna tell you this. You can't come back to my house no more and meet her [Dorothy] here." I said, "That is a no-no." [Morris said] *"Floyd!* Did you hear what she said? *Maaan,* what kind of—" I said, "Look." I said, "I don't play no two-time thing." I say, "I'm a one man woman." I say, "And I see that you is a one man *playin* woman!" I say, "You say you's married and have a wife?" I say, "And you with her [Dorothy] here in my house, and I'm thinkin, she's just your friend?" And I says, "Now, you have let me know that *you* plays around on your wife." I said, "Now if I'm gonna be *your* brother's friend, I'm not gonna be no *secondhand.* I'm gonna be *first.* And I don't want nobody behind me." I say, "I'm gonna be *it,* and it alone!" He said, "Ooh, man! She puttin down some strong *stuff* here now!" I said, "Well you know what?" I said, "My daddy always told me to be straight and plain, and give it out like it is. Don't beat around the bush." I said, "What you're doin, you're beatin around the bush."

So, Morris didn't know how to take it, and so, I got Floyd over to myself and I told him. He said, "You're right about that." He said, "My wife and I are separated and she has my children." He said, "But I takes care of my kids." He says, "I have allotment comin out of my check. I don't see it. It goes to her, for my two sons." I said, "Well, if you lyin to me, I don't want to see you no more." I say, "You know lies will always be found out." He said, "I'm tellin you the truth." And that's the way we got started, from *that* day *on.*

Chapter 31

FLOYD AND HIS SONS

So, I said, "Yes, I have a extra room. And you can use this room." Well, that's when I got to know *him* better. His wife had wrote and told him on the ship, "Don't come back to that house no more." He was overseas. He was so hurt. When he got off the ship, he couldn't go home to see his boys. She had wrote him a letter, "Don't come back there." He was in tears. And it's a hurtin thing when you know a person is concerned about their child and can't go [see him]. A lot of men dump 'em and don't care what happens to them. But that man was crazy about his two boys. He was crazy about those boys. And when he was tellin me he got the message "Don't come back," the tears started comin down out of his eyes. And he said, "You just have to excuse me." He said, "But, those boys is my boys, and I love my boys." And I said, "Well, that's OK." I said, "I know how you feel." I said, "I have boys, too."

☙

Floyd was *crazy* about his two boys. I hated so bad when he lost those boys. The man almost lost his mind. The baby boy I think was around about sixteen or seventeen when he overdose. And someone shot his older boy and killed him. He was older. Sang! He had tapes. I think he got some of them tapes now yet, where he was a spiritual child. Out of all the way his mother was treatin him, he was in a singin group from their church. He had the beautifulist voice you'd want to hear. We have some of his musics.

The oldest boy, his mother put him out. He was a sweet child. When he was killed, I'll always believe that it was Floyd's brother's son that killed him. It was over a girl. It was some argument over a girl! I don't know exactly how it was, but it was a conflict there. And his son came up shot. And they never did find out exactly who did it. But Floyd had said that—and I'm hopin he'll never find out—he said if he *ever* would find out who did it, he was gonna get them. And I told him, I said, "Well I hope you never find it out, because that wouldn't solve the problem."

The youngest boy lived with us for awhile. He was with his dad for awhile, helpin with the truck. And his *young* son—a smart kid— oh I had him in school in San Francisco. That boy was makin A's! He was in chemistry, that boy. I just knew he was gonna grow up to be a doctor or a scientist. He was good, but the child got on that *dope*. Oh Lord, I hated it so bad. I called him my boy because I lost a boy. I had three sons, and I lost one. I said this is my son I lost, that was my boy. And he was *smart*. In his high school, he was one of the smartest ones in the chemistry class. And he would come home sometime, and I says, "Ricky what is wrong with you?" "I'm so tired, I've been workin hard all day in that chemistry room." He could really fix it up there and you would believe it. But then, when we first got him, I was takin care of a cousin of mine in San Francisco and he was sick, so we didn't have enough room. The lady across the street said, well, she had a room, and we rented that room for him. So he'd come over to the house and eat his breakfast and everything and all. He got to where he was slippin kids in her place, and they was usin dope.

So I went over to his room one day to clean it up. I was gonna change his bed and everything, and I found somethin over there, and I didn't know what it was. So I called my cousin Marie, and I said, "Marie," I said, "I found somethin in this child's room. I don't know what it is." I said, "But he been comin in here lookin mighty *funny*," and I says, "One day he came in, he just sit down at the gate." [We] had a little, little fence and a little short gate, and he just sat down. And now I told him, I said, "Ricky come on in the house!" "I'll be there after while." And he sit there, and then he put his head down. I said, "Oh there's somethin wrong with that child." So I went out there, I said, "Ricky get up and come on in the house." I said, "You not supposed to sit out here." I said, "Police come by here and he'll think you're drunk." [He] said, "Oh let me get up." He got ready and he got up, but he couldn't hardly stand, and I got him in the house. I said, "Ricky, what is you doin?" I said, "Is you usin somethin?" "Mom, you know I wouldn't do that to you. I love you." And he just started to huggin me. I said, "No," I said, "somethin is wrong." Because I had done stepped on the thing then. So he said, "Mom, I wouldn't do that to you for nothing, you've been so sweet to me." Which I had.

∾

His mother told him [Ricky] to go to his dad. 'Cause after they had separated and he was with me, she said, "Go to your dad." And he was a smart kid in school when he was with her. So she was doin everything she wanted to do, and he'd sit down and told me, he'd say, "You know why my mama sent me to my dad?" I said, "No Ricky, and I don't want to know." "Well I want to tell you." I said, "Ricky I don't want to know." "I want to *tell* you." He said, "I want you to *know* why my mama sent me to my daddy." I said, "Well Ricky," I said, "do you think it'd be fair for you to tell me?" He said, "'Cause you been my mama now. I think you should know. You're my mom." He said, "Can I talk to you with whatever I want to talk to you about?" And I said, "Yes Ricky." And I didn't want him to be sad. I didn't want him to feel like nobody gonna hear him. And he said he never could talk to his mother about nothing. She wouldn't listen to nothin. So I said, "Yes Ricky, you can talk to me." So he said, "You know the reason my mama sent me to my dad?" I said, "Why?" "'Cause she didn't want me to see what she's doin. I'm tellin you, my mama is a cat with a case of the claws. I'm gonna tell you what, my mom party, party, party." I said, "Oh she do?" "Yeah, my mama really party, mmm. My mama gets dressed up, and if she doesn't have that party at home, she goes out partyin, and she has herself a ball!"

I knew it was the home trainin was causin him to be like he was. He wanted his mom, but when she told him to go to his dad, to get out, she didn't want him in her way, that let him know that what she was doin was more important to her than he was, and that made him feel bad.

But when he came to me, his little sack that he had his clothes in, I almost went in tears when I saw it. She sent him to me. Floyd's out at sea. I had a store that was a government store, and my second husband had gotten me a card where I could go in and shop. And, so, I told him, I said, "Well, we goin over and shop. We goin over at that store. He went in that store, and he went to pickin out. I said, "I want you to pick out some clothes." He looked at me, he said, "You gonna buy these clothes for me?" I said, "Mmm hmm." "For real?" I said, "For real." He was shocked. So, he went in there and picked out the clothes, and he looked at me and he'd get out something, and he'd say, "Can I have this?" I said, "Try it on. You wanna get something that you can wear." I said, "And somethin you don't want to fit tight now." I say, "You want to grow to it and have a space of growth." He said, "OK." And when I dressed that kid up and came out of that store, he put his arms around me, and he started cryin. And I said, "Ricky, why are you cryin?" He said, "Nobody has never . . . my mother never did this for me." He said, "I always had to beg Mama to get somethin for me, but she never carried me to a store, and told me to pick out." I said, "Well Ricky," I said, "I am not your mother." I said, "But I love you." I said, "I want you to remember that I love you."

Chapter 32

LITTLE EDITH AND LULA MAY

I taken her [Edith] away from her mother [Lula May]. Her mother was on dope, and I knew there was somethin goin on, but I didn't know just what it was. And my son had agreed for her [Lula May] to come, if she stayed with me. And she [Lula May] said she was, but when she got there, she didn't want to be with me, because of what she was doin. And the way I got Edith away from her then, someone came and told me that they saw her in the park at night. I said, "At night?" Say, "Yes," say, "her and that little girl was sittin out there in the middle of the park." And this park is where the drugs all dealt around. When I questioned her [Lula May], she said where she was stayin they throwed her out. And I asked her why did they throw her out from where she was. She gave me some kind of fragile remarks about what they didn't allow her to do. They didn't want her to have no company or anything. So I told her, I said, "Well," I say, "If you're the mother, you wouldn't have company over your daughter." I says, "What kind of company?" "Ma," she out and told me, "I have to do somethin to make a livin!" And I knew then just what she was talkin about.

~

She was in this park. And someone came and told me that they had saw her. So, when I questioned her about it, she told me it wasn't true. So I ended up with her in the house with me, and I was workin every day in the beauty shop. So, I told her, I says, "Sis, whatever you do," I said, "don't have people runnin in and out of my house." I says, "I don't mind you stayin here," I said, "but when I'm gone, I don't want people in and out of my house." 'Cause I was workin in the beauty shop. So I got worried that someone passed by my house and she was havin herself a party. And she would always call up the beauty shop, "Mom, how you doin?" That was keepin in touch with what I was doin. So, I told her, the proprietor of the shop, I said, "If she ever calls for me, you just tell her I'm out." I said, "And if she asks where, say, 'Well, she said she was goin home.'" That way it would make her clear the house.

So that worked for a little while, but then they got bold enough to come to the house when I was there and ask for her. And one young man come knockin on the door. "Open the door, open the door!" And I went there and I said, "Who are you lookin for?" "Uh, uh, uh, uh, where's the lady of the house?" I say, "You lookin at the lady of the house." 'Cause, see, she had done told them she was livin there. She was the lady of the house. He said, "No, you're not the lady of the house. You're not who I've been seein." I said, "Well, whoever you been seein, it wasn't the lady of the house." And I say, "I know who that was," I say, "that's my daughter-in-law." I say, "And I'll appreciate it very much if you don't come back here lookin for her any more." I said, "That's my son's wife, and that's their child." He looked at me and put his hands on his hip, and he told me off but good. "Well, as long as she and I is on terms, I don't care what you say." I said, "Well I'll tell you what, don't come back here lookin for her anymore." I said, "because she won't be here. If you come back, she'll be out." I said, "Because if you come back one more time, and I see you," I say, "you and her both won't be here anymore." Man, he looked at me and he blowed and blowed, and he said, "Well, will you tell me just what do that mean?" I says, "Son," I said, "my son is this child's father. *My* son is this woman's husband." I say, "And she come to me," I says, "and I love her, and I love my grandchild." I said, "Now if you think that she don't have a husband, and if she told you that," I said, "she's told you the wrong thing." I said, "As far as I know, they haven't separated yet." I say, "And if they have, that child is *my* grandchild." I say, "And don't come back to *my* house lookin for her anymore." I said, "The best thing for you to do is try to find you somewhere else to go." He looked at me, and he got *so* mad, he just puffed and blowed for awhile, then he turned around and stomped his foot, and off the porch he went.

ଦ୍ୱ

CHAPTER 32

And I had got her [Lula May] in a school where she could go and finish up her high school, and that's why I was keepin the baby, tryin to let her progress. And that's what she did. She went to that school enough to get in touch with the dope addicts and everything. Then I ended up findin some funny pills. She made a hole on a mattress on the bed. It was a fold-out bed, and it come out into the living room part. She had made a hole in that mattress, and where it was big enough for her to put her hand down in it, and that's where she was hidin dope in it. So one day, she didn't come in, and I put Edith to bed. And I was layin there talkin to her and playin with her, and my elbow went down. So, I started feelin, and that's when I felt and saw this hole. Something said, "It's time for you to strip this bed." So I got up and I pulled the sheets and things off the bed, and I had a pad on there, so in case Edith *would* have accidents, it wouldn't go through. I had a rubber pad. So I taken it up. I got so angry, I didn't know what to do. I said, "Well Lord," I say, "I'm tryin to help this girl, and she just makin a fool out of me." So I put my hand down there, and I found some little hard things in there, I didn't know what they was. It was what they call "rock." I took 'em out, and I opened it and flushed 'em through the commode. I said, "Well, if she come back lookin for this, she won't find it." I put my hand in there again, and I got about four or five of 'em. I don't know if I got 'em all, but every one I got out, I flushed it through the commode. And it looked funny! I just can't describe how the thing looks. And I said, "Now what do they do for that?"

So, it finally rocked on, rocked on, till one day, I come home and my neighbor across the street told me, she said, "Your house been full of people in and out, in and out." She said, "I started to call the police." I said, "I wish you had." She said, "Well, the lady that be there with you . . ." Well, I had the baby with me, and she was in the little preschool till around two o'clock, and then I would bring her down to the shop where I was workin. And I told the lady, I say, "Next time you see *anybody* come in this house and I'm not here and she's here," I say, "call the police. Please." So she said, "OK." But I guess she got in the wind. They stopped comin in the daytime. She would wait until I would get through and then she'd say, "Mama, I got to go to the store. I be right back." I say, "OK." Sometime she leave and I won't see her.

And so she got so bad, one day [she] told me she was takin her baby and she wasn't comin back there no more. She got a place with a friend of hers. And I say, "OK." I said, "If that's the way you want it, this is your child." I said, "I'm tryin to help you." I said, "But Sis, whatever you do, don't have no men over your baby." I said, "You have to watch over your child." I said, "Because they's some out there will rape this baby." I said, "And if I hear of it," I said, "you and them both gonna be dead 'cause I'm not gonna stop and just kill one, I'm gonna kill both of ya." "Mama, you know I take care of my baby." I said, "Well, I hope you will." But in the meantime, she was doin the same thing herself. She was sellin her body to get drugs, and whatever she could do to get the drugs she was doin it.

༄

And one time she went from Oakland and there to Sacramenta, someplace out of town. Here I gets a *long*-distance call. The phone woman [said], "Will you accept this long-distance call? Will you accept the call?" I said, "Well," Floyd was out, and I said, "I don't know if I accept this call." And I said, "Where is this call comin from?" And when she tell me, I said, "No, I will not accept that call." I said, "I'll accept the call from Floyd Hudley, from Everett H., and Andrew H." I said, "Anything else come in," I said, "*no*." I heard her say [chuckle], "Lady, don't get all upset with me." 'Cause I was tellin her off so nice. She said, "Don't get upset with me." She said, "I know sometimes people have trouble in their homes," she said, "but I'm just repeatin to you what was said to me. Will you accept the call?" I said, "No ma'am." [Laughs] She had left and she was tryin to get in touch with *me*, wanted me to send her some money to come back to Sugarland. So, I don't know how she got back—'bout two or three days after that she came. And when she got back in, she was ashamed to come around.

Edith was with *me!* I had Edith. I had Edith with *me!* And when she [Lula May] came back she was afraid to come to the house, because she didn't think I was gonna let her stay there anymore. But when she came back I was at work, and when I got home she was sittin on the steps. She couldn't get in. And she said, "Hi Mama." I said, "Hi. How you doin?" I said, "I'm doin OK. How you doin?" "Mama, I

Chapter 32

don't know how I'm doin. I'm sick as I can be." I said, "What is your trouble?" "I don't know what my trouble is. It's like the *world* is against me." She went to cryin and goin up. I said, "Sis, don't give me that." I say, "You know what?" I said, "You need to get your life together. You got a child to raise." I said, "But I'm gonna tell you one thing. If you don't get your life together," I say, "you gonna be outdoor, and you can't come in my house no more, and I'm gonna keep this child." "But that's my child, Mama." I said, "I know it." I said, "But you know what?" I said, "I have enough evidence on you right now that I could go to the court, and I could take Edith away from you." I said, "But you is her mother, and I don't want to destroy your love between you and your child." I said, "But if you keep this up, you won't have her." I said, "You goin to have to straighten up." I said, "I'm not gonna to have it." And Edith was so crazy about her mother when she was little.

∽

So, she [Lula May] left her again, and she didn't come back in 'bout three days—didn't know where she was, didn't call or anything. And when she did come, I said, "Where have you been?" I said, "You been in jail?" She looked at me, "Why would you ask me that, Mama?" I said, "Because you didn't call, and you didn't let your child know that you were still alive." And Edith was so attached to her that if she didn't hear from her mother she'd just sit down and she'd go to hummin her little song, lookin out the window. So I told her, I said, "You know," I said, "I hate to see you throw your life away." And I said, "I'm not gonna let you throw Edith's life away." So I told her, I said, "And if you can't straighten up your life," I said, "you can't be in my house. And I'm workin and people is seein people comin in and out my house." I said, "This can't happen." I said, "I want my *key* to my door. I don't want you comin in and out of the house. So if you leave, you'll just have to wait until I come." 'Cause the way she go out and lock the *door* behind her, but you have to have a key to come in. [Laugh] She was leavin me with my house unlocked—and I happened to come home one day and I found it unlocked—she caught herself playin me for a fool after I'd tell her what she could do and couldn't do and I'd taken my key. I said, "Now you can go out, but you'll have to wait till I come home to come in." But instead of her doin that, she would leave the door unlocked.

So she finally got so bad I told her, I said, "Sis," I said, "you can stay here, but your habits have to go." I said, "Now if your habits gonna stay with you, you'll have to go," I said, "'cause I'm not gonna have this in my house." I was payin for Edith to be in this preschool while I was workin in the beauty shop. And she [Lula May] had got enrolled goin to school to finish up and get her high school diploma. She went three or four days and that was it. And when I found it out, I told her, I said, "You can't stay here no more. You got to go." I said, "'cause I can't be workin with my mind back here on my house, and I got Edith and I'm takin care a her." "But that's my child. I'll take her and go." I said, "You know what?" I said, "I have enough evidence on you I can put you in the penitentiary." I said, "I don't want to do that." I said, "But before I see you take this child . . ." I said, "Baby, that's where you'll end up," I said, "'cause I'm not gonna let you *drag* her." I said, "Now I've given you the opportunity to finish and go back to school." I said, "And you tell me what you want to be, you want to be a nurse." I said, "I did too." I said, "Now I've told you I'll help you." I said, "So if that's the way you feel about it, and that's what you plan on doin," I said, "And you just gonna be a nobody." I said, "You can be a nobody by yourself, but not with this baby." And she got mad and she left. The woman packed up. She wrote somebody in Washington, D.C., and they sent her her fare.

～

I had a cabinet full of canned goods and stuff. She got to packin and packin. And I wasn't payin her too much attention, 'cause she had to go through the kitchen to go upstairs to the bedroom, and she had some things in there, and she was bringin them down. When that child left, she done packed up so much of my food! [Laughs] And I didn't realize it until after she'd gone. I went to look down in the cupboard for something, and Floyd had come in. I went to get somethin out, and I opened it, I said, "Oh my Lord!" He said, "What is it?" I say, "Yes, she gone." But I opened that cabinet like to look for somethin, I said, "Mmm, mmm, mmm." He said, "What's that?" I said, "That child done *cleaned* the cabinets." I didn't know she was packin all this food and stuff, but she carried enough food away from my house, I guess, to last her a month or more.

Chapter 32

She [Lula May] had got hooked on that dope, and she's just lettin that dope take a hold to her. So when I taken her [Little Edith], and [Lula May] left, she didn't get her back. And when she saw her again, her Daddy had come to see me, and he said, "Mama, don't let her have the baby back." I said, "Andrew, she birthed this baby." I said, "You and her need to get together and raise your child." "Well Mama, I done did all I can, and I ain't takin no more of this off her," and he was goin off on her. And I told him, I said, "Now look, you hush," I said, "because, if you had a did your part when this baby—" "Mama, you wasn't there, and you don't know what I did." I said, "I don't care," I say, "if you'd a been there and did your part, I wouldn't a had this baby." I says, "You and her would be together and ya'll would be raisin your child." So it ended up that I ended up with Edith, and I kept her till she was a big kid.

∞

So when she [Lula May] saw that I was really serious about her [Edith], she left, and I kept Edith, and I put her in school. And I started workin at Park Day School. I stopped workin at the beauty shop, started workin at Park Day School. But that's the way I got Edith. Now, Edith still calls me before she'll call her mother. She don't call me "Grandma," she calls me "Mom." And, anytime she has any problems— Christmas Day I had to talk to her for a long time—Christmas, she called me in tears. And I had to talk. Whenever her little problems come up, she won't call her Daddy, and he's right there in Virginia. She won't go into confidence in him. She gonna phone and call me. If she have to call me collect, she gonna call Grandma. And she calls me "Mom."

Chapter 33

REACHING OUT IN SALT LAKE CITY

So, I was just raised up in that bond of givin and reachin out. And like I told 'em at Calvary [Edith's church in Salt Lake City], we don't reach out enough to our young people. That's why we're losin so many of 'em. They got my picture—I've noticed that—they got my picture two or three times where I was standin up talkin to a young [person] and I had my arms this way [around the young person's shoulders] talkin. I didn't even know they were takin my picture. I see where they got me on the board, where I was standin up talkin.

◊

And they's a young man that joined the church not too long ago. He was baptized the other week. I talked to him at *Touched by a Angel* [television show filmed in Salt Lake using community people, including Edith, Floyd, and other church members]. I was workin on it, and I was talkin to him, and I said, "Do you attend church anyplace?" He says, "No." I said, "Well come in and visit our church." And I gave him a card and told him to come and visit church. By him comin and visitin the church, and me talkin to him, he has joined that church and was baptized. But if I hadn't a been workin with him, and askin questions and tellin him about the church I belong to and all, and *invitin* him. And every time he see me, he says, "You and your husband brought me to this church the first time I came to it." But, it makes me feel like, well, I may not be doin everythin that I should be doin, but I'm *tryin* to do, and children is my heart.

◊

CHAPTER 33

Now, if you want to see me rile up quick, let me see somebody doin somethin to a child. I remember one time, I went and taken a child out of a lady's arms. She was scoldin that baby and I went and *taken* that baby, and stop shakin it—up and down! [I said] "You don't do a baby like that! What's wrong?" The woman looked at me, and she said, "This is my child." But the thing about it was, the child had got on her nerves, and she had lost her patience. And it was good that I seen that in time, to go and take this baby, 'cause she was doin that [indicates shaking]. You shake a baby up and down like that, you can damage their brains! See, and my mother taught me, with my two little brothers under me, how you handle a baby, and everything. Huh! So, *children* is a part of my life. Now if you want to step on my toes quick, let me see you mistreatin a child. And, Floyd tells sometimes, "You need to keep your mouth shut." I said, "Floyd, cain't." [Laughs]

He don't see me all the time! [Laughs] Sometimes I'm by myself in places, and I says... I was in church one time, and this lady's baby just kept cryin and she was shakin that baby. [Whispers] "Hush, hush, hush." I said, "Can I help you with the baby? Let me have the baby for a little while." [Chuckles] Huh! She gave me that baby like that! She was tired of that baby. I takin the baby and picked it up and said, "Don't cry, don't cry." Put that baby up on my shoulder and started pattin that baby like this [motions]. That baby went to sleep. The baby was sleepy and tired! She didn't understand or hadn't thought of how long the baby had been awake. That baby was sleepy and tired. And he was cryin and frettin in the church. And I just tilted in after her and I said, "Let me hold it, can I hold your baby?" She said, "I don't know." I said, "Well, let me try." And when I taken that baby and started pettin, and I was doin it like this, in the church, on my shoulder, that baby stopped cryin and went to sleep. And the lady that was behind me, she looked at me. She said, "What did you do to that baby?" I said, "I didn't do anything. I just petted him." I said, "The baby knew I loved it." And I says, "And I just rocked the baby." But she was shakin the baby like this [gestures shaking]. And so, she said, "You must have a hand for babies." I said, "I come up takin care of babies. That was the biggest job I ever had."

Chapter 34

THOUGHTS ABOUT DEATH

Wendy, you know my oldest son, brought that [death] up one time. He said, "Mama," he said, "you have been through a lot." And he said, "Mama, is there's anything you want, special from me?" I said, "Well," I said, "only thing I want you to do," I said, "I'm fixin me some things up." I said, "I'm makin everything, arrangements and everything, and puttin it in paper," I said, "and I brought somethin I want you to sign." I said, "So if anything happen to me I want you to carry me back home and put me in close to my dad and my brother [Purcell] in the cemetery."

My mother wanted to be buried where my daddy is. But her mother wanted her to be in the cemetery with her family. So my dad's in the cemetery where his family is, and my brother that passed is in the cemetery. He's close to my dad. My sister, when she was in Houston, she bought a plot. But [laughs] she doesn't like all of us. So, she and her husband is in Houston. So I told Everett, I said, "I want to be close to my dad and my brother that was in the service." He's the one got hurt in the service and never did get over it. Here he come in that morning, he said, "Mama," he said, "put it all in paper." I said, "Then I don't want you to give me no real lavish funeral." I said, "Just put me away as comfortable as you can." I said, "You can take me some of my suits or my white dresses or whatever I wear in church." I said, "You can bury me in that. Don't come puttin no lockets in the ground." I say, "It's gonna stay there and rot." I said, "So." He—his eyes started to water. He said, "Mama, put all of this on paper [laughs] for me." And I said, "I'm gonna make everything out for you. So you can follow through."

Now, my husband [Floyd] has this service plot in Denver, and his two sons is buried there. So they could bury me there, because he's a vet. But I says, "I don't want to be put on top of any relations." 'Cause they put you on top. So, when he lost his two sons, they knew it was four, they put them down far enough for two people to be on top. So I told Floyd, I said, "Baby," I said, "that is for you and your two sons." I says, "I wants to go where my dad is." I said, "I want you to know that, where my dad and my brother [are]." He said, "Well, you get all that fixed out, and when you go out, you talk to Everett about it." I said, "I'll do that."

So when I told Everett, water started gettin in his eyes, and I told him, I said, "You know son," I said, "I need your word." I said, "Mama's preparin for this." And he got shook up. I said, "Well, you know Everett," I said, "I haven't been with ya'll since you came out of high school and college on a birthday." I said, "When I sent you all off to college, ya'll haven't been with me, and I haven't been with ya'll on a birthday of mine since." I said, "You never can tell when the time's gonna come." I said, "And Mama soon be seventy-seven." He said, "Yeah, Mama, I was thinkin about that." I said, "Well I want to be with you on my seventy-seventh birthday." I said, "Now, I'll be leavin after it." He said, "OK, Mama." He said, "You know, when you told me that, I got to thinkin." I didn't really want to tell him the reason why, but I could see it was worryin him after I got there. So I told him, I said "Everett," I said, "It's good to know than to think about it if you don't know." I said, "How long do I know if I'll be with you anymore?" I said, "I may not be here another year." I said, "But God has abled me to bring ya'll up." He said, "Mama, I looks back over and I thinks about from whence you come, and Mama, you done been through *so* much." Now maybe he realizes that. He realizes what I have been through.

Interlude 5

NARRATIVE

Now that the reader has heard so much of Edith's story, it seems fitting to reflect on the nature of her story as a story. In this interlude we consider questions about story genre, the practice of telling stories, the collaborative nature of this telling, and the developmental implications of adult storytelling.

What Kind of Story Is This?

Hudley's story fits within several scholarly categories. This is a life story, the story of Edith's life over the long term, told from her own perspective. It weaves together a series of oral stories of personal experience, each of which invokes a particular event in her life. Only rarely do people tell their life stories as comprehensively and as continuously as Hudley did for the purpose of this project. According to linguist Charlotte Linde (1993), people tell and retell their life stories in bits and pieces over the course of their lives. Each time narrators tell a piece of their story, they customize it to the occasion and the listener. Linde also emphasizes that life stories are subject to revision over time as people come to reenvision the past in light of later events.

Hudley's story is also an oral history, a spoken account that has been recorded and transcribed. As such, it exists within the lineage of African-American storytelling celebrated in the anthology *Talk That Talk* (Goss and Barnes, 1989). In the introduction to that volume, Henry Louis Gates, Jr., says, "Only black music-making was as important to the culture of African-Americans as has been the fine art of storytelling" (p.17). Although some of the contributors to *Talk That Talk* express how frustrating it is to try to translate their oral artistry into writing, Gates notes that black literary tradition, like every literary tradition, derives from oral and performative culture.

In addition to being a life story and an oral history, Hudley's story is a form of autobiography. It exemplifies the move within feminist and African-American scholarship to seek a more capacious definition of autobiography, one that resists the Eurocentric model of a lone, usually male author acting alone. Gwendolyn Etter-Lewis (1993), for example, argues eloquently for the need to enlarge our vision of autobiography to include variants, including oral genres, community-identified narrators, and narratives that incorporate multiple voices and realities. She says, "Autobiography is not an inert literary or historical mode, but a fluid pattern of discourse that assumes a specific configuration of features according to the culture and world view which shapes it" (p. 154).

Taken together, these various perspectives suggest that, in telling her story, Hudley expresses who she is, communicates her identity to others, and claims membership in particular communities and groups.

Who Is Edith Hudley?

What do we learn about Edith Hudley by listening to her life story? One of the most striking features of Edith's story is how densely peopled it is. She represents her life, throughout its many twists and turns, as inextricably bound up with the lives of others. One formal indicator of the depth of her social embeddedness is her copious use of quoted speech to represent her own and other people's voices. In keeping with Etter-Lewis's critique of the Eurocentric model, Edith does not imagine herself to be a solitary actor.

Equally striking is the moral and religious framework within which Mrs. Hudley situates the events of her life. We have already commented in the first interlude on Hudley's religious and spiritual commitments. Viewed from the standpoint of narrative, Hudley's story continues the tradition of African-American women telling spiritual stories, a tradition that is traceable to the slave narrative (McKay, 1988).

Many of the approaches to analyzing narrative recognize that narratives are freighted with ideological, if not specifically religious, meaning. Linde (1993) notes that life stories include "landmark events," such as choice of profession, marriage, and religious conversions and that religion is one example of a coherence system by which narrators order their accounts and render them intelligible to listeners. However, the white professionals whose life stories she analyzes rarely use religion as a coherence system. By contrast, in Etter-Lewis's (1993) analysis of the oral narratives of African-American women who were pioneers in their professions, religion emerges as a theme in the majority of cases.

Another work that recognizes religion as a possible ideological setting for self-narratives is McAdams' *Stories We Live By*. McAdams argues that each person creates a personal myth or sacred story that defines his or her identity. He claims that this is not a task that is limited to adolescence. Adults continue to form and revise their identities, and this is accomplished partly by the creation of "imagoes," characters that are constructed out of social roles and other aspects of the self. Imagoes are inspired by and built around significant others.

The imago of the caregiver is prominent in Hudley's life story, fashioned, one may surmise, from the models of her beloved mother and her "other mothers." Although this imago seems to valorize a traditional feminine role, the particular inflection that Hudley lends to it is distinctive. Hudley, as caregiver, reforms the Houston school that her sons attend; publicly resists the disciplinary policy in another school; contributes to the financial support of her family by working in the shipbuilding industry, where she delights in her mastery of her job; assumes the role of father to her sons when her husband reneges on his responsibilities; and comes close to shooting her husband when he abuses her.

Hudley also appears in the guise of teacher, sage, survivor, and truth teller. In the last case, it is evidently her father who provided the most compelling model. She remembers his story about the relative who was forced to withstand the sexual attentions of a white man and who ultimately bore and raised his son, Hudley's blue-eyed cousin. And when Hudley undertook to educate her sons about sex and romance, against the determined opposition of their father, it is hard not to hear the echo of *her* father, who equipped young Edith with concrete instructions about how to protect herself from predatory men.

INTERLUDE 5

Collaborative Narrative Revisited

In *The Norton Book of Women's Lives* (1993), editor Phyllis Rose explains that she included several coauthored works in order to broaden the range of women's experience represented in the book. One of these works is an excerpt from *Motherwit*, the life story of Alabama midwife, Onnie Lee Logan (1989), as told to Catherine Clark. Rose notes that *Motherwit* originated with Logan herself, "who, like many autobiographers, felt an almost painful need to get out her story before she died. 'I got so much experience in here that I just want to explode,' she told Clark. 'I want to show that I knew what I knew—I want somebody to realize what I am'" (p. 28).

The eagerness with which Hudley embraced the idea of a book about her life suggests that she harbored a similarly urgent need to tell her story. However, the collaborative nature of this telling deserves scrutiny, and so we return again to Gwendolyn Etter-Lewis (1993), who has thought a great deal about collaborative autobiography. She poses two fundamental questions about such hybrid texts: Who is the primary authority and does collaboration contaminate the process and products of autobiography? Etter-Lewis concludes that there is no definite answer to the question of authority. Even in the case of slave narratives, in which African-American women were not expected to be authorities of their own experience, narrators managed to exert some degree of authorship, if only by what they refused to say.

In the case at hand, Hudley was in control of her spoken account. She talked and we listened, rarely interrupting or asking questions. As younger women, we were cast in the role of attentive recipients of her story and her wisdom, an asymmetry that mimics the structure of female authority that has governed Hudley's life. Thus, the shape of the telling resembled a monologue much more than an interview. We assume that Hudley, like all narrators, shaped and pruned her account in response to her listeners, but we have no way of knowing exactly how our presence affected her story.

It is in the editing, the transformation of the transcript into a text, that we actively exercised authority as coauthors. Here we tried not to efface the spoken language. We tried to shorten without doing injury to Hudley's intentions and her distinctive voice. We are heartened that Hudley approved our editing, but we acknowledge that this is an arena in which she may not have felt so free to challenge, given our greater expertise with the written word.

In light of all of this, did our collaboration contaminate the process and products of Hudley's autobiography? Like Etter-Lewis, our answer is: not necessarily. We believe that this collaboration was based in relationships of considerable trust. At the same time, we recognize that had Hudley collaborated with someone else—a woman of her own age, a niece or daughter-in-law, an African-American social scientist—the process and the product would have been different.

Storytelling as Spiritual Practice

Most of the social scientific accounts of narrative have focused on the content of stories, treating stories as disembodied texts that offer windows into a person's life, identity, or meaning systems. It is much rarer to find works that address the practice of narrative, how people actually use stories in their everyday lives (but see, for example, Capps & Ochs, 1995; Heath, 1983; Miller, Potts, Fung, Hoogstra, & Mintz, 1990; Miller, Wiley, Fung, & Liang, 1997; and Ochs & Capps, 2001). Edith Hudley's experience of narrative, particularly her habit of retelling certain stories again and again, underscores the need to address this gap in our understanding.

How can we make sense of Hudley's practice of returning repeatedly to the story of being rescued from temptation by Mother Ewing? And what about her daily repetition of stories about her mother and father? These repeated engagements with particular stories exemplify what Peggy Miller and her colleagues have called "story attachments," strong and sustained emotional involvements with particular stories (Miller et al., 1993; Alexander, Miller, & Hengst, 2001). They found that young children sought repeated encounters with their special stories: listening to the story, talking about it with family members, enacting scenes in pretend play, dressing like the characters. Some of these attachments lasted for years (see also, Wolf & Heath, 1992). Mothers supported these attachments on the belief that they help children to manage their emotional concerns. Although this phenomenon emerges early in development, it apparently continues throughout the lifespan. Robert Coles' book *Call to Stories* (1989) includes many examples of how the medical students in his literature class became possessed by particular literary stories, and Kathryn Morgan (1989) says that family legends of her great-grandmother, a freed mulatto slave, continue to sustain her when some obstacle seems insurmountable.

Hudley, like these other individuals, has a set of personal stories to which she is deeply attached, but her use of these stories is distinctive. When she remembers her mother's death or her father's advice, she seems to be using stories as a form of prayer or meditation. These tellings are framed as expressions of gratitude for the blessings bestowed, "I thank the Lord that...." She offers herself and others these daily consolations, these constant reminders of what has been most important and most sustaining in her life. Apart from these always relevant stories, she revisits other stories from her life when they become pertinent to current circumstances. It is as though her own life story is so infused with religious meaning that it has become a sacred text.

We have been unable to locate any scholarly literature that addresses this use of personal storytelling as a spiritual and religious practice. However, Keith Basso's (1984) classic description of Western Apache narrative traditions is worth noting because it bears some resemblance to Hudley's practice. The Western Apache share a set of historical stories, each of which is known to have happened at a particular location in the natural landscape. As people go about their daily business, they move through a landscape that is saturated with moral tales, tales that "make you live right," as one informant put it (p. 21). At times, a member of the community might find it necessary to "aim" a story at an offender. If taken to heart, the story and the place with which it is associated will "stalk" the offender and promote beneficial change. Like Hudley's storytelling, these narrative practices are part of the fabric of everyday life, constantly orienting the person in a moral universe.

Storytelling as Legacy for Children

What does any of this have to do with child development? Several of the works that we have cited in this interlude take for granted that children are part of the scene when adults tell their stories. Etter-Lewis (1993) says that preparation for her book began in her childhood, when she sat on her great-grandmother's front porch listening to her stories. Speaking of the African origins of African-American storytelling, Pearl Primus (quoted by Goss and Barnes, 1989) says, "'Children sitting in the shadows of the house (where stories are told) are learning that greed, laziness, dishonesty, arrogance, and theft are all negative values which their society will not tolerate'" (p. 11). Morgan (1989) remembers that her mother told the legends of her great-grandmother while she was doing chores. Morgan had to follow her from room to room in order to hear the end of the story. Although these and other authors assume that such stories leave an indelible impression on children—transmitting values, shaping identities, serving as an antidote to the hateful images of African Americans that are at large in the dominant culture—developmentalists have paid little attention to the effects of adults' oral storytelling on children's development.

It is not the case that scholars of child development have been deaf to the importance of narrative in children's lives. In fact, in recent years many studies of young children's narrative development have been published, yielding important new insights into autobiographical memory, self construction, and socialization (for example, Bruner, 1990; Engel, 1995; McCabe & Peterson, 1991; Neisser & Firush, 1994; Nelson, 1989, 1996; Schweder et al., 1998). However, as Miller and her colleagues have pointed out, most of this work focuses on stories in which child and mother collaborate in telling stories of the *child's* past experiences (Miller, 1994). Far less is known about practices in which children are present as listeners, overhearers, or eavesdroppers when adults tell stories about their experiences. In Miller's (1994) study of white, working-class families in South Baltimore, such stories occurred at the remarkable rate of 8.5 per hour, on average, in ordinary family interaction. We know from Edith Hudley's own testimony that she was a "nosy child," who gleaned all sorts of useful information by monitoring the conversation of her elders. The privileging of co-narrated stories over stories told to or around children may reflect the assumption that it is only when children take on the role of narrator that storytelling influences their development, an assumption that implicitly treats the listening role as passive and negligible. Yet we know that in many cultures around the world children learn primarily through observation (Gaskins, 1999; Lancy, 1996; Rogoff et al., 1993).

It is likely that many African-American children grow up in families and communities in which oral storytelling is abundantly available in multiple forms. This is evident, for example, in Shirley Brice Heath's (1983) description of the fictionally embellished stories that are told in a community in the Piedmont Carolinas, Linda and Doug Sperry's (1996) research on early narrative development in the Black Belt of Alabama, and Marjorie Goodwin's (1990) account of older children's talk in west Philadelphia. In these studies African-American children emerge as remarkably avid and proficient narrators. Although Hudley says little about how she learned to tell stories, one can easily imagine the young Edith holding her family and friends spellbound. However, neither scholars of African-American narrative traditions nor scholars of child development have addressed the question of how children learn to weave stories of personal experience into overarching life stories. Both Linde (1993) and McAdams (1993) assume that this begins to happen in adolescence, but it remains to be seen how this is accomplished. Edith Hudley's storytelling also underscores how little we know about the continued development of storytelling during the adult years, yielding the kind of virtuoso performances that have become second nature to her.

References

Alexander, K.J., Miller, P.J., & Hengst, J.A. (2001). Young children's emotional attachments to stories. *Social Development, 10,* 373-397.

Basso, K. (1984). Stalking with stories: Names, places, and moral narratives among the Western Apache. In E.M. Bruner & S. Plattner (Eds.), *Text, play, and story: The construction and reconstruction of self and society* (pp. 19-55). Washington, DC: American Ethnological Society.

Bruner, J. (1990). *Acts of meaning.* Cambridge, MA: Harvard University Press.

Capps, L., & Ochs, E. (1995). *Constructing panic: The discourse of agoraphobia.* Cambridge, MA: Harvard University Press.

Coles, R. (1989). *The call to stories.* Boston: Houghton-Mifflin.

Engel, S. (1995). *The stories children tell.* New York: W.H. Freeman.

Etter-Lewis, G. (1993). *My soul is my own: Oral narratives of African-American women in the professions.* New York: Routledge.

Gaskins, S. (1999). Children's daily lives in a Mayan village: A case study of culturally constructed roles and activities. In A. Goncu (Ed.), *Children's engagement in the world: Sociocultural perspectives.* (pp. 25-61). New York: Cambridge University Press.

Goodwin, M.H. (1990). *He-said-she-said: Talk as social organization among black children.* Bloomington: Indiana University Press.

Goss, L., & Barnes, M.E. (Eds.). (1989). *Talk that talk: An anthology of African-American storytelling.* New York: Simon & Schuster.

Heath, S.B. (1983). *Ways with words: Language, life, and work in communities and classrooms.* New York: Cambridge University Press.

Lancy, D.F. (1996). *Playing on the mother ground: Cultural routines for children's development.* New York: Guilford Press.

Linde, C. (1993). *Life stories: The creation of coherence.* New York: Oxford University Press.

Logan, O.L. (1989). *Motherwit.* New York: Penguin.

McAdams, D.P. (1993). *The stories we live by: Personal myths and the making of the self.* New York: William Morrow.

McCabe, A., & Peterson, A. (1991). *Developing narrative structure.* Hillsdale, NJ: Erlbaum.

McKay, N. (1988). Race, gender, and cultural context in Zora Neale Hurston's *Dust Tracks on a Road.* In B.Brodzki & C.Schenck (Eds.), *Life/lines.* Ithaca, NY: Cornell University Press.

Miller, P.J. (1994). Narrative practices: Their role in socialization and self-construction. In U. Neisser & R. Fivush (Eds.), *The remembering self: Construction and accuracy in the self-narrative.* (pp. 158-179). New York: Cambridge University Press.

Miller, P.J., Hoogstra, L., Mintz, J., Fung, H., & Williams, K. (1993). Troubles in the garden and how they get resolved: A young child's transformation of his favorite story. In C.A. Nelson (Ed.), *Memory and affect in development (Minnesota symposia on child psychology)* (Vol. 26). Hillsdale, NJ: Erlbaum.

Miller, P.J., Potts. R., Fung. H., Hoogstra, L., & Mintz, J. (1990). Narrative practices and the social construction of self in childhood. *American Ethnologist, 17,* 97-116.

Miller, P.J., Wiley, A.R., Fung, H., & Liang, C. (1997). Personal storytelling as a medium of socialization in Chinese and American families. *Child Development, 68,* 557-568.

Morgan, K. (1989). Caddy buffers: Legends of a middle-class black family in Philadelphia. In L. Goss & M.E. Barnes (Eds.), *Talk that talk: An anthology of African-American storytelling.* (pp. 295-298). New York: Simon & Schuster.

Neisser, U., & Firush, R. (Eds.). (1994). *The remembering self: Construction and accuracy in the self-narrative.* (pp. 136-157). Cambridge: Cambridge University Press.

Nelson, K. (Ed.). (1989). *Narratives from the crib.* New York: Cambridge University Press.

Nelson, K. (1996). *Language in cognitive development: The emergence of the mediated mind*. New York: Cambridge University Press.

Ochs, E., & Capps, L. (2001). *Living narrative: Creating lives in everyday storytelling*. Cambridge, MA: Harvard University Press.

Rogoff, B., Mistry, J., Goncu, A., & Mosier, C. (1993). Guided participation in cultural activity by toddlers and caregivers. *Monographs of the Society for Research in Child Development*, 58 (Serial no. 236).

Rose, P. (Ed.). (1993). *The Norton book of women's lives*. New York: Norton.

Shweder, R.A., Goodnow, J.J., Hatano, G., LeVine, R., Markus, H., & Miller, P.J. (1998). The cultural psychology of development: One mind, many mentalities. In W. Damon (Ed.), *The handbook of child psychology*. (5th ed., Vol. 1, pp. 865-937). New York: Wiley.

Sperry, L.L., & Sperry, D.E. (1996). The early development of narrative skills. *Cognitive Development*, 11, 443-465.

Wolf, S.A., & Heath, S.B. (1992). *The braid of literature: Children's worlds of reading*. Cambridge, MA: Harvard University Press.

Epilogue

Edith Valerie Patton Hudley
Sunrise: October 2, 1920
Sunset: March 13, 2007

Edith lived for four more years following publication of *Raise Up a Child*. She and Floyd rented a small apartment in Denver, Colorado, near Floyd's niece. Edith disliked Denver's cold winters and missed gardening but quickly made friends with her neighbors, including a young mother for whom she provided child care. As her dementia progressed, however, her activity level and ability to care for herself and others declined. When she visited Wendy and her family in the summer of 2005, she would read *Raise Up a Child* to recall her stories and the details of her childhood and relationships with her parents, children, and grandchildren. Despite her dementia, Edith still was active, loving, and interested in others and her surroundings. And she thoroughly enjoyed the drive cross-country from Colorado to Illinois, the time together in the car with Wendy and Camilla, and the beauty of the prairie in summer.

On March 13, 2007, Everett called Wendy to tell her that his mother had "gone home." He and Andrew were able to spend time with her during her final days, which they all found to be enormously comforting. Edith, an independent spirit, was able to remain at home with Floyd as she wished until a final, brief hospital stay.

On May 12, 2007, Edith's friends and family gathered in Houston, Texas, for a celebration of her life. "Little Edith," now married and the mother of two, remembered with thanks the time in life that she "walked with" her grandmother. The pastor of Everett's church reflected on the importance of storytelling as a way in which Edith had remained connected to her parents and would remain connected to her family and friends. Everett created a DVD with pictures of Edith, the front cover of *Raise Up a Child*, a talk she had given at church, and some of her favorite songs, including "His Eye Is on the

Sparrow."The memorial service ended with another of Edith's favorite songs, "I Still Have Joy."

Following the service, Andrew shared with Wendy the importance of *Raise Up a Child* to his mother. Kathareen, now a mother and grandmother, expressed her profound appreciation that "Mama Edith got it right" in her book. After the reception, Wendy, Matthew, and Camilla were able to visit Kennard and Crockett in a forested area of east Texas, Edith's birthplace and home.

Appendix A: Chronology of Important Events in the Life of Edith V. P. Hudley

Childhood in Kennard, Texas, 1920-1935

1920 Edith Valarie Patton Hudley is born, the sixth living child of Aaron and Mamie Patton, on a small family farm in Kennard, Texas.
1926 Edith's brother Oliver is born.
1927 Edith enrolls and excels at an all-black elementary school.
1928 Edith's brother Willie Oscar is born. Mamie is ill as a result of complications from his birth. Under Mamie's supervision, Edith helps to care for the family.
1930 Mamie dies at the age of forty-one after bearing thirteen children. Edith continues to help care for the family, particularly her little brothers, and to attend school.
1931 The family home burns down. Extended family and community members take the family in and provide food and clothing.

Youth in Houston, Texas, 1935-1938

1935 Edith moves to Houston to attend eighth grade at Jack Yates High School while living with her older sister, Ruth. She also works as a maid and babysitter for Miz A. and her family. A family acquaintance tries to rape Edith. She outsmarts him using advice from Aaron.
1936 Edith is forced to leave school because of financial hardships and family responsibilities. She returns home to Kennard.

APPENDIX A

Life with Eugene, rural Texas and Oakland, California, 1938-1961

1938 Edith marries Eugene.
1942 Edith and Eugene move to Oakland, California, where Edith works as a burner in a shipyard.
1944 Mr. Bill, a white postman, attempts to rape Edith while she is visiting her father in Kennard, but she outsmarts him.
1946 Aaron dies.
1946 Edith and Eugene return to Texas, where they build and operate a store in a rural area outside of Houston.

Raising Everett and Andrew, rural Texas and Oakland, California, 1948-1969

1948 Edith's and Eugene's son Everett is born.
1948 Edith mothers Edna, a young woman who works in the store. Eugene rapes Edna.
1949 Kathareen, Edna's and Eugene's daughter, is born.
1950 Edith's and Eugene's son Willie Andrew is born and dies shortly after birth.
1951 Edith's and Eugene's son, Andrew Franklin, is born.
1956 Edith and Eugene move their family to Oakland in search of better schools and opportunities for their sons. Edith forms a close relationship with a deaconess of her church, "Mother Ewing."
1960 Edith is injured in a serious automobile accident with a train.
1961 Edith separates from and then divorces Eugene, who has become abusive to her.
1963 Edith marries Ellis, a sailor and wonderful stepfather to her sons.
1966 Everett graduates from high school and attends Howard University.
1968 Edith separates from and then divorces Ellis, who has become alcoholic and abusive to her.
1969 Andrew graduates from high school and goes to Howard University.

Later years in Oakland, California, and Salt Lake City, Utah, 1969-1999

1969 Edith marries Floyd, a sailor.
1972 Floyd's son Ricky dies of a drug overdose.

CHRONOLOGY OF IMPORTANT EVENTS IN THE LIFE OF EDITH V. P. HUDLEY

1973 Floyd's son Randy is shot and killed.
1976 Granddaughter Edith (Andrew's and Lula May's child) is born.
1978 Grandson Sterling (Everett's and Joan's child) is born.
1979 Granddaughter Courtney (Everett's and Joan's child) is born.
1979 Little Edith and Lula May come to live with Edith and Floyd. Lula May, who is addicted to drugs, leaves the family shortly thereafter.
1983 Little Edith returns to live with her father, Andrew, but remains in close contact with Edith.
1988 Edith and Floyd move to Salt Lake City, Utah, where Floyd works as a bus driver. Edith, a church deaconess, continues to take into her home children whose parents are struggling.
1997- Edith narrates her oral history to Peggy Miller and Wendy Haight
1999 in Urbana, Illinois, and Salt Lake City, Utah.
2000 Edith and Floyd move to Michigan, where Edith recovers from an illness while staying with Everett and Joan.
2002 Edith and Floyd move to Denver, where they live in an apartment near Floyd's family.

Appendix B: Important People in the Life of Edith V. P. Hudley

Part 1: Childhood in Kennard, Texas, 1920-1935

Edith Valarie Patton, 1920- (also known as Baby Rae, Ree, Valarie, Mama, Miss H.)

Parents

Aaron Franklin Patton, 1880-1946. (also known as Mr. Aaron, Daddy, Papa)
Mamie E. Scott Patton, 1889-1930. (also known as Sweetheart, Mama, Mother)

Siblings (surviving past infancy)

Ruth, 1908-1996
Andrew, 1913-
Purcell, 1915-1945
Mary Sterling, 1917-
Margie Louise, 1919-
Oliver Wendell, 1926-
Willie Oscar, 1929-

Other mothers

Mama Carrie (godmother)
Aunt Mollie (Aaron's sister)
Cousin Rena
Aunt Martie (Aaron's aunt)
Erma (neighbor who provided clothes for Edith after the fire)

Others

Aunt Sarah (ancestor raped by white man)
Uncle Shade (Aunt Sarah's husband)
Mr. Patton (Aaron's white "cousin")
Harvey (godbrother)
Mary (godsister)
J. C., Mutt, and Willis (neighbor boys befriended by Aaron)

Part 2: Youth in Houston, Texas, 1935-1938

Miz Cavanaugh and Mr. Goodwin (teachers)
Miz A. (employer)
Elizabeth (Miz A.'s young daughter)
Mr. S. (Miz A.'s elderly father, a retired minister)
Berta (former maid of Miz A.)
Bernice and Shirley (friends)
Thello (brother-in-law)

Part 3: Life with Eugene, rural Texas and Oakland, California, 1938-1961

Eugene (husband, also known as Gene, Sonny Boy, Mr. Gene)
Eugene, Sr. (father-in-law, also known as Sonny, Papa, Daddy)
Mary (mother-in-law, also known as Mae, Mama)
Bertha (sister-in-law, also known as Bert)
Big Mama (Mary's mother)
Mr. Bill (mail carrier)
Cousin Oscar
May and Sanett (friends in the shipyard)
Edna (young woman working for Edith and Eugene in the store)
Kathareen (Edna's daughter)
Miz DeFrance (landlady who befriends Edith)
Mother Pearl Ewing (Edith's mentor)

Part 4: Raising Everett and Andrew, rural Texas and Oakland, California, 1948-1969

Everett, 1948- (son)
Willie Andrew, 1950-1950 (son)

Andrew Franklin, 1951- (son)
Miz Bertha (PTA coworker)
Ellis (Edith's second husband)

Part 5: Later years in Oakland, California, and Salt Lake City, Utah, 1969-1999

Floyd (Edith's third husband)
Morris (Floyd's brother)
Dorothy (Edith's tenant and coworker, and Morris's friend)
Randy and Ricky (Floyd's sons)
Joan (Everett's wife)
Lula May (Andrew's wife, also known as Sis)
Edith (Andrew's and Lula May's daughter)
Sterling (Everett's and Joan's son)
Courtney (Everett's and Joan's daughter)

APPENDIX C:
NOTES FOR STUDENTS

Part 1

Many authors of social work, education, and psychology textbooks consider human development as resulting from the complex interaction of intrinsic, biological factors and extrinsic, environmental factors within particular cultural and historical contexts (for example, Cole & Cole, 2001; Ashford, LeCroy, & Lortie, 2001). Mrs. Hudley's childhood exemplifies these ideas. Her development in childhood was shaped by *biological factors,* including her excellent physical and mental health. Students might also consider how a physically or mentally ill child might have fared in similar circumstances, particularly given the quality of health care available to rural blacks in the 1920s. *Psychological factors* shaping Mrs. Hudley's development in childhood include the traditional ways in which she learned to cook, wash clothes, and care for her baby brothers, as well as the formal instruction she received in school. Students might consider the characteristics of Edith's home and school as contexts for learning. What are some contexts today in which children learn as apprentices through observation and participation with more experienced individuals? *Social factors* shaping Mrs. Hudley's childhood development include the relationships she formed while participating within her African-American family, church, and school. How might Edith have fared with less social and emotional support? *Historical factors* shaping Mrs. Hudley's development include the hardships of segregation and the Great Depression. Students may wish to speculate on how this historical context shaped the advice and guidance Edith's father provided on such topics as work and racism.

Part 2

Most textbooks that discuss adolescence include the physical, cognitive, and other psychological and social transitions central to adolescence (see, for example, Steinberg, 2002). Mrs. Hudley's youth exemplifies many of these issues. From a biological perspective, adolescence encompasses rapid physical growth and the development of secondary sexual characteristics (puberty). Students may wish to consider the social consequences of these physical changes, for example, how is Edith viewed by others at age ten versus age fifteen? From a cognitive perspective, adolescence encompasses improvements in logical thinking, hypothetical thought, and future planning. How are these developing cognitive competencies capitalized on at the Jack Yates High School? From a psychological perspective, Edith's identity, autonomy, sexuality, and achievement orientation continue to develop. Students may wish to speculate on the experiences Edith had in Houston that may have shaped her identity as an African-American woman. To what extent had Edith become emotionally, behaviorally, and morally autonomous from her parents? What experiences in Houston shaped Edith's emerging sexuality? What appear to have been young Edith's motives and beliefs regarding achievement? How might Edith's experiences at home have shaped these beliefs regarding education? From a social perspective, young Edith entered a number of new roles during her youth: high school student, employee working independently of her father, and a young woman with a much broader social life. How did Edith's relationship with her father change during this time, and how did it remain the same? To what extent do Edith's choices appear to have been shaped by her relationship with her parents? It also is important to consider how Edith's development was shaped within the particular historical context of Depression era Texas.

Part 3

Lifespan and adult development textbooks typically emphasize several roles and challenges of early adulthood (see, for example, Berk, 2001; Sattler et al., 2000). Some of these issues, especially establishing intimate relationships and finding adequate work, are in part 3. Students may wish to speculate on the factors that led to Edith and Eugene's decision to marry and the challenges of that relationship. What factors influenced employment opportunities for Edith and Eugene, and what did Edith's jobs mean to her?

Part 3 also provides the opportunity to consider a number of current social issues. First, the U.S. has the highest rate of divorce in the world with approximately half of all marriages ending in divorce (Berk, 2001). What impact did the dissolution of her marriage have on Edith? What social programs exist to support families experiencing divorce? Second, the sexual abuse of children and adolescents remains a significant and relatively common problem. Current estimates of the prevalence of sexual abuse of girls range from 6 percent to 62 percent (Conte, 1995). How did sexual abuse shape the life of Edna? What components would effective educational and social programs to reduce sexual abuse include? How can young women such as Edna be supported?

Part 4

Part 4 of the oral history touches on another important role for many adults: parenting. Becoming a parent can bring great joys and great challenges. Students may wish to speculate on how the transition into parenthood affected Edith's and Eugene's marriage. Also, how did the time and place affect Edith's child-rearing strategies?

Part 4 also provides the opportunity to discuss a number of current social issues. Today, approximately 25 percent of U.S. children reside in single parent households (Berk, 2001). What strategies did Edith, as a single mother, employ in raising her adolescent sons? What social programs exist to support single mothers and their children today? With the high divorce rate in the United States, blended families are increasingly common. The most frequent form is the mother-stepfather family (Berk, 2001). How did Edith's adolescent sons respond to Ellis? What did Ellis do to promote his relationship with his stepsons?

Alcoholism continues to plague many families today. Approximately 13 percent of men are heavy drinkers (average two or more drinks a day), and about one-third of these are alcoholics (Berk, 2001). How did Ellis' drinking affect his relationship with Edith and her sons? What are some effective interventions for alcoholism?

Domestic violence, commonly defined as physical, sexual, or psychological abuse of an intimate partner, is a dangerous problem in many families today. Over 1.5 million women are severely assaulted in their homes by their male partners (Davis, 1995). Social workers, educators, and others work both to support women who have experienced domestic violence and to develop preventative interventions for their children. How did Aaron's teaching of Edith affect her response when Ellis became abusive? To what extent is Aaron's advice to Edith relevant today?

Part 5

Part 5 of Mrs. Hudley's oral history draws our attention to a number of the challenges of adult development, as well as tenacious social issues that remain with us today. The death of a child by violence or drug addiction is devastating. Students may wish to consider how Edith and Floyd coped with the loss of his two adolescent sons, and how we might as individuals and professionals provide support to families who have lost a child.

Drug abuse remains a serious problem today, with devastating effects on families and children. How might Lula May's drug addiction have affected the development of her daughter, Little Edith? What is the role of grandparents in children's development?

References

Ashford, J., LeCroy, C., & Lortie, K. (2001). *Human behavior in the social environment* (2nd ed.). Belmont, California: Brooks/Cole.

Berk, L. (2001). *Development through the lifespan* (2nd ed.). Boston: Allyn and Bacon.

Cole, M., & Cole S. (2001). *The development of children* (4th ed.). New York: Worth.

Conte, J. (1995). Child sexual abuse overview. In R. Edwards & J. Hopps (Eds.), *Encyclopedia of social work* (19th ed.). Washington, DC: NASW Press.

Davis, L. (1995). Domestic Violence. In R. Edwards & J. Hopps (Eds.), *Encyclopedia of social work* (19th ed.). Washington, DC: NASW Press.

Sattler, D., Kramer, G., Shabatay, V., & Bernstein, D. (2000). *Lifespan development in context: Voices and perspectives*. Boston: Houghton-Mifflin.

Steinberg, L. (2002). *Adolescence* (2nd ed.). Boston: McGraw-Hill.

INDEX

Abell, E., 177
Adcock, C. R., 49
Adolescents, mentors and, 134-136
Adult development, mentoring and, 138-139. *See also* Child development; Human development
African-American children, oral storytelling and, 214
African-American churches
  benefits to children of, 51
  mentoring and, 137
African-American religious beliefs
  alternative systems of, 51-52
  dignity and worth of individual in, 53
  emphasis of community in, 52-53
African Americans
  Christian church and, 48
  nihilism and, 85
  preparing children to resist racism and, 82
  role of religion for, 48
  in Salt Lake City, Utah, 185-186
  spirituality and, 48
African-American storytelling, 207
  child development and, 214
Alexander, K. J., 211
Alternative belief systems, 51-52
Anderson, E., 134
Andrew Franklin (third son of Edith Hudley), 154, 160-162
Apache narrative traditions, 212
Arnold, M. S., 51
Autobiographies, 208
  collaboration in, 210-211

Bailey, B., 91
Bakhtin, M., xxvii
Barnes, M. E., xxii, 207, 213

Basso, K., 212
Baumrind, D., 174, 176, 177, 180
Becerra, R. M., 176
Becker, W. H., 51
Behar, R., xviii
Belief systems, alternative, 51-52
Berlin, S. D., 50
Best, K. M., 50
BEST programs, 137
Bishop, E. H., 2
Black, J. E., 182
Black Baptist church, 53
Black Panther Party, 143-144
Blyth, D., 135
Bornstein, M. H., 49
Bradley, C. R., 177
Briggs, E., 136
Broughton, V. W., 48
Brown, D. R., 52
Bruner, J., 213
Bullis, R. K., 49

Canda, E. R., 50
Capps, L., 211
Carlson, V., 178
Carson, C., 144
Cavanaugh, Miz (teacher of Edith Hudley), 61, 135
Chastisement of children. *See* Physical discipline; Spanking
Child abuse
  banning physical discipline and, 180
  vs. physical discipline, 178-179
Child development, xxii. *See also* Adult development; Human development
  context of oppression in, 81
  racism as risk factor in, 82

religious and spiritual experiences in, 50-51
role of spirituality and religion and, 49-50
storytelling for, 212-214
Churches, role of, 48
Cicchetti, D., 178
Civil Rights movement, 88, 143-144
Clark, C., 50, 210
Clifford, J., xviii
Cohen, P., 175
Colasanto, D., 135
Cole, M., 49
Cole, S. R., 49
Coleman, R., 185
Coles, R., xxii, 50, 51, 212
Collaborative narratives, 210-211
Collins, C., 48
Collins, P., 134
Colorism, 83-84. See also Racism
Comer, J. C., xxiii, 82
Community
in African-American religious beliefs, 52-53
importance of, 54
for positive development, 137
Congress for Racial Equality (CORE), 143
Contreras, J., 136
Corporal punishment. See Physical discipline
Cosgrove, J., 181
Costin, L. B., 179
Cowan, E., 135
Crawford, V., 48

Damon, W., 49
Davidson, W., 136
Davis, A., xxii, 135, 136
Davis, F., 84
Dead, visitations by the, 41-45, 48
Deater-Deckard, K., 177, 178
Death, thoughts about, by Edith Hudley, 205-206
Dimitriadis, G., 137

Discipline, physical. See Physical discipline
Dodge, K. A., 177, 178
Dodson, J., 48
Downs, S. W., 179
Dublin, T., 91
DuBois, D., 136

Ebert, L., 135, 136
Edith (daughter of Lula May), 196-202
Edna (mother of Kathareen), 120-124
Education, role of spirituality and religion and, 49-50
Ellis (second husband of Edith Hudley), 165-169
Emerson, C., xxix
Engel, S., 213
Etter-Lewis, G., xxii, 208, 210, 211, 213
Eugene H. (first husband of Edith Hudley), 91-92, 108-112
as father, 163-165
rape of Edna by, 120-122
Everett (oldest son of Edith Hudley), 146, 154, 160-162
Ewing, Mother Pearl, 92, 130-133
as mentor, 134-135, 138-139

Faith, community of, 52-53
Faith healings, 48
Fine, M., xviii, 87
Firush, R., 213
Fischer, K., 135, 136
Fisher, C., xxi, 81, 176
Fitts, L., 53
Foote, J. A. J., 47
Fowler, J., 50
Franklin, J., 48
Frazier, M. W., 81
Freedman, M., 134
Friedman, S. B., 175
Fung, H., 211

Gandhi, Mahatma, 144
Garmezy, N., 50, 135
Gaskins, S., 214

INDEX

Gates, H., xxii, 144
Gates, H. L., Jr., 207
Genre, story, 207
Giovannoni, J. M., 176
Goodnow, J., 49
Goodwin, M., xxii, 214
Goodwin, Mr. (teacher of Edith Hudley), 61
Goss, L., xxii, 207, 213
Gray, E., 181
Graziano, A., 175
Great Migration, 91-92
Griffith, E., 48
Grossman, J., 136

Haight, C., xvi
Haight, M., xvi
Haight, W., xvi, xxii, 53, 84, 136, 181, 182, 185
Hale-Benson, J., xxii, 52, 53
Harris, P., 50
Harris, V., 83-84
Heath, S. B., xxii, 88, 137, 211, 214
Hengst, J. A., 211
Holden, G., 174
Homeless phenomena, 49
Hoogstra, L., 211
hooks, b., xv, 52, 84
Houston, Texas, 59
Hudley, Edith Valerie Patton, xiii-xiv. *See also* Patton, Aaron (father of Edith Hudley); Patton, Mamie (mother of Edith Hudley)
  birth certificate story of, 96-100
  car accident of, 125-130
  as caregiver, 209
  on chastising children, 154-159. *See also* Physical discipline
  on childhood racism, 34-40
  church activities of, 203-204
  community unity and, 30-33
  concern for other's children and, 170-172
  consequences of oppression for, 88
  death of mother and, 19-24
  early childhood of, 1-4
  early discipline training of, 15-18
  early employers of, 64-68
  in eighth grade, 61-63
  family of, 5-9
  interviewing, xviii-xix, xxv-xxx
  life story of, 208-209
  loss of home by fire and, 28-30
  marriage problems of, 108-112
  marriage to Eugene H. and, 91-92, 94-95
  meeting Floyd Hudley and, 187-191
  moral training of, 73-75
  Mother Ewing and, 130-133
  other mothers of, 25-27
  power of love and, xv
  predators and, 69-72
  relationship with mother and, 10-14
  religious faith of, xiv-xvi
  resisting stereotypes by, 86
  role of oppression in development of, 82-84
  role of sexism in development of, 84
  schooling of children and, 146-150
  school teachers and, 151-153
  segregation experiences of, 76-80
  shipyard job of, 101-105
  storekeeping experiences of, 117-119
  teachers of, 61-63
  thoughts about death and, 205-206
  visions of the dead and, 41-45
Hudley, Floyd (third husband of Edith Hudley), 185-186
  meeting Edith and, 187-191
  sons of, 192-195
Human development, xxii-xxiii. *See also* Adult development; Child development
  role of spirituality and religion in, 48-49
Hurd, E. P., 51

INDEX

Husbands, of Edith Hudley
   Ellis (second husband), 165-169
   Eugene (first husband), 91-92, 108-112, 163-165
   Floyd (third husband), 185-195
Hyman, I., 180

Integration. *See* Segregation
Interviews, of Edith Hudley, xviii-xix

Jackson, J., xxi, 81, 176
Jaffe, A., xxvi
Johnson, C., 50
Johnson, D., xxii
Johnson, P., 2

Kathareen (daughter of Edna and Eugene), xxx, 122-124
Kelley, M. L., 177
Kennard, Texas, 2
Kessler-Harris, A., 92
King, Martin Luther, Jr., 144
Kolko, D. J., 178
Konopka, G., 139
Korbin, J., 179
Kornblum, W., 134
Kotlowitz, A., 88
Kozol, J., 87-88
Krause, N., 48
Ku Klux Klan (KKK), 2-3
Kuschnick, Louis, 82

Labov, W., xxii
Lamar, J., 87
Lamb, M. E., 49
Lancy, D. F., 214
Leadbeater, B. J., 85, 87
LeCroy, C., 49
Lee, J., 83
Lerner, G., 60
Levine, A., 134
Levinson, D., 134, 138
Liang, C., 211

Life stories, 207, 208-209
   religion in, 209
   use of repetition in, 211-212
Lincoln, C. E., 51, 52
Linde, C., 207, 208, 214
Logan, O. L., xvii, 48, 210
Long, C. H., 52
Lortie, K., 49
LoSciutp, L., 136
Love, power of, xv
Lula May, 196-202
Lykes, M. B., 87
Lynchings, 2-3

McAdams, D. P., 209, 214
McAddo, H., 48
McCabe, A., 213
McCormick, J., 87
McFadden, E. J., 179
McLearn, K., 135
McLloyd, V., 88
McPartland, J., 136
Mamiya, L., 51, 52
Mangelsdorf, S., 136, 182
Marcus, G. E., xviii
Martin, E., 134
Martin, J., 134
Maston, A. S., 50
Maton, K. I., xxii
Matthews, A., 185
Mendelsohn, J., 91, 144
Mentoring, 134-136
   adolescents and, 134-136
   adult development and, 138-139
   African-American churches and, 137
Miller, P. C., xvi, 50, 211
Miller, P. J., 211, 213
Mintz, J., 211
Mitchell, E. P., 52, 53
Moore, C., 51
Moore, T., 48, 52
Morgan, K., 212, 213

Morrison, T., 47, 83, 84
Morson, G. S., xxix
Mosby, L., 176, 182
Moss, B., 48
Munch, J., 135

Neisser, U., 213
Nelson, K., 213
Nettles, S., 136
Neville, H., 136
Newton, Huey, 143
Nidiffer, J., 134
Nihilism, 85

Oakland, California, 91
Ochs, E., 211
Ogbu, J., 177
Oppression
  consequences of, 88
  context of, and child development, 81
  critical consciousness of, 87-88
  in development of Edith Hudley, 82-84
  resistance to, 81-82, 84-85
  strategies for resisting, 85
Oral histories, 207
Oral storytelling, African-American children and, 214
Othermothers, 134

Paley, V., xxix
Pastor, J., 87
Patton, Aaron (father of Edith Hudley), 1, 5-9, 136
  death of, 92, 106-107
  practice of truth telling of, 85-86
Patton, Mamie (mother of Edith Hudley), 1, 10-14, 82
  death of, 19-24
Patton, Purcell (brother of Edith Hudley), 28-29
Peterson, A., 213

Physical abuse, 178-179
Physical discipline, xxi, xxix, 154, 173-175. *See also* Spanking
  banning, 179-183
  different values about, 175-177
  Edith Hudley's early training in, 15-18
  effects of, 176-178
  foster care and, 181-182
  vs. physical abuse, 178-179
  public welfare systems and, 181
Polite, K., 175, 177
Poll taxes, 2
Potts, R., 47, 48, 211
Poussaint, A. F., 82
Poverty rates, 88
Primus, P., 213
Public welfare systems, physical discipline and, 181

Racism, 34-40
  colorism and, 83-84
  defined, 82
  as risk factor, in child development, 82
Rajala, A., 136
Redner, R., 136
Religion. *See also* Spirituality
  defined, 47
  in life stories, 208-209
Religious beliefs, African-American
  alternative systems of, 51-52
  dignity and worth of individual in, 53
  socialization of, 53-54
Repetition, use of, by Edit Hudley, 211-212
Resilience, role of spirituality and religion and, 50-51
Resistance, 84-85. *See also* Oppression
Rhodes, J., 135
Rogers, R., 51
Rogoff, B., 214
Rose, P., 210

INDEX

Rosengren, K., 50
Rutter, M., 135

Salt Lake City, Utah, 185-186
Schmitt, B. D., 179, 180
Schoen, C., 135
Schoenberg, S. K., 175
Schweder, R. A., 213
Seale, Bobby, 143
Segregation, 2, 76-80
Sexism, role of, in development of Edith Hudley, 84
Share croppers, 2
Sheridan, M. J., 49
Shuman, A., xxii
Slaughter-Defoe, D., xxiii
Smith, A. D., xxvi
Smith, R., 135
Smitherman, G., xxii, 48
Sobel, M., 47
Socialization, of religious beliefs, 53-54
Social work, role of spirituality and religion and, 49-50
Spanking, xxiv, 154, 174. *See also* Physical discipline
Sperry, D., xxii, 214
Sperry, L., xxii, 214
Spirituality. *See also* Religion
  defined, 47
  importance of, and African Americans, 48
Spirituals, 52
Stack, C. B., xxii-xxiii, 52, 137
Stereotyping, 86
Story attachments, 211
Story genre, 207
Storytelling, xxx, 207
  African-American, 207
  African-American children and, 214
  Apache tradition of, 212
  as legacy for children, 212-214

as spiritual and religious practice, 212
Straus, M. A., 175
Strommen, E., 139
Sullivan, A., 135, 136, 138

Tata, L., 182
Tatum, B. D., 87
Taylor, A., 136
Teachers, of Edith Hudley, 61-63. *See also* Mentoring
Tenant farmers, 2
Tierney, J., 136
Townsend, T., 136
Tran, T. V., 48
Truth telling, 85-86

Villarruel, F., xxi, 81, 176

Watson, W. H., 48
Way, N., 84, 86
Welfare systems, physical discipline and, 181
Wells, S., 178, 179
Werner, E., 135
West, C., 84, 85, 144
Wiley, A. R., 211
Williams, D., 48, 52
Williams, K., 51
Williams, T. M., 134
Wolf, S. A., xviii, 211
Work, W., 135
Workman, C. L., 182
Wright, L., 185

Young, J. L., 48
Young, V. H., 52

Zambarano, R., 174
Zangrando, R., 3
Zimmerman, M. A., xxii

234